Confessions of a Baseball Purist

Confessions of a
BASEBALL
PURIST

What's Right—and Wrong—with Baseball,

as Seen from the Best Seat in the House

updated edition

JON MILLER

with Mark Hyman

The Johns Hopkins University Press

Baltimore and London

Original hardcover edition published by Simon & Schuster Inc., 1998
Copyright © 1998, 2000 by Jon Miller and Mark Hyman
All rights reserved
Printed in the United States of America on acid-free paper

Johns Hopkins Paperbacks edition, 2000
2 4 6 8 9 7 5 3

The Johns Hopkins University Press
2715 North Charles Street
Baltimore, Maryland 21218-4363
www.press.jhu.edu

Library of Congress Cataloging-in-Publication Data

Miller, Jon (Jon W.)
Confessions of a baseball purist : what's right, and wrong, with baseball, as seen from
the best seat in the house / Jon Miller with Mark Hyman.—Updated ed.
p.   cm.
Originally published : Simon & Schuster, 1998.
Includes index.
ISBN 0-8018-6316-3 (alk. paper)
1. Miller, Jon (Jon W.)   2. Baltimore Orioles (Baseball team)
3. Sportscasters—United States—Biography.   I. Hyman, Mark.   II. Title.
GV742.42.M55A3   2000
070.4′49796′092—dc21
[B]   99-039409

A catalog record for this book is available from the British Library.

For Janine, with all my love—
which I'd say more often
in person if I were ever home.

—J. M.

For Peggy, Benjamin, and Eli, my home team.

—M. H.

ACKNOWLEDGMENTS

Friends and family helped to make this book a reality, and the last year a lot of fun. I'd like to thank Mike Krukow, Duane Kuiper, and Ted Robinson, my partners on radio and TV in San Francisco, whose love for the game made my move to the Bay Area truly gratifying; Janine, my wife, who already has read the book three times, for her much appreciated feedback and support; Holly Miller, my daughter, who gave me the non-purist and nonfan point of view, assuring me this book would be perfect for anybody on your shopping list, baseball fans or otherwise; and my parents, Jerry and Winona Miller, who insisted upon speaking English properly and having good enunciation, and who politely looked the other way, if not outright encouraged, a ten-year-old wannabe baseball broadcaster.

—J. M.

This book reflects the contributions of many who supported Jon and me with their time and encouragement.

Bob Rose of the San Francisco Giants responded promptly and cheerfully to our countless research requests. Phil Orlins and Diane Lamb of ESPN served as archivists for our queries concerning *Sunday Night Baseball.* Ken Singleton and Jim Gott shared key details of memorable days at the ballpark. Olwen Price and Joy Rhodes tackled the imposing task of transcribing our tapes.

Along the way, we also leaned on Jack Gibbons and Steve Marcus of the *Baltimore Sun,* Michael Bryant, Jeff Helman, Franklin Branch, David Richman-Raphael, Gene Bratek, and the Epstein family of Tempe, Arizona.

Thanks to literary agent Scott Waxman and to lawyer Ron Shapiro for guiding us through a sometimes formidable process. We owe a major debt of gratitude to Jeff Neuman, our editor at Simon & Schuster, and to Frank Scatoni, his assistant. Jeff improved the manuscript with each suggestion and, most important, laughed in all the right places.

Finally, thanks to my parents, Tony and Evelyn Hyman of Freehold, New Jersey, who, against their better judgment, allowed me to spend the entire summer of 1969 holed up in the basement playing APBA Baseball.

—M. H.

CONTENTS

A
BASEBALL
PURIST

Hello, I'm Jon Miller.

And I'm a baseball purist.

Jon Miller, purist.

Kind of has a regal sound to it, doesn't it?

"That's right, Jon Miller, former ambassador to Morocco, one-time U.S. Middle East peace envoy, six-time national speed-skating champion, and now . . . now, baseball purist."

I like it!

Actually, I wasn't even aware I was a baseball purist until the surprising news was broken to me a few years ago on one of our telecasts of *ESPN Sunday Night Baseball*. And the man I have to thank is baseball's longtime—perhaps even permanent—"acting" commissioner, Bud Selig.

This once-in-a-lifetime event occurred on June 13, 1993. Joe Morgan and I were at County Stadium in Milwaukee for a Brewers-Yankees game. We invited Mr. Selig, also the Brewers' owner, to come by the booth for a discussion of the serious issues facing baseball. One of the most serious at the time was interleague play.

"What's new on that front?" I asked.

Mr. Selig didn't hesitate.

"Jon," he replied, "I know you're a purist . . ."

I'm what?

Those were the first words out of Mr. Selig's mouth: *Jon, I know you're a purist.*

I was taken aback by this pronouncement, but I didn't let on as Mr. Selig explained that the owners were very interested in interleague play. Their polling data, he said, indicated that fans were clamoring for it.

"It's time to move beyond narrow ideas and give the fans what they want," Mr. Selig declared, in so many words.

I couldn't believe it—Mr. Selig calling me a purist on national TV. At one time, the label "baseball purist" could've been worn as a badge of honor. Any legitimate fan would've been pleased to be thought of as a purist. But I suppose that to Mr. Selig, a purist was a lonely old man hunched over a windup Victrola, thumbing through a 1929 *Who's Who in Baseball,* fretting that the game just hasn't been the same since the Babe retired.

Not to sound defensive, but I don't even own a Victrola.

The baseball owners and Mr. Selig, it seemed to me, have turned *purist* into a code word. I've heard and read many owners using the word *purist;* they use it in much the same way as Rush Limbaugh uses the word *liberal.* In other words, each became a label whose rough translation would be "someone who is responsible for just about everything that's wrong with our country today" (or in the case of a purist, someone whose refusal to let go of his old-fashioned notions of the game has plunged baseball into its current sorry state).

So, if a person is labeled a purist—as Bud Selig labeled me on *Sunday Night Baseball*—it's essentially a license to declare, "This person's opinions are irrelevant. Don't listen to them."

I've always thought it was a shame that the owners took that position. It eliminated so much debate regarding the game's future, debate that might have been healthy. My stance has always been that change in baseball could be a positive, but let's first think about, as George Will puts it, "the law of unintended consequences." If baseball makes a radical change in the game—even for all the right reasons—might that change have an unintended consequence that could hurt the game? This is a question that should be asked and even studied. The more dialogue there is about change, the better the chance of that change, if undertaken, truly being in the game's long-term best interest.

Now, we purists have traditionally left the owning of major-league franchises in the usual hands, those of brewing companies, media conglomerates, and affluent attorneys. But outside the boardrooms and the owners' suites at the ballparks, there's a lot of baseball wisdom floating around—and I'm not referring to the pearls of a certain baseball broadcaster. Every baseball fan has about six ideas he or she is dying to share; no owner has a shortage of fans telling him what to do. So when big changes are being considered, instead of hunkering down into a siege mentality, the owners ought to consider the implications of those moves a little more carefully. And they ought to get away from the box seats sometimes and talk to the fans in the cheap seats—and not just by commissioning a poll.

I've been going to major-league parks since my dad took me to my first game at Candlestick Park in 1962. Almost four decades later, I still remember the winning pitcher (Billy O'Dell), who hit the home runs (Willie Mays, Felipe Alou, and Jim Davenport), and the game's totals:

LA 8-15-3
SF 19-12-1
Att: 32,819

Yep, it made a big impression.

I'm as much of a fan of baseball now as I was then, only now I don't have to ask my mom and dad for a ride to the park. The game itself has always fascinated me: The strategy, the statistics, the pennant races. Always the pennant races.

But the best part of any trip to the ballpark is the people you meet. In this book, I'll share stories about some of my favorites. You'll find a chapter on some of the most memorable people I've met in baseball, including some whose reputations aren't that good. There's a chapter about my eight years with *ESPN Sunday Night Baseball* and my travels with colleague and friend Joe Morgan. If it gets past the publisher's lawyers, you'll even find out which owner brilliantly assembled three world-championship teams but blew his stack if the front-office phone bill exceeded thirty bucks.

There are some serious subjects, too. Early in this project, I decided I wanted to tell for the record the real story of how I came to be the radio/TV voice of the San Francisco Giants after fourteen wonderful years with the Baltimore Orioles. I'll also offer my opinion on interleague play and radical realignment.

It's very difficult to write a book on these subjects without mentioning the executive director of the players' union, the general counsel of the umpires' association, and the owner of the Chicago White Sox. But you won't find their names mentioned here. I've omitted them intentionally, because I've noticed that these names are an instant turnoff for baseball fans. And, hey, you're a baseball fan, one that I hope will recommend this book to other like-minded fans and maybe even a baseball purist or two.

Thank you very much.

In fact, this book should be mandatory reading for all baseball owners and executives . . . and players, coaches, and broadcasters . . . and all fans and . . .

Sorry. I guess I've had to read too many ticket promos over the years. You know, "Say, fans, plenty of copies of my new book are still available—low, ball one—be sure and pick one up soon. And don't forget—swing and a foul back to the screen—my book makes a great gift item, be sure to pick one up for all your friends—low, outside, ball two—and their relatives."

But now let's get back to the action.

Mr. Selig might be surprised to hear this, but I like interleague play. I really do. Revoke my purist's membership card! Report me to the central committee! But I think the concept has real potential.

The best thing about interleague play is evident when it accentuates intracity and other geographic rivalries, for these matchups excite the fans. I love that. Interleague play instantly gave us some very powerful rivalries: the Cubs and White Sox, the A's and Giants, the Dodgers and Angels, and the Yankees and Mets.

Although I wasn't there, I'd bet that the most exciting interleague games were the matchups between the two New York teams. For a lot of fans, those games must have brought back memories of the Giants and Dodgers, battling in an all–New York scenario. Yankee Stadium was sold out for all three midweek games—an interleague record of 168,719 for a three-game series ("you could look it up!"). The joint was rocking, just as it had been the previous October when the Yankees won the World Series.

Purist though you know I am, I took great delight in broadcasting the *first* interleague game. In my capacity as voice of the San Francisco Giants, I was at the microphone on June 12, 1997, when the Giants met the Texas Rangers in Arlington, Texas.

A sellout crowd of 46,507 filled The Ballpark; an October electricity coursed through the stadium. Though it was an early summer game, it had all the trappings of a seventh game of the World Series, from the red, white, and blue bunting festooning the ballpark to the players lining up along their respective foul lines as the teams were introduced during pregame ceremonies.

So much about that night was special. For me, it was a thrill to watch Barry Bonds, a major star in the National League, introduced in an American League ballpark where the fans never had seen him in a regular season game. (Bonds had played in Arlington once before, in the 1995 All-Star Game.)

In the same vein, it was fun seeing the former Giant star Will Clark introduced to a lusty ovation as he trotted out to the foul line to do battle against his former team for the first time.

Even the first-ball ceremony was memorable: Former Ranger great Nolan Ryan was introduced to a huge roar, and another all-time great—and former Giant—Willie Mays was brought out to just as loud a cheer. It was goose-bump time!

The game proved to be a beauty, which only contributed to the excitement. The Giants put together a dramatic three-run seventh-inning rally to overcome a 3-1 deficit and post a 4-3 victory for the first interleague win in the 115-year history of the Giants franchise—or any other franchise's history. (For the record, veteran Mark Gardner got the win and Rod Beck, with a perfect ninth inning, saved it. Stan Javier hit the first interleague home run.)

Of course, many of the highlights that night were ceremonial, which is something baseball should remember if it thinks interleague play is some kind of magic bullet. There was a novelty to playing this kind of game for the first time—and that novelty no longer exists. In 1998, you could invite Willie McCovey and Jeff Burroughs to throw out the first pitches, but once the game begins, for the most part, it will be just a game between two teams with no natural rivalry or special reason for playing each other.

Even the first year of interleague play wasn't all pomp and ceremony. Sometimes it was more like confusion and disarray.

The most blatant misstep was the flubbing-up of the major-league schedule, a prime example of the owners falling in love with the concept of interleague play without attending to the details. It provides a beautiful illustration of the revenge of unintended consequences.

As the owners envisioned interleague play, each team would play fifteen or sixteen interleague games every year. The rest of the games on the 162-game schedule would continue to be played against opponents from within each team's league.

Apparently no one thought about how to make room on the schedule for the interleague games. Unless the major leagues were going to play a 177-game season, 15 or 16 games versus same-league opponents would have to be removed from the existing schedule.

As much as the owners wanted the glitz of interleague play, many balked at sacrificing the attraction of lucrative home dates against top draws in their own leagues, teams like the Yankees and Dodgers that helped fill up their ballparks. So a compromise was reached, to the ultimate satisfaction of no one: Clubs in both the National League West and American League West divisions had eight two-game interleague series crammed into their schedules. In the four other divisions, teams added five three-game interleague series.

And, bowing to the pressure of some owners, no series were actually removed from the schedule. To make room for the new games, the owners instead lopped off a game here and a game there from what had been three- and four-game sets.

This decision turned out to have major, and unforeseen, implications. For the players, the exponential rise in the number of two-game series meant more overnight flights, more five A.M. arrivals, and more afternoons spent trying to catch up on lost sleep. For the players, 1997 was the Year of the Yawn. The Giants went from five two-game series in 1996 to twenty-six of them in 1997.

Traditional weekend series were also sometimes disrupted. Instead of the old Friday-night-to-Sunday-afternoon format, some series began on a Saturday and ended Monday night. The players really winced about that one, because now they were forced to travel overnight on Monday instead of having a leisurely getaway on Sunday afternoon.

Mr. Selig, it seemed, was as concerned as anybody about these travel problems. Before the 1997 season was over, he and a few other baseball executives had a new plan to address the scheduling snafus and take baseball, they said, into the twenty-first century. Their plan was characterized as "radical realignment"—as indeed it was.

Under this plan, travel burdens would be greatly eased. To accomplish that, however, they would nuke the two leagues and reorganize them along strict geographic lines. The new National League envisioned by Mr. Selig and his allies would be a Chicago-and-points-west league, while the new American League would be the eastern-time-zone league.

Compared to this, interleague play looked like kids' stuff. Radical realignment took your breath away.

You're telling me that we're going to blow up the American and National Leagues as they've existed since 1901 and start over with as many as fifteen teams switching league affiliations? This, in turn, would mean that in reality, all thirty teams would be in a league unlike any they'd played in before.

Radical enough yet?

And after that, we'd still have interleague play!

This truly made no sense. Let's think it through for a minute: The owners are pleased with the promotional lift they got from interleague play, those games that were special because of the crossing of the traditional lines of demarcation between AL and NL. And so, like a kid who wants every day to be like Christmas, they want to obliterate the two leagues, change the entire organization of the game, and in so doing *destroy the exact thing that made those games special.* An interleague game in this setup would be as meaningless from a promotional standpoint as an interconference game is in pro basketball or football. The whole idea wouldn't merely kill the goose that had just laid the owners a golden egg; it would spend a lot of energy driving down the value of that gold, too.

It didn't take a purist like me to realize this structure would see the Giants playing interleague games against teams like the Phillies, Reds, and Braves—teams they've been playing throughout their entire history. Or imagine being in Chicago, with the White Sox trying to drum up excitement about a big interleague showdown with . . . the Cleveland Indians! What a novelty, eh?

Geographical realignment is an intriguing idea. It has merits, but the plan before the owners in 1997 obviously wasn't the right one. The owners overwhelmingly voted it down and instead approved a smaller-scaled version, which moved just one franchise—Bud Selig's own Milwaukee Brewers—from the American to the National League.

But before I leave this subject, I'd like to make one more point: When supporters of realignment make the argument that a bold step is needed to reinvigorate interest in baseball, they make it sound as if baseball is dying. *It's not.*

Leonard Koppett, a respected sports columnist enshrined in the writers' wing of the Baseball Hall of Fame, has written, forcefully and repeatedly, that the decline of baseball is a myth.

Want to measure that by attendance? Well, paid attendance per game in 1997 was the second-highest ever for a full season—exceeded only by 1993—in the history of Major League Baseball. Koppett also points out that attendance—on an average, per-team basis—at major-league games is 50 percent higher than it was just twenty years ago.

Overall, according to Koppett, the sport's revenues have mushroomed from $200 million twenty-five years ago to *$2 billion* in 1997. So the problem, says Koppett, is not that too little revenue is being generated—far from it. Baseball is producing incredible revenues.

The problem is how the owners share those revenues with one another and how they divvy them up with the players. Thus, says Koppett, any plan that doesn't address these two central problems misses the point.

Baseball would be wise to put aside the radical proposals for a few years so it can see how the changes already in place fare with its fans over time. Interleague play had a very good rookie season, in my mind, but we don't know, and won't know for several years, whether those games will be just as appealing to fans when the novelty wears off. Will the atmosphere be super-charged for this season's Giants-Rangers games at The Ball-park? Or will it be just another series on the schedule? We may learn much about the ultimate viability of the concept during the 1998 season.

I'm confident that some interleague games will remain big attractions, and the ones I'm betting on are the games between natural rivals. Of course, the annual matchups between the Yankees and Mets or Cubs and White Sox should always be big with the fans. There could also be a rivalry evolving between two teams from bordering states, the Cleveland Indians and Pittsburgh Pirates. On Labor Day, 1997, the Pirates and Indi-ans drew a rollicking crowd of 45,298 at Three Rivers Stadium in Pittsburgh. I didn't realize how good that was until I learned that two years ago on Labor Day, the Pirates had hosted the Colorado Rockies in front of a meager gathering of only 9,513. (Much of that increase may have come from nearby Indians fans buying up tickets to Three Rivers after getting shut out when Jacobs Field sold out for the season, but that fact alone could lead to a great promotional opportunity in Pittsburgh—"Hey, Bucs fans! Are you gonna let those Clevelanders overrun our stadium?"—and a rivalry's got to start somewhere.)

For us purists, there's nothing better than a great baseball game between two true rivals. Whether they're rivals for geo-graphic reasons or historical ones, or maybe just some recent bad blood, those games where everyone cares just a little bit more give us the best of what baseball has to offer.

On September 18, 1997, a beautiful sunshiny day in San Francisco, the Giants and the Dodgers, two ancient rivals, took the field at 3Com Park at Candlestick Point.

With ten games left in the schedule, the Dodgers had a one-game lead over the Giants. The night before, in front of 56,625 fans, the Giants had escaped a desperate situation for a thrilling 2-1 victory. It was great baseball theater, and the kind of game that draws everyone to the sport.

On this day, these two teams made "thrilling" seem much too tame a description. The Giants, having blown a 5-1 lead, had been taken to extra innings by the first-place Dodgers.

Rod Beck, the Giants' ace closer who recently had fallen upon hard times, took the mound for the tenth inning. He promptly allowed three consecutive singles to load the bases with nobody out.

The crowd of more than 52,000 was in an uproar. Thousands of fans implored Giants manager Dusty Baker to remove Beck before it was too late. Thousands more were angry with Baker for having brought Beck in in the first place. And still others were urging Beck to just shoot himself and take the decision away from Baker.

As Dusty Baker headed to the mound to talk to his veteran righthander, the stadium was a cacophony of angry sounds. Once on the mound, Baker told the beleaguered Beck that he had complete confidence in him. Forget about everything; just focus on getting the job done—which, Dusty reminded him, Beck had done so many times before.

With the problems he'd been experiencing, and now this terrible situation in front of him—his own fans, his own crowd turned against him—it was just the kind of pep talk Beck needed.

With many in the huge crowd having almost lost the ability for rational thought, so delirious were they with fear of impending doom for the upstart Giants, the Dodgers' Todd Zeile stepped into the batter's box. But Beck, after Baker's visit, was a new man. Throwing a combination of fastballs and split-fingered pitches, he got Zeile to outguess himself, and froze him on a knee-high fastball for a called third strike.

As one, the 52,000 roared in approval, as if Beck had been their choice all along. Right on, Rodney!

Then another worry: the great future–Hall of Famer Eddie Murray came off the bench to pinch-hit for the pitcher. Murray was not only one of the great RBI men of his era, but had a lifetime batting average of better than .400 with the bases loaded. In the booth, I was especially nervous for Beck, because in my years in Baltimore I had seen Murray deliver in spots just like this many times before.

As he had with Zeile at the plate, Dusty Baker ordered his infield pulled in all the way around. Beck again made a brilliant pitch, throwing Murray a split-fingered fastball that Murray got on top of and chopped to Jeff Kent at second. Kent threw home to force out Mike Piazza coming in from third, and catcher Brian Johnson fired over to first—TWO! A double play! Incredible.

Against all odds, the Dodgers had been kept off the board. The exultant roar that emanated from Candlestick has been seldom heard in any ballpark, in any game. But who could be surprised by that? After all, it was the Giants and the Dodgers.

It didn't seem possible then, but the roar grew even louder in the twelfth inning when Johnson, who had been acquired by the Giants' canny young general manager, Brian Sabean, got only the third Giant hit of the game's final seven innings, hitting the first pitch of the bottom of the twelfth into a strong wind in left field for an unforgettable game-winning home run.

The Giants won a fabulous game, a game whose great moments will be talked about for many years.

As the Dodgers' Eric Karros said later when the Giants proceeded to roll to the division title, both teams' seasons seemed to turn around with the bases loaded and nobody out in that tenth inning. The Dodgers were never the same after that.

It was another bit of lore to be carefully written and then placed into that rather large, gilded book of exquisite and breathtaking moments that we've come to recognize as being uniquely "The Giants and the Dodgers."

The two teams hadn't been thrown together by radical realignment; nothing whatsoever had to be done except for these two to play the games that had been scheduled against each other for more than 100 years. You can't manufacture that kind of history, and you tinker with it at your own risk.

Yes, there's something to be said for accentuating rivalries, whether their origins are geographical or historical. So, instead of radically altering the two leagues for geographical purposes, let's start by giving the fans more of the great rivalries that already exist. More games between the Giants and Dodgers, the Yankees and Red Sox, and the Cardinals and Cubs. Until the 1993 expansion, the Giants played the Dodgers eighteen times a season. Last year, they met twelve times. These teams should be playing more often, as they used to.

And I'll go a step further.

In October 1997, with the first season of interleague play in the books, Mr. Selig predicted that eventually, geographical realignment would have to occur. His point was that under the current system, you can't have it all. An acceptable number of interleague games plus all the series against all the teams in your own league is impossible.

But under the current system, a percentage of interleague series are wasted dates, as far as I can tell. Detroit at Montreal generated no interest in Montreal in 1997. Cincinnati at Minnesota proved to be anything but compelling—attendance of 43,078 for the three-game series was the lowest of interleague play.

I say, why not try a different form of interleague play, one that would showcase the games the fans want the most and at the same time help reduce those scheduling problems?

My concept: natural-rivalry interleague play. Under my plan, each team would have a "natural rival" in the other league, and that would be the only team it would meet in interleague play. This could be in the form of two three-game sets, one apiece in the home city of each team.

If you sit down and try to come up with a workable scheduling format, you understand why Mr. Selig is proposing radical realignment; with sixteen teams in one league and fourteen in the other, there's no way to schedule any all-interleague periods without having two teams sit and watch. Even in my natural rivalry-proposal, the idea comes more easily than does the implementation.

Nevertheless there are a good number of obvious geographical natural-rival matchups right now: Yankees–Mets, White Sox–Cubs, A's–Giants, Angels–Dodgers, Rangers–Astros, Royals–Cardinals, Orioles–Phillies, Indians–Pirates, Blue Jays–Expos, Devil Rays–Marlins, and maybe even Red Sox–Braves. (The geography doesn't always work out perfectly, though the history in the last case is a fine substitute.) The rest, which isn't ideal, could go Tigers–Reds, Twins–Brewers (Mr. Selig forced this one on us), and Mariners–Rockies. But that leaves us with the Padres and the Diamondbacks each without an interleague series—ah, there's the rub. For the natural-rivalry concept to work, four National League teams would have to play only one three-game interleague series, and two American League teams would play one three-game series against each of two different National League clubs.

Granted, natural-rivalry play creates some scheduling disparities. The Mets would play the Yankees six times; the Marlins, playing in the same division as the Mets, would have it easier, for a while at least, matching up in interleague play with the expansion Devil Rays.

But that's okay; the 1997 interleague schedule wasn't perfectly balanced either. Teams in the same division played common interleague opponents, but while the Orioles played all three of their games with the Braves in Atlanta in 1997, the Yankees had their three at home. That type of home–road disparity is even more pronounced on the 1998 schedule, extending to matchups of teams in the same league.

The natural-rivalry concept allows room for an increase in important intradivisional matchups, giving fans what they really want: games that mean something in a pennant race.

And interleague play remains in the mix, too. (The concept would allow each team in the NL West to play its intra-divisional rivals seventeen times. In the AL West, teams would meet teams within their division eighteen times. If you really want more details, see me at the ballpark.)

If you ask most purists, you'll find that, in fact, they don't think every aspect of the game should be set in concrete. What they want is change that makes sense and that recognizes and enhances the game's virtues rather than just grafting something on because it has worked somewhere else.

For example, the question of the pace of baseball games has been talked about for decades. Well, let's pick up the pace of games.

Baseball already has a twenty-second pitch rule, one that in theory requires the pitcher to deliver a ball to the plate at regular intervals. The rule is almost never enforced by the umpires, and I totally understand why: who wants to stand in front of 56,000 fans arguing whether the elapsed time really was twenty-one seconds or nineteen?

I say, take the matter out of the umpires' hands. Post a clock in every major-league ballpark, NFL-style. If the clock runs down before the pitcher releases the pitch, he's penalized—a ball is added to the batter's count. At the same time, make the batter stay in the box; if the pitcher throws within the twenty seconds, make the pitch count whether the batter is there or not.

The present twenty-second rule isn't in effect with runners on base, and I see no reason to change that. There are legitimate reasons for pitchers to be more deliberate with runners on base. Besides, I'm not trying to ruin anybody's pickoff move.

Baseball also needs to get tough on the matter of meetings—unscheduled, impromptu, whenever-you-feel-like-it meetings. You know what I mean: The third-base coach who jogs halfway to home plate to whisper instructions into the batter's ear. The catcher who is constantly trotting out to the mound. It's an annoyance to the fans, and it's not necessary.

In the NBA, the point guard calls the play and the other players are supposed to know what he means. In fact, plays are constantly being called on the move. The rule book should require baseball players to do the same.

We can't prevent a catcher from going to the mound, nor should we. But we can limit the number of visits per game by issuing time-outs, like they do in the NBA and, for that matter, the NFL. Stop the game, use a time-out. Stop the game again, use another time-out.

I'm not sure how many time-outs each team would receive. Four sounds about right. Maybe three is enough. Hey, I'm open to suggestion.

The time-out system not only would improve the tempo of games, but it would also add a new layer of managerial strategy. A smart manager would want to conserve most of his time-outs for the late innings, in case he needed to call a mound conference in the eighth or ninth inning. If he has none, he's out of luck. Next time, maybe he would use his time-outs more judiciously. Also, the catcher may feel he has to go talk to his pitcher in a crucial spot in the game. Fine, call a time-out and go chat—but make sure you still have one to use later.

Nothing I've suggested here changes the game itself. The game is great. The game is the reason we're all at the ballpark or listening on the radio. All I'm saying is, no one comes to the park to watch the catcher and the pitcher confer. Those are baseball moments we could do without.

Hey, Mr. Selig—not bad for a purist, eh?

Life
WITH CAL

People who know I spent fourteen years watching Cal Ripken often ask me whether there is a key, a secret to his consecutive-game streak. I think they expect to hear that Cal is physically indestructible—like a rock, as they say on Cal's Chevy commercials.

That's true, to a point. Cal seems to suffer fewer colds, fewer hamstring pulls, fewer broken bones—fewer of just about everything that keeps other players out of the lineup.

If physical prowess is a key, though, I've always thought *the* key to Cal's streak is his love of competition. Cal is the most competitive person I know, in everything he does, everywhere he goes. On the field, in the clubhouse, even on the Orioles' charter flights.

I learned this one day while flying over Utah.

In 1984, I accompanied the Orioles on a cross-country flight from Baltimore to, if memory serves, Anaheim. It's a five-hour trip, which is just time enough to eat a three-course meal and squeeze in a feature-length motion picture—with two hours to spare.

To kill time, players often travel with diversions of one sort or another—stereo headphones, playing cards, games. (Though I never saw an Etch A Sketch.)

In 1984, veteran slugger Ken Singleton's game of choice was

Trivial Pursuit. Singleton and I took on all comers, retiring as undefeated champs. The only real competition came from a couple of other Orioles whose minds, like ours, were overloaded with useless junk, pitchers Mike Boddicker and Mike Flanagan. We played for a couple of hours, until everyone was sick of it. Then we went looking for something else to pass the time.

That's when I reached under my seat for the ultimate time-killer-in-a-box: Strat-O-Matic Baseball.

In the first game, a Singleton-managed team met a club skippered by Flanagan. I don't remember which team won. I do recall that Wayne Gross, the O's third baseman of the hour, walked by and posed a pretty good question.

"This game is supposed to be pretty accurate, right?" he asked. "What if I'm facing Bob Stanley? In real life, I wear this guy out—four-forty lifetime batting average. If he's pitching against me in this game, do I wear him out?"

Be real, Wayne, I advised. This is a board game, not a reenactment of the next trip into Fenway.

"Then it's a horse[bleep] game," Wayne announced, and walked away.

Cal approached next. When he found out what we were doing, he immediately wanted in. He chose a club to manage, the Orioles, and Flanagan as his pitching coach.

Me? I'm not stupid. I picked the Tigers, the hottest team in the majors that year. I was directing a cardboard powerhouse.

I started a righthander who allowed Cal's Orioles to go ahead early in the game, then I brought in a lefty, Willie Hernandez, for the middle innings. Cal responded with a string of pinch hitters even though it was early, about the fourth inning. He pinch-hit Dan Ford for Jim Dwyer, Gary Roenicke for John Lowenstein, Rick Dempsey for Joe Nolan, John Shelby for Al Bumbry, and Floyd Rayford for our disgruntled friend Wayne Gross.

It cost Cal. Late in the game, my Tigers pushed ahead, and I went to the bullpen for my ace right-handed stopper, Aurelio Lopez. Thanks to his quick trigger, Cal was caught with a batting order filled with right-handed swingers; the only bats remaining on the bench were Benny Ayala and Lenn Sakata, and they were right-handed hitters, too.

After the game, I reached for the ballpoint pen I'd been using to keep the scorecard. Grasping it like a microphone, I said in my best Howard Cosell cadence:

"The Ore-e-oles lost this gay-mah because manager Calvin E. Ripken made some ill-advised moves in the middle innings and used up his bench. . . . Ladies and gentlemen, in the waning moments of the game, Manager Ripken had absolutely no one to whom he could go."

Cal was perturbed. He was upset about losing a meaningless Strat-O-Matic game he'd never in his life even heard of until then.

But Cal wasn't angry with me. Cal was upset with Cal.

Politely, he asked if he might borrow the score sheet. I handed it over. Then Cal made his way to the back of the plane, where his dad was sitting. (Cal Sr. was the Orioles' third-base coach at the time.)

For the next fifteen minutes, the Ripkens sat in row 36 reviewing the score sheet together. From Row 9, I couldn't hear them, though glancing over my shoulder, I could see Cal Jr. pointing and Cal Sr. gesturing. Whatever they were doing, I know it was very serious; I say that because I noticed Cal Sr. putting on his eyeglasses. Cal Sr. only dons his eyeglasses when matters are very serious.

Meanwhile, up in Row 9, the mood was jubilant. I celebrated my momentous victory by leafing through the in-flight magazine and treating myself to a bag of cocktail peanuts.

In a while, Cal returned, score sheet in hand. He looked me straight in the eye and he said, "I know what I did wrong. Let's play again."

It was more than an invitation and less than an order. Anyway, we played again—and this time, Cal's Orioles won. You better believe they won (and with flawless managing!).

My dominant memories of Cal aren't what you might expect—the great defensive plays or the clutch hits, though Lord knows there have been plenty. For me, the purest Cal moments are the ones that reflect his competitiveness, his drive.

For years, Cal never missed infield practice or batting practice. In late July, the Orioles would be on their swing through Kansas City and Texas; the nights were hot and humid, and just standing on the field was enough to sap your strength. At various times in their tenures, Oriole managers Frank Robinson and Johnny Oates urged Cal to skip batting practice on those nights. "Conserve your strength. Relax a bit, get dressed in the clubhouse, and then play ball."

Cal flat-out refused. To him, this was ridiculous. Not only did he take batting practice and participate in infield practice, he'd horse around with teammates and run all over the field shagging fly balls.

He drove a lot of Orioles managers nuts.

Finally, in 1991, at age thirty-one, Cal agreed to skip an occasional BP and infield. Even then, he felt squeamish about it—on those days, he'd studiously avoid Cal Sr., knowing his dad didn't approve of such slacking off.

Were it not for Cal's competitive fire, we wouldn't be talking about the streak. I'm pretty sure of that. But eclipsing Lou Gehrig required more. That's where Cal's physical toughness comes in.

As tough as he is, and he is amazingly tough, I'm not sure Cal is even the most durable member of the Ripken family. In that department, I'd have to give the nod to Cal Sr. Talk about indestructible—Cal Sr. may be the toughest man alive.

I've seen Senior do things Junior wouldn't even dream of . . . that Evel Knievel wouldn't dare try. Once I saw him play catch with only his bare hands and a block of wood. I'm not kidding: Senior used his right hand to trap the baseball against the block in his left. This went on for fifteen minutes. *Thwack . . . thwack . . . thwack.* I wasn't sure what the point was, but it impressed the heck out of me.

Cal is blessed with his dad's resistance to pain, and with some pretty amazing recuperative powers of his own. Countless times over the fourteen seasons I spent with the Orioles, I'd watch Cal pound a foul tip off his ankle or foot. After such blows, most players would walk around with a big purple welt for a month. Not Cal. The next day, Cal wouldn't have a mark.

For several years, Cal was part of a well-publicized brother act on the Orioles. His kid brother Bill, a fine major leaguer in his own right, played a sparkling second base for Baltimore back in the late 1980s and early '90s before departing for the Texas Rangers.

When Bill left the club, this raised an interesting question for me, and when I saw Billy in Florida the following spring, I put it to him.

I set up a hypothetical situation in which Billy was a baserunner headed for second to break up a double play. In my hypothetical, the infielder he'd be bearing down on would be Cal.

"What about it?" Bill asked.

"Given the streak and all that, would you go into him hard, even though you might injure him?"

Bill didn't flinch. "Are you kidding?" Bill shouted. "I'm counting on it happening! My whole life I've been waiting for the chance to come in hard and knock him right out to left field."

"Why?" I wondered. "I don't get it."

Bill pointed to a little scar on the left side of his face, near his ear. "See that scar? Cal gave me that scar."

It seems that when he and Cal were little kids, Cal invented a game called "Sack the Quarterback." According to the rules of the game, Bill was always the quarterback and Cal was always the rushing defensive lineman trying to sack him.

There were no other players in the game.

Play after play, Bill would pick up the football and try, unsuccessfully, to avoid getting sacked by Cal.

The only way for Sack the Quarterback to end was for Bill, who was four years younger, about a foot shorter, and forty pounds lighter than Cal at the time, to get totally pummeled, over and over again.

"So, yeah," Bill said. "Given a chance, I'd wipe him out."

In my years of streak watching, there really have been only two instances in which an injury seriously threatened to put Cal on the bench.

Both times Cal suffered leg injuries. But in each case, Cal had shaken off the pain in a matter of hours, and was in the Oriole lineup for the next game.

Perhaps the closest call occurred on June 6, 1993, when Mike Mussina plunked Mariner catcher Bill Haselman with an inside pitch. An ugly brawl that lasted nearly twenty minutes erupted. Benches cleared, punches flew, and near the pitcher's mound, a dozen players formed a pile of tangled knees and elbows. At the bottom of the pile was Cal, who suffered a severely twisted knee. That afternoon, he could barely walk. That night, he hardly slept.

The next night, Cal was back at short.

Eight years earlier, a busted pickoff play nearly ended the streak in its infancy. On April 10, 1985, with the Orioles in Baltimore against Texas, Mike Boddicker whirled and threw to Ripken as he swooped in to cover second. As he reached for the ball, a Ranger base runner slammed into Cal, who came away from the bag limping severely.

When the inning was over, Cal's ankle was so swollen that Ralph Salvon, the late Orioles trainer, wanted to send him to the hospital right then. Cal objected. Instead of engaging Cal in what surely would have been a losing argument, Ralph insisted that Cal prove he could walk without a limp. Cal did. Ralph then taped Cal's ankle heavily and let him stay in the game.

After the game, the ankle was swollen so badly that Cal was taken to a nearby hospital for tests. The injury was diagnosed as a severe sprain, and he was given strict orders to stay off the leg.

The next day was a scheduled off day for the Orioles, though the team did travel to Annapolis for an exhibition game against the Naval Academy baseball team. Cal listened to his doctor and stayed home on crutches; had the Orioles been scheduled to play that day, Cal wouldn't have been able to play.

The following day, April 12, when the Orioles went back to the regular schedule, Cal was in the lineup. He even got two hits, a single and a double. He also scored one run, drove in another, and handled three ground balls flawlessly as the Orioles beat Toronto, 7-2.

In Baltimore, Cal watchers have been debating for years whether an occasional day off for the Iron Man is a good idea. The discussion really heats up when Cal drops into one of his periodic batting slumps.

The popular wisdom goes that Cal slumps when he's fatigued, and that he's fatigued because he's playing every day. I've never bought that; Cal is a streaky hitter, prone to prolonged dry spells—but the world is full of streaky hitters, and fatigue is only one of hundreds of possible contributing factors.

There were years when Cal started out the season in a slump, stumbling out of the blocks batting only .200 five weeks into the season. That early in the season, fatigue surely wasn't a factor. I mean, Cal had just had five months of rest. In other words, slumps happen; the reasons are always mysterious and defy easy explanation. But for the Iron Man, any slump is followed inevitably by cries of "It's the streak! He's tired! He needs a day off!"

Cal often says that he views the streak in 162-game increments: Play 162, take five months off. Play another 162. Another five-month interlude. Look at it that way, Cal says, and it's hard to establish a link between his slumps and the streak.

Almost to a man, the baseball people I know consider the streak, and Cal, remarkable. When he was managing the Oakland A's, Tony LaRussa told me that the longer he was around baseball, the more he thought the streak was the most impressive feat he'd ever seen on a ballfield. Tony said the quality he most appreciated in a top player was the determination—the inner drive—to be in the lineup every single day.

"The top guys are the ones on your ballclub you're looking to win ballgames. And they're the ones teammates are looking to not only to win ballgames, but to set the standard for what's expected of everyone," Tony told me. "Now, here's Cal. You never have to ask, 'Is my key guy going to be able to play today?' He's in there, every day, against every pitcher, no matter how tough. Randy Johnson, Roger Clemens, whomever. There's never a question. What a luxury for a manager."

Cal's managers, from Earl Weaver to Frank Robinson to Johnny Oates, have echoed those sentiments. In so many words, most have said how much they appreciated having Cal in the lineup every day, because his was the one position they didn't have to worry about from March to October.

A notable exception was Davey Johnson.

Davey believes in utilizing his full roster—inserting a player in the late innings here, giving a seldom-used reserve a start there. It's Davey's way of keeping all twenty-five players on his roster prepared. At times, Davey's style and Cal's style clashed, with unfortunate consequences.

In 1996, the Orioles were carrying on their roster an inexperienced young infielder, Manny Alexander, whose natural position was shortstop. Given an opportunity, they thought Manny might be a very good shortstop in the big leagues, but because of the streak Davey could never get Alexander into the lineup at short.

The Orioles had offered Alexander in various trades, but there was never much interest because no one had really seen

Alexander play shortstop at the major-league level. Apparently, no one was willing to bet on the chance that he could.

In May, B.J. Surhoff, then playing third base for the Orioles, went on the disabled list. Davey went to Cal and, in a private conversation, broached the subject of Cal moving to third and inserting Alexander at shortstop—just for a couple of weeks, until Surhoff was healthy. Davey said he thought this would help the ballclub defensively at third base and give them a chance to get a look at Alexander at shortstop for a while.

Cal, who was getting ready for batting practice and the game that night, was reluctant. He felt he wasn't adequately prepared to play third base, not having played the position for many years.

"I'm not telling you I'm going to do it," Davey said to Cal. "I'm just asking you to think about it."

Cal agreed to give it some thought, and the two planned to talk about it again the next day.

Within an hour of the so-called private conversation, it seemed that everyone at Camden Yards knew about Davey's proposition. We used the story on the broadcast that night, after Davey told it to me.

After the game, Cal was surrounded at his locker by writers, all asking about his impending move to third base. Cal was astounded, still thinking the conversation had been private. "We had a private conversation, and we agreed we'd talk about it again tomorrow," Cal told the assembled media.

At which point Cal was depicted in the media as being unwilling to make a move the manager felt was best for the team. One *Baltimore Sun* columnist openly questioned whether Cal truly was a team player, or if that was all some sort of myth.

The irony was that Cal was never asked to move to third while Surhoff was out. Davey kept delaying the change until one day, with the Orioles in Seattle, he filled out a lineup card with Ripken at third base. *Bill* Ripken.

"You thought I meant . . . Cal?" Davey joked.

Davey explained that he only went public because he assumed reports of the meeting with Cal would become known anyway, leaks within baseball organizations being what they are. The only problem was that he'd neglected to tell Cal.

I know Davey respects what Cal accomplished in breaking Lou Gehrig's record. But after he was named manager for the 1996 season, his attitude toward the streak was pretty much that it has to end sooner or later, so why not sooner rather than later? To everyone around the club, Davey and his coaches made it known that the streak was something they intended to end, probably after the All-Star break in '96.

Even so, that left room for a run at still one more iron-man record, the "world record" of 2,215 consecutive games, set by the former star third baseman of the Hiroshima Carp, Sachio Kinugasa. Cal broke the record on June 14, 1996, at Kauffman Stadium in Kansas City with Kinugasa-san in attendance. Naturally, the scene was considerably different from the electricity that pulsed through Camden Yards on September 6, 1995, when Cal passed Gehrig. This game was not sold out, for one thing, although a larger-than-normal crowd of 28,502 did attend.

When the game became official after the fifth inning—meaning the true world record now belonged to Cal—they held a miniature version of the previous year's Baltimore observance. The Royals' fans gave Cal a very warm standing ovation, and as they cheered, Cal went to the box seats near the Orioles dugout, where he and Kinugasa shook hands and embraced. It was a memorable moment, the two iron men from different cultures sharing something special through the game of baseball.

Davey Johnson apparently was not all that moved. After the game he offered a wry comment: "Has anyone checked to make sure that all the records are accounted for now? There's no surprise record in the Italian league, is there?"

After that comment, I guess I'm surprised that Davey didn't end Cal's streak while he was managing the Orioles. But history tells us that the streak did not end after the All-Star break in 1996, nor at all. Through the 1997 season, the consecutive-game number was at 2,467!

If the streak is both a luxury and a dilemma for Ripken's managers, some of them have handled it better than others. On that score, I give the highest marks to Frank Robinson, the Orioles' manager from 1988 to 1991. With Frank around, there was never a question of who would make the determination on a daily basis of whether Cal would sit or play: that was Frank's job, and he never ducked it.

I know Cal appreciated Frank's decisiveness because he thanked Frank publicly—and profusely—in his recently published autobiography, *The Only Way I Know.*

When it comes to managing the streak, I give a lower grade to Johnny Oates, who managed Cal from 1991 through 1994. Once while Johnny was the Orioles' manager, he made a statement that there was no way he would or could stop Cal's streak. I don't recall Johnny's exact words, but they were something like "The only way Cal isn't in the lineup this year is if he comes to me and asks out. The streak is bigger than Johnny Oates and even bigger than the game itself!"

I know Johnny well and I like him, but to me, that was a terrible statement for a manager to make—and a very unfair burden to place on Cal's shoulders.

Johnny's comments probably reflected the fact of the matter. I understand that. And I sympathize with Johnny's position; any manager even thinking about taking Cal out risked being torn limb from limb by an angry mob.

But the point of the streak was Cal's goal of being dependable and ready to play every day. When Oates did some research showing that Gehrig, when hurt, had made token appearances in a few games, he told Cal that he'd like to do the same thing occasionally to keep the streak going but at the same time get Cal a little rest. Cal told Johnny he didn't want to keep the streak alive just for its own sake; if Oates thought he needed to sit, Cal said, just sit him and end the streak.

Throughout the streak, Cal has said time after time that he wanted to play every day, he hoped to play every day, and he expected to play every day—but, Cal added, ultimately the decision whether he played every day was up to the manager.

Johnny Oates was the manager of that ballclub. The manager makes out the lineup card and decides who plays and who doesn't. It's the manager's job to get the best production from his roster. I think the proper thing for Oates to have said would've been something like, "I want Cal to play every day as long as he's able to. If I think it's best for the ballclub for him to get some rest, I'll give him a day off."

It wouldn't have changed anything. He still would've let Cal play every day. It just would have eliminated the cop-out.

In 1995, as Cal inched closer to Gehrig's record, it seemed the whole world was watching the Orioles. The media attention was intense. *The Baltimore Sun* published a season-long series about the streak, with *Sun* reporter Brad Snyder devoting a weekly article to successive seasons of the streak. Elsewhere, newspapers in all the major-league cities kept daily track of the streak, and were filled with Ripken stories when the Orioles came to town.

The most curious article I can recall was one that appeared in no less a journal than *The New York Times*. Maybe Robert Lipsyte, the author and one of the country's most highly regarded sportswriters, was simply trying to be provocative. If that was the plan, it worked: Lipsyte wrote that before Cal reached Gehrig's record, he ought to sit out a game in deference to Gehrig.

The point of Lipsyte's article, as I recall, was that Gehrig was one of the all-time great players, whereas Cal was not as great a player. Therefore, Lipsyte argued, it would be a magnanimous gesture on Cal's part if he were to sit out a game in tribute to Gehrig.

The article caused quite a buzz for a day or two. But Cal very calmly and, I thought, rationally explained why his take on the streak—and how it should end—was very different from Lipsyte's.

"This whole thing was never about a record, tying or breaking one," he stated. "It was just about being reliable and professional, going out to play every day.

"If I intentionally stop shy of the record, it will mean that it—the streak—was the goal, when it was never about that. The way to truly pay tribute to Gehrig is to do what he would have done—keep playing."

Cal was exactly right about that. Gehrig didn't stop when he was about to pull even with the old record, Everett Scott's 1,307 consecutive games. I doubt the thought even crossed his mind, unless Lipsyte was writing for *The Times* back then.

Later, Gehrig's wife, Eleanor, suggested to her husband that he end the streak at 1,999 games, a number that would be remembered forever and, she guessed, never equaled. It was a nice thought, but Gehrig apparently wasn't impressed.

If Cal's wife, Kelly, ever lobbied Cal to quit the streak at a nice round number, we never heard about it.

One of the many things I admire about Cal is the way he's balanced the demands of baseball and family. September 6, 1995, is as good an example as any. The world well remembers Cal high-fiving his way around Camden Yards that evening, having finally, and emotionally, eclipsed Gehrig's record.

Fewer people know how Cal's September 6 began. It was Rachel Ripken's first day of kindergarten. And Daddy drove.

Kelly and Cal now have two children. Rachel is eight and a very poised young lady. Her little brother Ryan, a lefty, is three.

When Kelly was pregnant with Ryan, the Ripkens faced a family dilemma that not many people really focused on. Unlike Rachel, who was born in November, Ryan was due to arrive smack in the middle of the baseball season, in mid-July.

When the baby came, which would it be for Cal, shortstop or the delivery room?

In spring training that year, I bumped into Cal and Kelly going to the movies at a shopping mall in St. Petersburg, Florida. We talked about the baby, and what would happen if the Orioles were on the road when Kelly went into labor. Would Cal end the streak to be in the delivery room?

I thought of it as a movie love story. The superstar. The woman he loves. And the streak. It would be an incredibly romantic way to end the streak, I said to them. Imagine how they'd depict it in the movie version: The streak ends for love. There wouldn't be a dry eye in the house.

I even had a few ideas about the cast: Meg Ryan as Kelly. Nicolas Cage as Cal. (I couldn't decide on an actor for the film's key role, the debonair team broadcaster.)

Kelly warmed to the idea immediately, but Cal had a worry. "If I end the streak to be with Kelly at the birth," he mused, "wouldn't it be unfair to the baby?"

It was obvious Cal had analyzed the situation carefully.

"It's not easy being the child of a celebrity," he went on. "But what if you're the reason your dad didn't break Lou Gehrig's streak?"

And that was a good point, too. Just ask Pete Rose Jr. or Mike Yastrzemski, each the son of a living legend without the father's talents.

Baby Ryan arrived on July 26, 1993. And Cal took the day off . . . along with the rest of his teammates, as the Orioles weren't scheduled to play. Even the Lord wanted the streak to continue, it seemed—so Cal was spared the tough decision *and* was there for Ryan's birth.

Cal's streak can't go on forever. At thirty-seven, he'll be fortunate to have three, maybe four more seasons of good play. The question comes up: What's next for Cal Ripken? If he's interested, maybe broadcasting. Perhaps even politics. (How'd you like to run against him?) Cal has a skill essential for either profession: poise as a public speaker.

I wouldn't have said that fifteen years ago. Back then, Cal was anything but polished when he spoke in front of crowds. He was very shy, and the words that came out were halting and uncertain. Cal was very much on shaky ground.

But in typical Ripken fashion, he changed that. He worked on his delivery, his lines—and his nerves. I make a fair number of speeches at banquets, and Cal has been a head-table guest at many of them. Many's the time that he picked my brain for advice or inquired about the telling of a particular anecdote.

"I've heard you tell that story three or four times before, but tonight you told it differently," I remember him remarking at a banquet a few years ago. It wasn't the common postbanquet comment of "I've heard that story a thousand times but I always love the way you tell it." Cal was analyzing my delivery, trying to get inside my head. That's a trait of Cal Ripken: learning everything there is to know.

Nowadays, Cal is far more at ease speaking in front of crowds—not totally relaxed, but enough so that he's been able to deliver speeches smoothly in situations where it seemed the whole world was watching, like the night at Camden Yards when Gehrig's record fell. Cal delivered that speech like a pro.

Cal's transformation into the poised, confident public figure that fans see now really struck me as Cal was closing in on Gehrig's record.

One night after a game in Minnesota—totally unexpectedly—Cal popped out of the dugout. In his full uniform, he started signing autographs. Fans were stunned, but not so much so that they weren't eager for the chance to get something—a hat, a program, a scrap of paper—signed by him. The line snaked around and around the stands. Cal stood there for forty-five minutes, signing for everyone.

The Orioles went on to Kansas City. The scene repeated itself there. Then home to Camden Yards. Cal must have signed on two or three different nights after games in Baltimore. One night, he signed until after one in the morning—before stadium security stopped him, he must have signed two or three thousand autographs that time.

Those scenes were surreal. The games were over and the stadium lights dimmed, but thousands of fans remained in the park for the chance to spend a moment with Cal Ripken. It seemed like more than one person should be expected to handle.

One night, Cal decided not to sign. Thousands of people had already lined up and were waiting. A few got really angry, as if Cal had violated some promise to send them home with an autograph. It was sad: here Cal was, extending himself beyond what any other ballplayer had ever done, and there were actually a few people who thought that in addition to seeing the game, their tickets entitled them to shake hands with the record-breaking shortstop. It takes all kinds, I suppose.

I've always thought Cal would make a good manager, and I'll tell you why: The guy never tires of talking about baseball strategy, about moves a manager made, and, if they didn't work out, moves he should have made.

Cal isn't one to impose his views on you. He doesn't want to stand on a stage and lecture about it; that's not Cal's way. He'd prefer to have a discussion, one that he can win. Like I said, with Cal, everything is a competition.

The thing about Cal is, he's not going to pull rank. He knows who he is and what he's accomplished in the game, but you never feel he's lording that over you, that he's a know-it-all.

Cal's view is that baseball is a constant learning process. You play, you learn; you talk with knowledgeable people, you learn some more. But just because you've been playing the game all these years doesn't mean you know it all, or know even most of it. Earl Weaver also believed that, and he was one of the greatest managers who ever lived. In fact, the title of Weaver's autobiography is *It's What You Learn After You Know It All That Counts.*

Some of the most spirited baseball discussions I've ever seen have involved Cal Ripken. He loves the back-and-forth, the intellectual stimulation.

I remember one time when Cal challenged me about a play he'd seen on one of our *ESPN Sunday Night Baseball* telecasts. We had an exciting game in Seattle, an extra-inning thriller between the Yankees and Mariners.

We were deep in extra innings, into the last of the thirteenth inning. The Mariners had the potential winning run—in the form of Matt Sinatro, a journeyman backup catcher—on third with one out. The Yankees brought the infield and outfield in to try to choke off the run coming in.

The next hitter sent a bloop into shallow right. The Yankee right fielder, Jesse Barfield, came in, but had to play the ball on a hop. Or try to—the ball bounced off his chest and rolled a few feet away.

The game should have been over, and would have been, except that Sinatro had inexplicably gone back to third to tag up, and then belatedly headed home. Barfield, who had one of the great arms in the game, quickly retrieved the ball and fired a strike to the plate. Sinatro was out by ten feet.

We were all over Sinatro. Joe Morgan asserted in no uncertain terms that Sinatro had made a terrible mistake. With Barfield playing shallow, Joe explained, there's no reason to tag up, because if he catches the ball, you're not scoring anyway; the play is to come down the line toward the plate in case the ball isn't caught.

The next day, when I rejoined the Orioles in Anaheim, Cal grabbed me. He wanted to talk about Joe's criticism of Matt

Sinatro. "Joe's wrong when he says there's never a reason to tag on that play," Cal said. "What if the guy dives and catches the ball? He's rolling around on the turf. The fact that you tagged means you can score."

"But if the ball falls in front of the outfielder, you've got to score. Your scenario is the most unlikely of all the things that could happen on that play," I told Cal. "You've got to score if Barfield doesn't make the catch. Doesn't that seem like the key?"

This went on and on, with neither of us giving an inch. Finally, as we were headed out of the clubhouse, Cal spotted his dad—who'd taught two generations of young Orioles how to run the bases properly—and decided to put the question to him.

Cal Sr. didn't hesitate a moment.

"You always teach a player to go halfway on that ball," said Senior, who'd watched the game on television. "When I saw him go back to the base, I wanted to throw up."

Thanks, Senior. I couldn't have said it better myself.

You'd figure that that would have ended the discussion. All it did was start another discussion, this time between Cal and his father.

And that's really the point: Cal can put up a good fight, and he can be contrary, but for the most part, it's a game with Cal—and a way to learn. Take a position and be ready to defend it—like it used to be at Sunday dinner at the Kennedy compound in Hyannisport. It's too bad they don't give an award to baseball's best debater, because Cal would be in a league of his own.

He'd be a good manager, all right, but a reluctant one. Managers live the same nomadic existence as their players: hotels, airports, suitcases, and countless holidays away from home. Cal has lived that life for a long time. In his next life—at least in his current frame of mind—he'll be home in time to tuck the kids into bed at night.

I'm also guessing that at some point, the lure of the game will bring him back. And then, I think he'll become a great manager.

Since I left the Orioles after the 1996 season, the controversies swirling around Cal, injuries, and the streak haven't ended.

The latest occurred late in the 1997 season when Cal suffered from a herniated disk in his back. The pain apparently was affecting him at bat and limiting his range at third base, his new position for the 1997 season. He couldn't sit, so he knelt or stood leaning against the wall of the dugout.

Through it all Cal quietly played on, not disclosing his condition to the media. I can imagine what he was thinking: "If this gets out, I'll need a police escort to get past the writers camped out at my locker."

Eventually, word did get out. And Cal came in for some pointed criticism.

A few in the Baltimore media questioned whether Cal was keeping the streak alive at the expense of the team. They argued that the prudent course would be for him to take a few days off and allow his back to heal.

The debate gained momentum in the last weeks of the season, after the Orioles clinched a spot in the playoffs. At that point, the critics argued, Cal was playing in meaningless games, risking an injury that might keep him from playing in the most important games of all—the World Series.

Reasonable points—but points that begged a response not from Cal, but from Davey Johnson.

During the regular season, Davey said publicly that to keep his job, he believed the Orioles would have to go to the World Series. Anything less and Davey was gone. That was Davey's own assessment. (And in a sense it came true, but not exactly the way Davey expected.)

Yet despite the supposed risks, Davey continued writing Cal into the lineup right through game 162. It was the perfect opportunity for Davey to end the streak, if that's what he wanted. It would be all in the name of getting the Orioles to the World Series. Who could have argued?

But Cal started every regular-season game. Each time, it was Davey who wrote Cal's name on the lineup card. So maybe Davey wasn't *that* worried about Cal being fit for the World Series.

As for Cal, he never asked for a day off. His point was that a few days off wouldn't cure his back problems, but they might screw up his timing at the plate. He'd rather gut it out.

He made a pretty good point. In the postseason, he played every inning of all eleven Orioles games. And he played brilliantly.

Cal's postseason batting average? Just a team-leading .385.

The
GOOD OLD DAYS
ARE NOW

Twenty years from now, when baseball fans look back at the 1990s, they'll have a name for this era: they'll call it Baseball's Golden Age.

You heard me, the Golden Age.

I can hear them now. And I can hear the reverence in their voices.

"The problem with the game today is there's absolutely no hitting . . ."

"To win a batting crown in the nineties, you had to hit three-seventy. That's right, three-seventy! And if Tony Gwynn got in one of his grooves, three-eighty. Three-eighty!"

And . . .

"Power. In those days, we had some *real* sluggers in the game. In the nineties, Frank Thomas batted three-fifty and hit four-hundred-fifty-foot homers; Albert Belle hit ninety-eight home runs in two years—and still batted three-hundred; Mark McGwire hit fifty-two home runs one year and fifty-eight the next; Ken Griffey Jr. hit fifty-six home runs, batted three-oh-four, and robbed a guy of a home run every game! And I haven't even mentioned Alex Rodriguez, who had the best hitting year for a shortstop of all time!"

This is not a joke. These are transcripts of actual conversations that will take place in the year 2018.

Let's make a resolution. Let's start giving proper respect to baseball in the 1990s. It's as good as it has ever been, and maybe even better.

"Modern stars are healthier, bigger, and they receive better individual instruction."

Oh, yes. That quote, which I'm totally agreeing with, was uttered by Cincinnati Reds general manager Gabe Paul . . . in 1956!

There's no comparing the physical conditioning of players today and players of sixty years ago—or even thirty years ago. Today's players are bigger and stronger. Mostly stronger.

Peter Gammons, ESPN's fine baseball commentator, made an interesting point a year or two ago along these lines. In the 1920s and '30s, Jimmie Foxx was called "The Beast" because of his size and strength. According to *The Baseball Encyclopedia*, Foxx was six feet tall and 195 pounds. That's just about the same size as . . . José Offerman! Jim Leyritz! Randy Velarde! What a brute!

A few years back, Mark McGwire approached me before a game at the Oakland Coliseum. He'd heard my ESPN partner, Joe Morgan, ruminating about reasons why home-run production was on the rise. McGwire was mildly annoyed that Joe kept talking about juiced baseballs and watered-down pitching instead of giving credit to sluggers like him.

"Joe keeps talking about why there are so many home runs," Mark said. "Well, here's the answer."

With that, he held out his right arm and flexed it. I'll never forget that flex; his biceps muscle looked like a high-rise condominium—it was gigantic.

McGwire is a big believer in weight training. He lifts weights during the season as well as in the off-season, and his program is closely monitored to ensure that he maintains his flexibility as he builds muscle.

For Mark, and many of today's players, pumping iron is only part of the training drill. Hours before a game, they're down in the catacombs of the ballpark, pounding baseballs in the indoor batting cage. After a half hour, they disappear into the video room for another twenty minutes to study replays of their swings, looking for the smallest flaws.

That's during the season. In the off months, the routine hardly changes. Players still get their swings, in batting cages they've set up in their backyards or garages. A few even follow the cost-is-no-object example of Cal Ripken, who on his Maryland estate built a full-service gymnasium, complete with batting cage and regulation-size basketball court.

Thirty years ago, baseball was more a seasonal job. At least, the players saw it that way. Brooks Robinson once told me his one regret about his Hall of Fame career was that he didn't keep himself in shape during the off-season. Every winter, Brooks said, he'd put on ten or fifteen pounds, then spend most of spring training trying to shed the weight.

Now, trainers and conditioning coaches monitor players year-round. These health professionals are highly skilled; many have advanced degrees in specialties ranging from nutrition to physiology. Back in Brooksie's day, the main job of the trainer was to give a decent massage.

Stronger, better-conditioned players have forced adjustments throughout baseball. One of the most important is that pitchers have had to rethink the way they get hitters out.

Al Jackson, a fine pitching coach and, before that, a pitcher on the original expansion "Amazin'" Mets of '62, once told me about pitching in the horseshoelike Polo Grounds, home of the Mets for their first two seasons. No ballpark was as oddly shaped: 279 feet down the left-field line, 258 feet to right, and a cavernous 483 to dead center.

But in those days, Al said, everybody tried to pull the ball. So, to be successful at the Polo Grounds, a pitcher had to keep the ball away from the hitters to make them hit the ball straightaway, to the big part of the ballpark. The porches in left and right were so absurdly short, he said, that if a hitter pulled the ball he could get a really cheap home run—and send the pitcher to an early shower.

Today, Al went on, that style of pitching wouldn't work at the Polo Grounds. Nowadays, hitters lunge into the ball and take the outside pitch the other way instead of trying to pull it. Today's power hitters would take that outside pitch and flick it into the short porch in the opposite field at the Polo Grounds, he explained.

"Jon, you can't believe how much stronger these guys are than when I played," Al said.

I was happy to hear Al say that. Hey, I'm happy whenever I hear an old-timer say something complimentary about baseball players today; it doesn't happen often. Many ex-players are very stingy with their praise of current players, which is too bad—too bad for them because it tends to paint them as sour old men, but mostly, it's too bad for the game.

You may agree with the following assessment:

"The great trouble with baseball today is that most of the players are in the game for the money."

You've probably said those words yourself. It's a common lament about today's game and today's players. Except that this criticism was uttered by Ty Cobb—in 1925!

Baseball is damaged when ex-players, especially those who are still in the game as coaches, scouts, or broadcasters, deride the present-day players. I don't have any doubt about that. It's lousy public relations. It's confusing to fans. And as far as I'm concerned, it's unsupported by the facts.

If ex-ballplayers have some things they want to teach the younger guys, fine: Why don't they put the uniform on and come teach them? Base running. Bunting technique. All the lost arts that you hear the old-timers complaining about. But as for making vague, unsupported claims that today's players are unwilling to work, lacking in the fundamentals, and the rest of it, well, that's a bunch of baloney.

It's human nature for the generation on the way out to knock the generation on the way in. At a banquet in Nashville, Tennessee, in 1956, Gabe Paul felt the need to defend the game against the verbal assaults of old-timers such as Cobb.

In May 1952, Cobb penned an essay entitled "They Don't Play Baseball Anymore" for *Life* magazine. In Cobb's opinion, the game's decline was so severe that "There are only two players in the major leagues who can be mentioned in the same breath with the oldtime greats." He named Phil Rizzuto and Stan Musial. (No Ted Williams; no Joe D., who had just retired—not even those newcomers Willie, Mickey, and the Duke!) Cobb also wrote, "There are too many joke teams, like last year's Browns. In far too many games they fall behind by scores like 12-2 around the fourth or fifth inning . . ."

Paul, at that Nashville banquet in 1956, defended the current game—the game of the 1950s—by expressing a sentiment that could be voiced in any era. "You know what?" he said. "Around 1975 they'll be saying the players of that period aren't as good as they were in the fifties."

Come to think of it, in 1980, I was speaking with Clyde King, a highly respected scout then with the Yankees, and he unwittingly made a prophet of Gabe Paul. Clyde had been in the game forty years, and had pitched in the big leagues in the 1940s and '50s. It was clear that he was totally unimpressed with what he was seeing in the late 1970s and early '80s.

"I see a lot of games, Jon," Clyde told me. "And there isn't a night when I don't see five or six mistakes made at a minimum—it's awful!"

No doubt Cobb would have agreed with that assessment.

Cobb had been a symbol of the dead-ball era, when speed and "scientific hitting" dominated. When Babe Ruth ushered in a new era of home runs and offensive punch in the 1920s, the old-timers held their noses. They were baffled by the Babe.

"He isn't scientific at all," they brooded. "He just tries to hit it over everybody's head."

Yeah, it was so terrible that the fans loved it and came out in record numbers.

But then Cobb's predecessors of the 1890s thought that *he* was overrated, too.

It's like former ballplayer Bill Joyce once said: "Baseball today is not what it should be. It makes me weep to think of the *men* of the old days and the boys of today. It's positively a shame—and they are getting big money for it, too."

Bill Joyce said that in 1916.

In my line of work, I meet a lot of ex-players. And we talk a lot about how the game has changed over the years.

I love these guys. They're good people and, generally speaking, smart people. Many I consider friends. But on this subject, I've found that many have a blind spot—a huge one. The idea that the game today might be superior to the game they played makes them very, very uncomfortable.

In that category, I put one of my good friends: Joe Morgan.

Joe is entitled to his opinion, and any opinion Joe has, I pay attention to. There's nobody I've met who understands baseball as thoroughly as Joe Morgan.

But Joe's human. And Joe falls into the old-timer trap. His memories of the old days tend to be rosier than the reality of the old days. I'm forever finding things from Joe's era that weren't as great as he remembers.

It happens to all of us. We remember the great plays and the great players more than the ordinary plays and ordinary players. But, in Joe's case, there's another factor: loyalty. Joe is fiercely loyal to his ex-teammates and is the biggest booster for his former teams. If you run into Joe, please ask him to name the greatest team of all time. I have a good idea what he'll say, since he's said it to me countless times: the 1975–76 Cincinnati Reds.

Joe may be right; the Reds of the Big Red Machine era were an awesome offensive club, one any right-thinking person would agree belongs with the very best. Whether they *were* the best is beside the point. I think Joe's main point is to keep alive the memories of that team and the players on that team—Davey Concepcion, Tony Perez, Ken Griffey, Johnny Bench—that whole Reds lineup.

Joe should be a booster for the Big Red Machine. If Joe weren't waving the flag for his old buddies, who would?

But in 1976, when the idea of the Reds being baseball's greatest team was floated, there were outraged cries that the 1961 Yanks with Maris and Mantle or the 1927 Yanks with Ruth and Gehrig were far better. The '76 Reds weren't even in the same ballpark with those teams, it was said.

To me, it's a remarkable coincidence that the best teams are always the ones from twenty years ago. Win the World Series tomorrow, you're a footnote to history; win the World Series in 1965, and you're knocking on the door to immortality. Does this bother anybody else?

Back in 1985 or '86, the Orioles were playing the White Sox at old Comiskey Park in Chicago, and I got to talking baseball with Don Drysdale, the late, great Dodger pitcher. At the time, Don was broadcasting for the White Sox, a club that had been hit hard by injuries to key people. As a result, the night we were in town, the Sox were fielding a decidedly nondescript lineup.

Drysdale was put off by the whole thing: not just the weak starting eight, but by how this anemic lineup reflected the woeful state of the game in general. It was a recurring theme I'd been hearing since I was eight years old.

As usual, I couldn't stay out of the discussion. And, as usual, I stuck up for the current guys.

I reminded Drysdale of his own world-champion Dodgers of 1965. Was it not true, I asked, that the leading home-run hitters for the Dodgers that year—"Sweet" Lou Johnson and Jim Lefebvre—each had crashed a total of twelve big flies?

Wasn't it true that Willie Davis, the Dodgers' third-place hitter—the spot usually reserved for the team's best, most potent bat—had a batting average of .238?

And—I was on a roll now—wasn't it true that the Dodger with the highest slugging average during the vaunted '65 season was . . . Don Drysdale? At .508, his slugging average was the only one on the team above .400. With seven home runs to his credit, Drysdale should have been hitting cleanup on that team. (Actually, I didn't bring up this point with Don—I just looked it up. And I'm sad I can't bring it up to him now; he was a good man and I miss him.)

Finally, I asked Drysdale whether after the Dodgers won the World Series that year, many of the old-timers of the 1930s and '40s had cried out about how this proved that the current state of the game (in the sixties) was in the toilet? You know the quote: "Back in the old days, if you didn't hit three-hundred, you got sent out to the minor leagues. Look at these Dodgers today. Nobody knows how to hit the ball. It's a disgrace." Yet, just twenty years later, there was Don saying almost the same thing about a club in Chicago. Ah yes, the more things change, the more they remain the same.

For years, Joe Morgan and I have had a running disagreement about whether the ball is juiced. Joe believes it is. I don't know—and I don't especially care.

First, let's define our terms. A ball is said to be "juiced" if it's been changed somehow so that it has more resiliency and will travel further. Maybe the yarn under the cover is wrapped more tightly than it should be. Maybe the ball's cork center is bigger. Who knows? In theory, a juiced ball flies further than one that hasn't been fiddled with. That's good for hitters, and it's especially good for home-run hitters.

Joe's belief is based on the numbers: There are more home runs hit in the big leagues today than twenty years ago. Juiced baseballs are one way to explain it. But so is stronger hitters and smaller ballparks. So, probably, is better lighting, or maybe El Niño.

Why does an increase in home runs have to be explained? So home runs are up. Why does this indicate something's wrong? The fans love it.

The same complaints were heard in 1961 when Roger Maris hit sixty-one home runs, and in 1927 when Ruth hit sixty. Is there a trend here?

"There is no doubt at all in my mind that the old-time ballplayer was smarter than the modern ballplayer. Now the game is all power, lively balls, and shorter fences."

Such were the views of "Wahoo" Sam Crawford, a Hall of Fame outfielder, who offered that opinion in 1960. Seems the game hit the skids after Wahoo Sam hung up his spikes . . . in 1917.

On *Sunday Night Baseball,* it's usually a home run that draws Joe and me into one of our juiced-ball discussions. A light-hitting infielder with three career homers might suddenly pop one out; it might even be an awkward or an off-balance swing. The ball jumps off the bat, and it's gone.

Joe played in the big leagues for twenty-two years. He's in the Hall of Fame. A homer like that just doesn't sit right with him.

"Jon, could be that one was juiced," he'll say with a smile, knowing we're headed for the abyss of another debate on the subject.

I just don't see it his way. I think the hitter deserves credit. If the swing was off-balance, well, maybe he's strong enough to reach the seats with less-than-perfect form. As long as the ball meets the bat at the center of percussion—with sufficient bat speed—why shouldn't it be a home run?

Such questions go on and on. Once you start doubting home runs—which ones are legitimate and which aren't—it's difficult to stop.

Unconventional home-run swings aren't new. In the '71 All-Star Game, the great Roberto Clemente hit an opposite-field upper-deck home run at Tiger Stadium on a high, inside pitch that most hitters wouldn't even have gotten their bats on.

Clemente's homer came up during one of our Sunday night discussions. I asked Joe whether he thought the ball was juiced that night in Detroit, and he said no; he believes that Clemente was such a fabulous hitter that he was capable of hitting that ball out with that swing.

Fabulous hitter that he was, Clemente was listed at 5-11, 175 pounds, about the size of the lightest-hitting infielders today. (Just try to find an outfielder that small in today's game!) And, obviously, Clemente wasn't doing weights, ever. More evidence, perhaps, that it's not the ball that's juiced these days, it's the hitters.

The criticism I hear most often from old-timers is that the present-day players aren't as well schooled in the fundamentals as players from other eras. They'll point to outfielders who don't hit cutoffs, base runners who get poor leads, and pitchers who fall behind in the counts. I know Joe feels this way; it's a point he has made many times on *Sunday Night Baseball.*

I contend that today's ballplayers make no more mistakes than the players of Joe's era. And I'm constantly trying to come up with evidence to support my case.

In my memory, perhaps the most exciting game of the 1960s was the third game of the 1962 National League playoff between the Giants and Dodgers. Two of the best teams of the era, loaded with many of the best players: for the Giants, Willie Mays, Orlando Cepeda, Harvey Kuenn, Felipe Alou, and Juan Marichal; for the Dodgers, Maury Wills, Sandy Koufax, Don Drysdale, and Tommy and Willie Davis. I was just about to turn eleven years old when that game was played. My exact recollections of what was then a huge event in my life were sketchy, at best, though I remember a tense, well-played game. But I listened to an audio tape of the radio broadcast of the game recently, and I was surprised by what I heard thirty years later.

The game was tense enough, all right, but hardly well played. The Dodgers threw the ball all over the park. They booted ground balls, botched rundown plays, and missed cutoff men. In the third inning, the Dodgers made three errors—and could have been called for a fourth. They had two Giant runners hung up and didn't put out either one. And with all that help, the Giants scored . . . twice! That's right, all that help and only two runs.

The Giants' dramatic ninth-inning rally—they trailed 4-2 going into the inning—consisted of two hits (one an infield chop off the pitcher's glove), one error, one wild pitch, and four walks. The winning run scored on a bases-loaded walk.

Somebody had to win, and the Giants did. But it was a less-than-compelling advertisement for baseball in the sixties.

I couldn't wait to play the tape for Joe.

"You told me they didn't make those kinds of mistakes in the old days?" I chided. "Neither one sounds like a major-league team."

Joe wasn't moved.

"Just one game," I remember him saying with a smile.

I don't know if today's ballplayers make more mistakes or not. But I do believe that we're more aware of their mistakes than we ever were before. And for that, we can thank TV.

In the 1950s, very few games were on television, and next to none on network TV. When an outfielder threw to the wrong base, who knew? Only eight thousand spectators at the park witnessed it—or even knew about it. Today, that mistake would be shown on local TV at least, with two or three replays fully revealing the screwup. Then that same mistake would get replayed fifteen more times on *SportsCenter* and *Baseball Tonight*, local TV newscasts, and Cable News Network. Now, if you make an error, you're infamous in Samoa.

Baseball is the best arguing game. If you're passionate about baseball, you argue. It's not even optional. Everything is a potential argument in baseball. Were the seventies better than the nineties? Were the fifties as good as the seventies? Will there ever be a season as glorious as 1961?

Do football fans ever argue about the old days? Or even discuss them? I mean, who'd bother comparing the NFL of 1995 with the NFL of 1955? Every player at every position in the NFL today is seven inches taller and outweighs those old-timers by 100 pounds. They're not even playing the same game.

The difference in basketball is even more dramatic. Look at film of the NBA in the fifties—it's laughable. Two-handed set shots. Vertical leaps of a foot. It was slow, it was earthbound—it was basketball before the Wright brothers, before we learned to fly on Air Jordan.

But baseball retains much more of its old character. Basically, baseball hasn't changed; you can defensibly compare Ken Griffey Jr. to Mickey Mantle. You can compare their batting styles, you can compare them as center fielders. Their careers were almost thirty years apart, yet it's the same game, there's a real connection. But that connection, for all but the very best players, makes the differences in size, speed, and strength very apparent.

Some baseball arguments last a lifetime. I remember Larry King telling me about a dispute he has with his best friend, Herbie Cohen. Larry and Herbie have been friends since they were six years old—despite the fact that when they were growing up in Brooklyn, Larry was a Dodger fan, while Herbie rooted for the Yankees.

Since the 1950s, Larry and Herbie have been arguing who was the better center fielder, Mantle or Duke Snider. Now, Larry is the host of the most-watched talk show in the world, and Herbie is a best-selling author. It's fifty years later. And they're still arguing who's better, Snider or Mantle.

Reggie Jackson is one of the names that always seems to get a discussion going. When I was working for the A's in 1974, one of the coaches was a serious detractor of Reggie's.

"Reggie [bleep]ing Jackson!" he would say, spitting out the words. "What's so great about Reggie [bleep]ing Jackson? This guy wouldn't even have gotten an at-bat for the old Yankee teams.

"I mean, this guy is so overrated. He strikes out all the time. He doesn't hit his cutoff man. Reggie [bleep]ing Jackson my eye!"

I'm not mentioning this coach's name for two reasons. The first is that when he said these things to me, I doubt he expected to read them in a book twenty-four years later. The second is that the quotes don't hold up under the test of time. I mean, how overrated could you be if you hit 563 home runs and were so good in the clutch they named you "Mr. October"?

That coach was way out of line, but he wasn't the only one in the A's organization with doubts about Reggie. The big knock against him was that he wasn't committed to the game, that he didn't work hard enough on his skills.

When Reggie first came up, he had all the tools: great speed, tremendous range, and a powerful arm. A lot of people thought he was capable of being a Gold Glove outfielder. As it turned out, Reggie got progressively worse as an outfielder. By '74, many of his A's teammates were complaining privately that Reggie didn't care about playing the outfield and that he wasn't the world's most alert base runner.

Joe Rudi, the talented left fielder on those A's teams, could become exasperated by Reggie. In 1974, Rudi was having his best year in the big leagues—a season in which he'd go on to lead the league in doubles.

One night in Cleveland, Rudi was at bat with Reggie on first. Joe launched a deep fly ball over the head of the right fielder, a sure double—or so it seemed. But Reggie, for some inexplicable reason, had gone back to tag up at first base. When the ball sailed over the outfielder's head, Reggie belatedly took off for second, but not before Rudi, unaware that Reggie was still hanging around first base, had almost passed him.

Rudi ended up with a single, and after the game he was really steamed about Reggie's gaffe. I remember him telling me, "Here I have a chance to lead the league in doubles, and he costs me one—because he's not mentally in the game."

Reggie wasn't always contrite about the mistakes he made, or pleased when they were pointed out. On a Sunday afternoon at Shea Stadium—the home of the Yankees during the '74 and '75 seasons while Yankee Stadium underwent renovations— Reggie was in right field. With a runner on second, a Yankee batter rolled a single into right.

Reggie charged in, picked up the ball, and without hesitating a moment, threw home—which would have been the right move, except that there was no play on the guy coming home, and no hope of one. It was so obviously the wrong move that it hadn't even occurred to anyone that Reggie might throw home. The first baseman hadn't even set up a cutoff. The guy who hit the ball ended up at second when he should have been held at first; thanks to Reggie's inattention, he'd gotten a gift base.

"Reggie threw to the wrong base on that one," I said on the A's broadcast, stating the obvious. "He's allowed the Yankees to take an extra base when a proper throw would have held the runner at first."

The next afternoon, in Baltimore, I was with the A's in the lobby of what is now the Omni Hotel, waiting with a group of players to get on the team bus. And off the elevator strolled Reggie.

He didn't look at me. But I knew he was speaking to me.

"Well, Charlie Finley called me last night here at the hotel. And Charlie said, 'Hey, Mr. Superduperstar, my broadcaster said you made a stupid throw. Yup, my broadcaster said my highly paid superstar doesn't know where to throw the ball.'"

Reggie was quite the orator. He sounded like a Pentecostal preacher delivering a fiery sermon to his flock. But Reggie didn't stay angry long. At the ballpark, I stopped at Reggie's locker and we talked.

"You don't know the whole story, what was really going on

out there," Reggie told me. "When Dick Green is playing second base, he keeps me in the game. Before each pitch, he'll tell me where to throw the ball if this happens, if that happens. I just follow what Greenie says.

"Yesterday, Ted Kubiak was playing second. He doesn't keep me in the game the same way."

"So," I reasoned, "if the same thing happens again, to get it really accurate, I should say on the air, 'Reggie threw to the wrong base because Dick Green isn't in the game to tell him where to throw it?'"

Well, not exactly.

That was Reggie then. Today's Reggie is in the Hall of Fame. He's a senior statesman, an establishment figure. Back in 1992, Mark McGwire was having a terrible year in Oakland. Reggie had retired after the 1987 season and was with the A's as an instructor and television analyst.

I'll never forget Reggie's comment about McGwire that year: "The problem with the young guys today," Reggie declared, "is they make mistakes and you can't talk to 'em. They won't listen. I'm trying to help the guy and he won't listen."

I laughed about that. Twenty years earlier, some veteran ballplayer on the A's was making the same exact statement about Reggie Jackson. Now Reggie was carrying on the tradition. Years from now, I can imagine Albert Belle making the same criticism about a new crop of players in the twenty-first century: "The thing with these young players today is they don't hustle and they have an attitude problem," Albert will say.

Why not? There hasn't been a time in baseball history when retired players gave the current players their due.

"The present crop of big leaguers does not think enough. He feels he has arrived. The result is less intelligent baseball and a bit of laziness."

That was Hall of Famer Tris Speaker, in 1926.

• • •

It's interesting turning the tables on these comparisons, to talk with current or recent players about the players of the past. I've talked to several. For the most part, they're incredulous that anyone could think baseball players were better fifty years ago. Every player I've ever talked to finds that notion so ludicrous as to not even be worthy of discussion.

Once, I was having this discussion with Jim Dwyer, a utility outfielder and accomplished pinch hitter whom I knew when he played for the Red Sox and later the Orioles. Jim and I talked about baseball in the 1920s and 1930s, when it was not unusual for the better hitters to bat .400.

"The pitching must have been terrible," Jim commented.

"How could that be?" I replied. "Walter Johnson and those guys supposedly threw as hard as anybody has ever thrown."

"Then they didn't throw sliders and forkballs," Dwyer said.

We talked some more. And Jim finally said, "Jon, how could those guys have been better than us? That was seventy years ago! How could they have been better than us?"

For Jim Dwyer, it was impossible to take seriously the proposition that a guy could hit .424—as Rogers Hornsby did in 1924—if the pitching then had been as good as it is today. In other words, when the athletes in every sport are bigger and stronger and faster than ever before, how could the best baseball players have *finished* their careers in the twenties and thirties?

"Leo Durocher [says] that Willie Mays was the greatest ballplayer who ever lived. Evidently Mr. Durocher never saw Mr. Cobb, Mr. Ruth, or Mr. Harry Heilmann. [Mays] is a great fielder and he can run, but he couldn't carry the bat of many a player."

Lefty O'Doul, who played against Mr. Ruth, Mr. Cobb, and Mr. Heilmann, said that in 1960.

I've made some blanket generalizations in this chapter. Some are true; others I should qualify. Of course it's not accurate to say that every old-timer believes baseball was better in the past than it is now. Many do, but I know of several who are extremely fair-minded on this issue.

I've already told you about Al Jackson. I'll also mention Tommy Henrich, Old Reliable. Mr. Henrich played for some of the great Yankee teams pre– and post–World War II. By all accounts, he was a great player and a gritty player. A clutch one, too: His home run in the ninth inning of Game One of the 1949 World Series gave the Yanks a 1-0 win over Don Newcombe and the Dodgers, and is a great Series moment.

A few years ago, I spoke at a charity banquet in New Jersey honoring Gene Michael, who has had the rare honor of working for the Yankees as a player, scout, manager, and general manager. Tommy was one of the head-table guests at the affair, and afterward, we happened to share a limo from some country club in Jersey back into midtown Manhattan, a forty-five-minute ride.

The whole trip, we had a discussion about the players in the old days and the players of today. Tommy agreed with me entirely: There were a lot of outstanding players in the game today who could have played in any era, he said.

Tommy was proud of the teams he played on and thought that the Yankees of his era could have competed with anybody. But he was very willing to give the current players their due. He was very impressed with them and still enjoyed the game as a fan.

I wanted to ask him if he believed in juiced baseballs, but I thought better of it.

I began this chapter by talking about how the players of the nineties will likely be viewed as better, stronger, and probably smarter than the players of 2018 or so. I believe that baseball is better now then it's ever been. But there's one more thing I can predict with absolute safety: When we say these things in 2018, we'll be just as wrong as everyone has been in every era. In sports, athletes only get better. The Golden Age is now. Always.

This
BOY'S LIFE,
IN REEL TIME

A career has to start someplace. My someplace was the bedroom I shared with my brother, Paul, in my parents' home in Hayward, California, an Oakland suburb.

When I was ten, I saw in the back of a magazine an ad touting a tabletop baseball game. The game was called Strat-O-Matic, and it sounded like the most fantastic toy I'd ever heard of.

You sent away your ten or fifteen bucks, and a couple of weeks later, a long, flat box arrived in the mail. Inside were enough charts, numbers, and statistics to befuddle an IRS agent, or so it must have seemed to my poor parents. But for me, Strat-O-Matic proved to be the perfect outlet for my two rapidly developing passions: baseball and talking.

The idea behind Strat-O-Matic is simple: you roll the dice, refer to player cards, and recreate a baseball game, all in a half hour. If you're really dedicated—and have six months to kill—you can replay an entire season, all on your bedspread. Every year the company puts out a new game based on the previous year's statistics, so it never gets old.

From my first roll of the dice, I was hooked on Strat-O-Matic. One year—1966, I believe—I played an entire National League schedule, all ten teams, all 162 games. It was unbelievable. I was crazed.

As time went on, I began to think about the larger baseball issues, like expansion and realignment. But only within my private Strat-O-Matic world. Baseball, I decided, was ready to go global, so I put a team up in the Hudson Bay area, with a ballpark right on the shore of Hudson Bay. A lot of seagulls and cool breezes. It was an open-air stadium; even then, I didn't care for domes.

I put a team in Rome—the Rome Cardinals. This would be one of the great moneymaking franchises in history, I decided. I'd build the ballpark right in St. Peter's Square. Every Sunday, I'd schedule a doubleheader, and between games the pope would come out to give a blessing. What a promotion! Every Sunday, I figured on five or six hundred thousand fans in Cardinal Park at St. Peter's Square.

I put a team in Wembley Stadium in London—the London Fog. I put a team in the mountains of Peru, in Machu Picchu. Called them the Machu Picchu Incas. A real interesting stadium there: a blending of the ancient ruins of the Machu Picchu city with all the state-of-the-art modern amenities. A little bit like The Ballpark in Arlington, Texas.

It was a heck of a trip to get to Machu Picchu Park, but it didn't matter. It was Strat-O-Matic baseball.

Strat-O-Matic changed a lot of things in the Miller house. For one thing, I never left my room. My mother, Winona, has been quoted saying that, at that age, Strat-O-Matic was all her wayward son "lived, ate, and thought about."

I suppose that's true.

The other thing that changed around our house were the sounds coming from behind my bedroom door, which was always shut tight. My mom refers to them as "those awful noises." My dad, Jerry, says there were many times when he'd walk by and wonder whether I was having "some sort of heart attack."

Fortunately, I wasn't ill; I was merely strange. After I'd been playing Strat-O-Matic for a while, I started broadcasting the games. Let me be clear about this: I wasn't broadcasting on the air. I was broadcasting into thin air. Of course, I had a stable of the finest broadcasters handling my Strat-O-Matic games. I'd be Vin Scully on one game, and then, on the second game, I'd be Russ Hodges. If Russ couldn't make it, no problem—I'd be Chuck Thompson. "Ladies and gentlemen, ain't the beer cold here in St. Peter's Square this afternoon . . ."

When people walked in on one of my games, it was a bizarre scene. There were charts and tables all over the place. And there was the noise. I'd do PA announcers, broadcasters, infield chatter. I'd make the crowd noise with my breath—one way for a big weekend crowd, another for a small Thursday-afternoon-in-April crowd. Anything was liable to happen; if somebody hit a three-run homer, without notice I'd jump off the bed and start doing one of my huge stadium cheers: *AAAAAhhhhhhh!*

I loved doing the game descriptions in my room. But after a while, what I really wanted was to be able to play back my "broadcasts." I decided I had to have a tape recorder, and I broke the news to my parents.

What a huge event, the day I set out to buy that baby. My dad drove me to a jewelry store in downtown Hayward. I opened my own charge account and, for thirty dollars, returned home with the gadget of my dreams. I paid for it with my allowance.

When I had my tape recorder, I began experimenting with other kinds of re-creations. I wasn't limiting myself to Strat-O-Matic anymore, or even to baseball.

One of my more ambitious undertakings was a re-creation of an NBA playoff game between the Warriors, our local heroes, and the St. Louis Hawks. One of the games, in St. Louis, was being televised back to the Bay Area. I decided I had to do a play-by-play description of that game.

Doing a decent-sounding broadcast is difficult when you're fourteen, but I wanted to try. Next to my bed, I set up a portable television so I could see the game, which I'd broadcast as I followed it on the TV. Then I commandeered my dad's huge Webcor reel-to-reel tape recorder, with microphone. (My dad was then a schoolteacher, but after hours he was also a musician and a member of a Kingston Trio–type folk-music group called the Profs. The band appeared all over the Bay Area, and my dad used the big—and even then obsolete—Webcor to record the Profs' rehearsals and to hone the act.) I would be doing my play-by-play into that.

On the bed, I carefully arranged two other portable reel-to-reel tape recorders—no cassettes yet. One was cued to play normal crowd noises that I'd taped at a Giants game at Candlestick Park. The other had sounds of a loud cheering crowd—I'd captured that at Candlestick after somebody hit a long home run. The normal crowd noise was background sound for when I did my play-by-play. If the Hawks did something good, I punched on the cheering crowd. And if the Warriors did something good or a Warrior player committed a particularly hard foul against a St. Louis player, I'd hit the cheering-crowd tape, but then put my finger on the feed reel to slow it down so that it sounded like booing.

My room was a maze of wires and plugs. It looked like the after-Christmas sale at Radio Shack. But on top of everything else, I decided I needed a phonograph: at halftime and during time outs, I'd need to play organ music, so I found an LP of organ music.

With a free hand, I kept score.

Afterward, I listened to that tape—you know, as a critique of my "broadcast." My assessment was, "Man, this is fantastic broadcasting!" Yes, I was fourteen years old and ready for the big time. I was even planning to apply for broadcasting jobs—and plotting ways to conceal my age.

Within a week, the dream had died, at least temporarily. My brother got out that big reel-to-reel and decided he had to tape something—he and his eleven-year-old buddies singing obscene lyrics to the tune of Beatles songs. In the process, he inadvertently taped over my historic broadcast. I wanted to kill him. Fortunately, I'd already played parts of the tape for everyone in our neighborhood—and over the telephone for anyone with a listed number. (My brother now claims he erased my tape as a favor to hundreds of angry people.)

I thought about doing another game, but every time I did it just seemed like it would be so hard. I never got around to it.

In 1968, the A's moved from Kansas City to Oakland, and my baseball-watching habit got a big boost. With the A's in town, it was even easier to see a major-league game, for the ballpark was much closer to our home than Candlestick, and I'd just turned sixteen, so I could borrow one of my parents' cars and drive down. Sometimes I'd take the bus, the A.C. transit bus, and I was there.

I wanted to broadcast a game right from the ballpark—go down there with a tape recorder and do a game. If I could handle it in my room, hunched over a portable TV, I could certainly do it at an actual game, with the action unfolding right in front of me. It seemed like a snap. So I started preparing myself. I knew I needed statistics; you couldn't do a broadcast without statistics. And the latest statistics were in the Sunday newspapers.

These days, every paper in a major-league town carries team-by-team stats. If you know where to look, you can find any player on any team—and not just home runs and RBIs, either. Papers run even the more arcane stats, from CS (caught stealing) to GIDPs (grounded into double plays).

Thirty years ago, that was unheard of. The Sunday paper carried one long list of hitters and another long list of pitchers. The hitters with the highest averages were at the top of the list, the weakest at the bottom. Pitchers with the lowest ERAs led the pitching list, and the guy with the 12.75 ERA was usually last.

The statistics ran in a column as long as the newspaper page, a page that could take fifteen minutes to peruse. I'd go through that list picking out players for the two teams in the game I would be doing. It took a good, long while, but I felt I had to do it. My statistics had to be current. The listeners had a right to expect that, didn't they? So I'd save box scores from Friday's and Saturday's games—which weren't included in Sunday's list—and the night before the game I was doing, I'd use them to update my stats.

A lot of players didn't appear in those long columns. You had to have a minimum number of at-bats or, for pitchers, a minimum number of innings pitched or decisions. That really screwed me up, since I had nothing on the players who didn't qualify. I had to hope they didn't get in the game, and if they did, I rooted against their coming up in crucial situations, where it'd be obvious if I omitted a key piece of information.

At the Oakland Coliseum, my broadcast booth was the right-field bleachers—top row, in a corner under the overhang of the upper deck. A great spot. There was a modicum of privacy—nobody wanted to sit up in no-man's-land—and the entire playing field stretched out in front of me. I'd have a seat on the wooden plank, which is what the bleachers were then, and spread my stuff out all around me.

Usually, I took the entire radio crew—by that, I mean a friend came with me. My friends from high school—Lol Sorensen, Ray Melville, Bill Hatcher, and Chris Lauritzen— liked to go along. They thought it was cool to do a broadcast, even if it did mean being the No. 2 man in the booth (or, in our case, Row QQ). I loved the idea of working with somebody else; you're not really doing a major-league broadcast if you don't have a partner.

My broadcasts were always loaded with commercials. I couldn't get the kind of commercials that advertisers pay for— when your listenership is about four, that's tough. But I had some really unusual ones, usually borrowing something I'd seen in a magazine or the newspaper.

At the time, the *San Francisco Chronicle* had just announced it was going to carry dispatches from Reuters, the British news service. The *Chronicle* was running full-page ads touting this new partnership and explaining how great it would be for readers.

I got the bright idea to bring in Reuters as a sponsor for A's baseball. Never mind that Reuters wasn't a brewery, a car dealer, or a deli-meat company, the usual baseball sponsors. Never mind that the idea of a worldwide news service buying time on a ballgame was preposterous. I wanted Reuters, so I got Reuters.

"Reuters, it's Jim Pagliaroni's news service, shouldn't it be yours?" Or, "Hi, I'm A's pitching ace Lew Krausse, and when I want the latest on Cambodia's Prince Sihanouk, I rely on Reuters." Catchy stuff like that.

We read the commercials before the game and between innings. My friends were really into that; reading the commercials was the part they liked most. I'd let them read a few, and if they showed promise, I'd even give them play-by-play assignments for a couple of innings—say, the third, fourth, and seventh.

Hey, I owed them. They kept my stats from blowing away.

I must have been a sight, with my tape recorder balanced on my lap, reams of statistics, announcements, and commercials flying everywhere. Fans never gawked at us, nor did they complain about our constant chatter, bless their hearts. If any fans sat near us, I'd explain what I was doing—what was I doing?—and say that I hoped we didn't disturb them. That seemed to keep everyone happy.

We never had any really serious problems during our broadcasts—we never got chased away by the ushers, and our batteries never went dead. The worst thing that happened was boom boxes: if somebody brought a boom box to the game to listen to the actual A's broadcast, and they were sitting close by, we were off the air. You couldn't do a broadcast sitting five feet away from a boom box.

Soon, I started looking for other outlets for my strange hobby, and at Hayward High School I found one. When I was a senior, I appointed myself the official voice of the boys' basketball team. The drama class got a big sheet of muslin and made up a banner for me, just like the KSFO sign at the 'Stick in front of Russ Hodges's booth or the KNBR banner in front of Bill King at the Warriors' games. In big block letters, they sewed on the "station's" call letters: KMIL.

KMIL. Clever, eh?

I'd set up a little table next to where the official scorer sat, right at courtside, and I'd take my banner and drape it over the table. Now fans sitting on the other side of the gym could see it, which was the whole point of having the banner. I was proud of that banner; with it, we looked very professional.

When the basketball team went on the road, KMIL went too. I'd call the other school and tell them I was with the radio station at Hayward High, that I needed a table at courtside because I'd be broadcasting the game the next afternoon. The first time, I was a little nervous; I thought, "The principal is going to realize this is a crock. There is no student radio station at Hayward."

But I'd show up at the high school, and there, waiting for me, would be my broadcasting table. There'd always be a note taped to the top: RESERVED FOR JON MILLER, HAYWARD HIGH SCHOOL RADIO STATION.

My basketball game tapes were very big on the room-to-room intercom at Hayward High. The morning after a game, I'd do a recap for the students, playing back highlights, key baskets, and whatnot as part of my report. The basketball players appreciated this service: these intercom flashes improved their chances with the girls and generally put them in a good frame of mind before chemistry exams. But I think most of my classmates thought I was nuts, which mystified me. I felt I was the most normal kid in the school.

Broadcasting was fun. And a number of people were telling

me I was good at it. But as a high-school kid, you don't know where you're headed with your life—and even if you do, you only have the vaguest idea how to get there. All that applied to me until I met Lon Simmons when I was in college.

Lon was the longtime broadcaster for the Giants, and one of my heroes. I listened to him and Russ Hodges, his partner, all summer long. I considered him a member of the family, nothing less than a favorite uncle.

A professor of mine at the College of San Mateo arranged for the two of us to go to Candlestick and to go into the booth to meet Lon before the game. For a kid, just nineteen, it was heady stuff. Lon was gracious; he sat with me for a bit, answering questions, and he took one of my baseball tapes and agreed to listen to it.

A few weeks later, I heard back from him. Lon said he definitely thought I had a lot of talent, but that, obviously, I needed to start my career someplace where I could learn about broadcasting, at a small station in a small town. But the point Lon made that was so important was that in his opinion I was ready to go to one of those small markets right then.

Other people had offered me support, saying I was going to do this or that, that I had this God-given ability. But now that Lon Simmons was telling me this, somehow it was true.

Year later, I ran into Lon at Fenway Park. By that time he was doing A's games, and I was doing the Red Sox broadcasts with Ken Coleman. I reminded Lon about meeting him at Candlestick Park, about how he'd listened to my tape and had given me all that encouragement. I thanked him and explained how he'd had such an impact on my career, my life.

It was news to Lon. He had no memory of it. Later, I realized he'd probably been asked to see hundreds of college kids during his years in broadcasting—and probably had said similarly pleasant things to most of them. Maybe all of them.

That didn't matter. I appreciated the time Lon gave me. Then and now. (By the way, Lon now claims he does remember our meeting—and that he advised me to get into another line of work.)

Today, I'm in the position Lon was then. I get the letters from the eighth graders with the tape recorders and the big ambitions, the earnest high school kids come to the booth to see me. It's wonderful. They're all dreaming precisely the same dream that filled my head thirty years ago: to sit behind a microphone at a major league ballgame.

I wish there were some wonderfully sage advice I could pass along, some magic formula that would put these young people on the path to broadcasting baseball, or any sport for that matter. My advice is always the same: Get a college education. Study English literature. Read the great books. Learn to use the language. The language is our most important tool to do this job well. It's what can set you apart from the rest.

Many former ballplayers look to move into the booth. They bring name recognition and a great knowledge of the sport, but unless you played in the majors, what you have to offer must be your facility with the language and, of course, some talent.

Back in '71, I was sure I was going places. Lon's comments filled me with confidence, and I was hot to get out in the job market, maybe even land a paying job. But that wasn't the only exciting thing going on that summer. My beloved Giants were in a furious pennant race with the Dodgers. Needing a victory to clinch the division, the Giants were in San Diego on the next-to-last day of the season. The Padres beat them, so now the Giants needed to win the next night, the last day of the season, to clinch.

As the Giants were losing this penultimate game in San Diego, I was in Hayward with my friend Ronnie Cardenas. We were sitting there in my mother's kitchen, late at night, talking about the game. At about one o'clock in the morning, one of us said, "Let's go down to San Diego, see the final game, and see them win the division."

As usual, we were supremely confident.

I arranged to borrow my mother's car. An hour later, in the dead of night, we were on the road. We had a lot of—how should I say—mobility at the time.

The only thing I remember packing is my tape recorder. The next afternoon, we got down to San Diego, bought tickets for the game, and looked around the city a little bit. Then we went to the ballpark. Our seats were way out in the left-field stands, which were totally empty except for Ronnie and me. Perfect. Not a boom box in sight.

We did have an usher problem. This gentleman apparently was under orders not to let anybody sit out in the left-field stands, and from the looks of things, he was doing a pretty good job of it. Then I explained to him, "Look, I'm a college student. I'm just trying to make a demo tape, an audition tape. I need a little space."

"Fine, sit wherever you want. I'll make sure people leave you alone."

It was perfect. They had the largest crowd of the season in San Diego that night, 35,000 fans. I saw the Giants clinch the division, and I "broadcast" the game—won by Juan Marichal—into my tape recorder, from the left-field stands.

With that tape, I got my first real, paying job. A UHF television station in Santa Rosa hired me as the sports director. And I was on my way.

Thanks, Lon.

Everything I Needed to Know
I LEARNED FROM
MY TRANSISTOR

I'm lucky. Over the years, I've met most of my heroes—the broadcasters I worshipped growing up in Northern California. I've even worked with a few.

If I had my way, I'd arrange one more introduction: I'd so love to spend some time with the late Russ Hodges.

Russ was the first broadcaster I heard on a ballgame. By far, he was the one who made the biggest impression on me. From 1949 through the 1970 season, Russ was the booming, baritone voice of the Giants, in New York and then in San Francisco. You couldn't imagine a Giants game without him.

Russ's broadcasting days ended before mine began. Our paths did cross one time, twenty-eight years ago at Candlestick Park. I was a punk kid, a student at the College of San Mateo; Russ was, well, Russ.

One night, I went out to Candlestick to broadcast a ballgame into my tape recorder. That was not unusual; I went to the ballpark a lot to talk games into my tape recorder.

This night, I decided to splurge. Instead of sitting in my usual spot in the upper deck, I treated myself to a ticket in the mezzanine—Candlestick's high-rent district. Mezzanine tickets were $6.60; I was used to paying $2.50.

For a do-it-yourself broadcaster, the mezzanine held allure. You not only got a seat on the same level as the press box, but there was a table in front of you, just like in the broadcast booth, on which I could spread out my stuff—my clippings, notebook, recorder, etc. It was more private than the upper deck—and you could actually see the game. All in all, not a bad deal.

I'd been to Candlestick dozens of times. I knew it better than the ushers. But this was my first venture to the mezzanine. I decided to have a look around, and, on my walk, I discovered a narrow concrete corridor.

A man with a friendly and familiar face strode through. I'd never seen this man in person, but I knew that face. He was bundled up in a big, heavy windbreaker. And he was right there.

I couldn't speak. As the big man shot by me in the hall, I managed to get the words out:

"Hi, Russ."

He looked back.

"How ya doing?"

The words reverberated off the concrete walls, as if we'd met in an echo chamber.

How ya doing.

How ya doing.

How ya doing.

It was perfect. Russ always opened the broadcasts the same way: "San Francisco Giants baseball is on the air . . .

"How ya doing, everybody?"

How ya doing, Russ.

Once I'd heard Russ Hodges on the Giants broadcasts, I don't think I ever considered another line of work. He had that much of an impact on me.

To me, Russ was the consummate broadcaster. His voice was not a classic, but it was rich and distinctive. He gave listeners a great picture of the game through the radio, and when things got exciting, Russ had this knack for getting excited, but in a very controlled way. Russ stayed under control.

Russ wasn't alone; there are a handful of broadcasters who steered me toward this passion of mine. Each one went about the job differently: Some openly rooted for their teams; others maintained a professional distance. Some had the deep baritones; others had their own unique sounds. All of them shared one gift: they brought baseball to life in every broadcast from April through October.

I was lucky to grow up where I did, when I did. San Francisco in the 1960s had a stable of local broadcasters that I doubt will ever be bettered. I listened to them all: Russ and his partner, Lon Simmons, with the Giants; Bill King on the Warriors of the NBA and the Raiders of the AFL; and Hank Greenwald doing both Warriors games and college basketball. As a young fan, each made an indelible impression on me, and I took lessons from them all.

With Russ and Lon, the lesson was about rapport: Russ and Lon had a genuine fondness for each other, and it showed.

Bill King, now the voice of the Oakland A's and a dear friend, is without peer in his game descriptions. With every broadcast, Bill taught me the importance of placing the ball on the court or the field for the listener.

When I was eleven, I thought Hank Greenwald was the funniest man alive—and I still rank him in the top eight. From Hank, I learned you can do the job and do it with humor.

Vin Scully also worked in the Greater San Francisco area—sort of. Dodger broadcasts came in loud and clear over the 50,000-watt signal from KFI Los Angeles, bringing with them Vin's precise, coolly professional calls of the Giants' hated rivals.

But for me, it all began with Russ.

Russ *was* the Giants. When Horace Stoneham picked up the Giants from New York and moved them west, Russ came with them.

In San Francisco, he was joined by Lon Simmons, who became No. 2 in the booth. Lon's voice was purer sounding than

Russ's; it was deep and bassy, cleaner and more authoritative. Russ had more of a rich, guttural sound. But both had great voices to listen to. It was maybe the best pairing of voices in a broadcast booth ever.

Russ and Lon were part of the scenery in San Francisco, like Herb Caen in the Sunday *Chronicle,* the Golden Gate, and sourdough bread. Giants fans knew the voices immediately—and they certainly recognized Russ's distinctive home run call: "*Tell it bye-bye, baby.*"

Tell it bye-bye, baby became so big that the Giants used the words to score their theme song. Imagine this to an upbeat tempo, The Village People doing the vocal:

"*When the Giants come to town, it's bye-bye, baby . . .*
"*Everytime the chips are down, it's bye-bye, baby.*"

On the Giants telecasts, we still use the instrumental version of that song to lead to commercial breaks after innings in which a Giants player has told one, "Bye-bye, baby."

Russ was very selective about when he'd use "Bye-bye, baby"—he'd only use it when the Giants hit a big fly. So we'd wait for Mays or McCovey or Cepeda to step into the batter's box, and then . . .

"Mays swings . . .
"There's a long, high drive . . .
"Deep into left field . . .
"Way back there . . ."
One thousand one, one thousand two . . .
"Tell it bye-bye, baby!"
I still get goose bumps.

If the Giants hit a homer and it wasn't accompanied by Russ's "Bye-bye, baby," you felt out-and-out cheated, something I experienced when my parents took me to my first game at Candlestick in April of '62.

The Giants beat the Dodgers, 19-8, and smacked three home runs in the process. My dad had the transistor—and was using an earphone—when the homers were hit. The hometown heroes were winning in a rout. And I was perplexed. Three booming home runs, but I hadn't heard a single "Bye-bye, baby." Something was missing.

In my mind, Russ and Lon were joined at the hip. It was nearly impossible to think of one without the other. On the air, they exuded warmth and friendship. A few times each game, Lon would make a remark that cracked up Russ, and they'd have a good laugh. But nothing was forced; it was obvious there was a genuine camaraderie between them. I particularly remember that part of their broadcasts—and I remember thinking how great it would be to someday have the same kind of rib-poking relationship with a partner.

Russ and Lon seemed so close that, as a kid, I made assumptions about their lives away from the ballpark, too. I envisioned Russ and Lon as inseparable buddies, like me and my pal Ronnie Cardenas. In my mind's eye, they went to games together, ate dinner together, stayed together in the hotel—probably put on their pajamas together.

This made absolute sense to me, as it would to any kid who wore pajamas and had a kid brother. When my parents took us on an overnight trip, we always stayed in the same room, and my brother and I always slept in the same bed. You couldn't tell me it was any different between Russ and Lon.

Russ and Lon worked together until 1971, when Russ opted for semiretirement. He was going to do about twenty-five games on TV, while Lon inherited the lead radio job.

Tragically, Russ's plans never materialized. On April 19, 1971, he had a heart attack and died suddenly.

Years later, I bumped into Lon Simmons at Fenway Park and we talked about Russ Hodges. It was one of the most memorable conversations I've ever had at a ballpark. There I was, chatting with my childhood hero, comparing my eleven-year-old fantasies with the real lives of Lon and Russ.

When Lon spoke, it was clear he had such affection for Russ, even all these years after he had died. Right then, I knew what I had heard on the radio as a kid was true: They really did have great affection for one another.

But not all of what Lon told me meshed with my storybook take on their lives.

Russ had been looking forward to a reduced workload, Lon said, to leaving radio and doing just the two dozen or so games on television. After all those years of grinding through a full schedule, Russ finally was going to be able to kick back, relax, and enjoy life a little more.

But, Lon said, when opening day of the '71 season came and Russ wasn't in a booth broadcasting baseball—he was sitting at home instead—Russ realized he'd made a terrible mistake. The thing that made him happiest in life was doing Giants baseball, and he wasn't doing it anymore.

Despite what the doctors said about a heart attack, Lon said he always believed Russ died of a broken heart. It was a sad story, and particularly moving the way Lon told it. Lon believes that Russ died when he handed over that microphone. And maybe he's right.

To this day, Lon is loyal to Russ, and quick to defend the memory of his old friend and partner. I know from experience.

During the off-season, I'm asked to speak at a number of sports banquets, affairs at which I'm expected to slip into my tuxedo and tell humorous baseball stories for fifteen or twenty minutes. One story in my repertoire is about the time my parents took me to a Giants game and we sat in the upper deck at Candlestick, a spot from which I could see into the Giants radio booth.

The thrill was indescribable. Not the game—forget about the game. The view of the broadcast booth was nothing short of breathtaking. From our seats, not only could I listen on my transistor to Russ and Lon, but I could see them work.

I've got the binoculars trained on the booth. I can see Russ's lips move. And, on the radio, I hear Russ say, "The pitch, low and outside for a ball, two and oh."

Incredible. Sensory overload.

Suddenly, the radio falls quiet. So I train the binoculars on the booth again, and what I see startles me. Russ has grabbed a big handful of french fries and has stuffed all these french fries in his mouth. Between pitches, he's wolfing them down.

"High, ball three . . ."

I actually can see Russ chowing down. Now, listening closely to the radio, I can hear chewing sounds.

The next pitch comes in.

"Ball four . . ."

I look again. Russ picks up a cup of soda, takes a big pull, and washes it all down.

At that moment, I remember saying to myself, "Now that's the life for me."

In reality, the whole story is a joke, and the joke is on me. I was just ten years old at the time; whether I saw Russ Hodges eat on the air, whether I saw Russ or Lon eat—look, I was ten years old, I really don't remember.

I tell the story simply because it's a good banquet story, with a good punch line. The point is, Hey, look what attracted me to broadcasting: free food in the press box!

It so happened that on one occasion when I told it, I was in the company of a reporter for *Sports Illustrated,* Franz Lidz.

Franz followed me around for a few days to do a feature for *SI* about me, a really nice piece. And he put this story—the Russ Hodges story he heard me do at a luncheon—in the article.

A week after the article came out, I saw Lon. You can guess what was on Lon's mind. He said, "I saw the story in *Sports Illustrated* about you watching Russ eat french fries." Lon was disturbed, but very nice about it. "Don't get me wrong," he went on. "It's a funny story and all that. But Russ has been dead all these years. He's somebody I admired, loved, and respected. So, when I saw the article, I wrote a letter to *SI* saying, as his former partner, I never once saw him eat anything while he was on the air."

As nicely as Lon was putting it, it was clear he was disappointed in me. I wanted him to understand my point. "Lon," I said, "the joke is on me, not on him. I'm really making fun of myself."

"I understand that," Lon replied. "But Russ is in the Hall of Fame. He hasn't worked in twenty years. All that's left is his memory. You never see his name in print except a rare time. And now *Sports Illustrated* has a big article, and the one thing it says about Russ is that he ate french fries on the air."

I really respected Lon for doing what he did. What a great guy, to come to Russ's defense, all those years later. Ever since, I've tried to keep Lon's feelings in mind. It's still a great banquet story, but now when I tell it, I drop Russ's name and use a generic broadcaster:

"I could see into the out-of-town broadcasters' booth. I don't know who those guys were, but man, they were starved . . ."

When I joined the Giants last year, the person I was replacing was Hank Greenwald. *The* Hank Greenwald! The guy I'd grown up listening to, the one who through some kind of high-frequency osmosis became an unofficial member of my family. (Starting in 1979, long after I'd left the Bay Area, Hank joined the Giants' broadcast team.)

In the back of my mind, I almost think of Hank as my favorite uncle. When the Giants called, it was as if my favorite uncle had retired and I had been anointed to move in and take over the family business.

In a way, it makes sense that I should follow Hank, because I've been following his example for more than twenty years. When I was in college, I worked for the school's UHF television station. If I had those tapes now, I'm sure I'd hear myself trying to be Hank Greenwald—trying to emulate Hank's sense of humor, but more than that, actually trying to sound like Hank, with the same vocal cadences and phrases. Hank had that kind of impact on me.

Ironically, I had almost no experience listening to Hank as a baseball broadcaster. Although he broadcast the Giants for sixteen years and was amazingly popular, I had long since moved east when he first got the job.

Hank came to San Francisco in the mid-1960s, when I was thirteen or fourteen. At first, he did the *Saturday Night Sports Special,* which featured a package of Warriors NBA games, Seals minor-league hockey, college basketball, and whatever happened to be around.

Hank doesn't have the big, rich voice of Russ or Lon. His voice is just friendly; it always felt as if he was talking directly to you. I was won over immediately, because Hank was so good. And he was so funny.

Hank's humor can be very subtle, and very dry. Many years ago—in the days when we had two divisions in each league—Hank was doing a broadcast in Houston. At the time, the Astros were leading the NL West and the Montreal Expos were the front-runners in the NL East.

"If the Astros and Expos win their divisions," Hank observed, "it will mark the first time in history that the National League playoffs will take place entirely in foreign countries."

For several years, Hank's partner on the Warriors radio broadcasts was Bill King. Together, they formed the best radio tandem on NBA basketball that I ever heard. I haven't heard everybody, but I can't imagine there ever being a better duo.

Bill was the best play-by-play man, an artist painting vivid verbal portraits of the action. And Hank was the perfect complement, adding bits of insight and humor. He always seemed to have a great line for a play or a player.

Hank was the first professional broadcaster I ever really met and spoke with.

I remember going to a game at the Civic Auditorium in San

Francisco. I couldn't have been more than seventeen or eighteen. Hank worked the game from a table at courtside, and afterward I stayed around, sat down right behind him to listen to him do the wrap-up show.

When he was done and packing up his briefcase, I introduced myself. At the time, I was either a senior in high school or just starting college.

I don't remember what I said or what Hank said to me, but I do recall that he was very friendly. My real memory of that meeting, though, was that Hank was the first celebrity I'd ever met, much less the first professional sports broadcaster. There he was, right in front of me. It wasn't like watching baseball broadcasters in their booth, way up there, inaccessible; in basketball, the broadcasters sat at courtside, right in front of the stands. I'd watched him do the wrap-up show, and now it was just the two of us talking it over.

Maybe it was the physical proximity to Hank that day, but the idea of getting a professional broadcasting job seemed more real to me after that. Until then, it had been a dream, and a fleeting one at that. "These guys are going to keep going another thirty or forty years," I thought. "I'll be an old man before I even get a shot behind a microphone."

After meeting Hank, I became more optimistic, though I couldn't tell you exactly why. Mostly, I think, it was just that Hank seemed like a regular guy. He wasn't physically imposing, and there was nothing unusual about him. He seemed like a next-door neighbor.

When I accepted the Giants job after the '96 season, I spent some time with Hank and his wife. It was probably the most time I've ever spent with them. I visited their home—the first time I'd been there. They took me to their favorite restaurant, but I didn't know it was their favorite restaurant at the time.

When you come down to it, I didn't really know that much about Hank. I thought I knew him; I felt a kind of intimacy toward him. But it was an intimacy I'd developed with my transistor radio as much as with Hank—because the Hank I knew was the broadcaster, not the person. Creating that illusion is part of what makes the best broadcasters special. You may not know what their interests are, what kind of food they like, what they do in the off-season, but in a very real way, you *do* know them. What you hear in the voice doesn't lie.

For a broadcaster, nothing is as important—or as difficult to master—as describing what you see. Placing the ball on the field or court, cluing in the listeners to where the fielders are and where they're going—painting the picture with words.

The best I've ever heard at game description is Bill King, the longtime voice of the Oakland A's, and before that, of the NBA Warriors and the NFL Raiders. Bill's basketball play-by-play stands as the most remarkable I've ever heard.

Using a staccato delivery that always reflected the tempo of the game, Bill would tell listeners who had the ball, where they were on the floor, who was guarding him, and who was setting a pick for him. When a twenty-foot jumper was on the way to the basket, you could follow its arcing flight because Bill would give you that extra moment in the middle of telling you—"He shoots a jumper from eighteen . . . two." He was truly an artist.

He was just as good describing Raiders football. Once, Ken Stabler threw a long pass downfield, and, while the pass was in the air, Bill told you not only that it was intended for Cliff Branch, but who was covering Branch as well!

You hadn't lived until you heard Bill describe how a Raiders running back raced through "the yawning chasm" that had opened in the defensive line. Or, with the crowd going crazy in New York after a dramatic run by the Knicks, Bill intoning, "The mighty jaws of Madison Square Garden open wide, threatening to devour the Warriors while leaving nary a crumb!"

A few times when I was about fourteen, I remember keeping score of a Warriors game while listening to Bill on the radio. I just wanted to try it out; I'd kept score listening to baseball a few times, and I'd found I enjoyed the game more if I kept score. You really have to pay attention to keep score when the game is on the radio—no sneaking away for an inning to ride your bike.

When those Warrior games were over, Bill would run down the official final statistics. I'd always check my stats against his. Usually, mine were close, if not identical, to the official tally. At the time, I thought this was due to superior scorekeeping on my part. Later I realized it was mostly Bill's doing: he'd given a fabulous description of everything that was going on—missed shots, offensive rebounds, blocks, assists.

Years later, as Bill and I became friends, I also came to know him as something of a renaissance man. For a time, he was quite the sea captain; reaching him anytime between the end of the NBA season and the start of the NFL season was virtually impossible—he was off on his sailboat. A few years ago, Bill became interested in art and started painting beautiful oils, mostly still lifes and landscapes. I've asked Bill to sell me one of his paintings, but he won't part with any.

Back in the 1960s, it seemed that my beloved Giants were embroiled in one endless pennant race with the Dodgers, one that stretched from my sixth-grade graduation until sophomore year at college. Or so it seemed. The Dodgers were on a very powerful station out of Los Angeles, KFI. Every night, those games would beam up to the Bay Area loud and clear.

The Giants, when they were at home, played mostly day games—Tuesdays and Fridays were the only night games at home. So, all summer long, we could hear the Giants during the day and the Dodgers at night.

Those Dodger broadcasts were my introduction to a new voice from Planet Baseball. At first, all I knew about Vin Scully was that he was sure no Russ Hodges. Not even close. On his best day, Vin never celebrated a home run with anything like Russ's signature, "Bye-bye, baby." Vin's home-run call was decidedly less theatrical: "It's gone," or, if he was feeling frisky, "She's gone."

I remember thinking, "This guy is reeeally dull."

I also remember thinking, "No wonder Scully's stuck in a jerkwater town like L.A. He'll never get out of there."

So at least I was right about one thing.

It wasn't until years later, when I was listening as a student of the art rather than as a Giants fan, that I began to realize how extraordinarily good Vin Scully truly is.

Scully's command of the language, his ability to create images in the listener's mind, is beyond compare. On Vin's broadcasts, a batter doesn't fall away from a high, inside pitch. He "hits the dirt like a folding chair." Vin creates an image so vivid that you can see in your mind's eye exactly what he's talking about.

In style and approach, Vin Scully and Russ Hodges were vastly different.

There's no better example of that than Russ's famous call of Bobby Thomson's "Shot Heard 'Round the World" from 1951, undoubtedly the most listened-to and replayed radio call in history:

"Branca throws . . . there's a long drive. It's gonna be, I believe . . . *The Giants win the pennant! The Giants win the pennant! The Giants win the pennant! . . . And they're going crazy. They're going crazy, hey ho.*

"*Bobby Thomson has hit a line drive . . . into the lower deck . . . of the left-field stands . . . And they're picking Bobby Thomson up, and carrying him off the field.*"

I remember hearing Vin Scully criticize Russ's call of the Thomson home run. It wasn't anything personal; Vin was simply referring back to his upbringing in the business. His mentor, Red Barber, always maintained that the broadcaster's job was not only to describe the event, but to maintain control, to be separated enough from the event that he could describe it clearly and articulately. If the broadcaster lost control—in Red's mind, and in Vin's—that was very unprofessional. He had ceased to do his job.

The day Bobby Thomson smacked his historic home run, Vin felt, Russ hadn't been at his most professional.

I never agreed with that criticism, and I'll tell you why: When you listen to that call, you can say Russ got hysterical. But, on the other hand, you can hear every word. He never became unintelligible. He never lost his train of thought.

That home run was the culmination of one of the greatest comebacks in history. On August 12, the Giants had been thirteen and a half games back with only forty-four to play. They managed to claw their way back to finish the regular season in a dead heat with the Dodgers, and split the first two games of a three-game tiebreaker series. They entered the ninth inning behind 4-1.

They scored once. And then, with two men aboard, Bobby Thomson made history.

I always felt that on that call, Russ captured the moment perfectly, the outpouring of emotion that erupted with the completion of one of the greatest—and most unlikely—comebacks of all time.

Back in 1969, I had one of my most memorable experiences listening to baseball on the radio. And I was listening to Vin Scully.

I had just graduated from high school, and had a job as a gas station attendant working the graveyard shift. With my newfound wealth, I had just bought a new car.

I also had a girlfriend, whose family had moved up to Eugene, Oregon, which is also where my grandmother lives. She—my girlfriend, not my grandmother—was headed up to Oregon, so I decided to give her a lift, see my grandmother, and head back to the Bay Area the next night.

I began the trip back at night, alone. I switched on the radio to the Dodgers game, coming in loud and clear on KFI. That night, I listened to the whole nine innings, the entire broadcast, from first pitch to final out. Now, I'd heard a lot of Dodger broadcasts, or rather parts of broadcasts. But before that night, I don't recall having ever listened to every pitch of a full Dodger game.

That night, I was all by myself, without anybody talking to me, without any interruptions. And it was absolutely the best broadcast I had ever heard.

What do I remember about that broadcast? Above all, I remember the stories. Vin had stories about everyone wearing a uniform that night. The Dodgers were playing Chicago, and the Cubs had a veteran shortstop, a gutty switch-hitter named Don Kessinger.

When Kessinger came to bat, Vin related that probably the only reason for Kessinger still being in the big leagues was his becoming a switch-hitter. Vin didn't just know the outline of the story, he knew the whole thing, down to the name of the guy who'd helped Kessinger develop his cut from both sides of the plate.

That's preparation.

The stories Vin told were impressive, but so was the manner in which Vin recounted them. You never had the feeling that, with Kessinger at bat, Vin was telling the obligatory anecdote: Came up in '62, hit only .215 that year, the following season was asked by management to attempt switch-hitting, and, seven years later, he's still making a go of it. Blah, blah, blah.

Instead, Vin turned the Kessinger story into a lively narrative. As he himself might say, "It was marvelous."

On the one hand, Vin was speaking to an audience of Dodger sympathizers whose only real concern about Kessinger was that he make an out right then—and sooner rather than later. On the other, Vin had you caring about Kessinger. He had you—perish the thought—rooting for the enemy shortstop.

Not only does Vin tell good stories, but he tells good stories that fit. The story is always relevant to what's happening in the game at the moment. A batter twice fails to get a bunt down and then, with two strikes and the bunt sign removed, hits a three-run homer. Afterward, Vinny says, "The late Walter Alston once said, 'Some of the best signs I ever gave were bunt signs I took off.'" Amusing, adding perspective, and relevant to the moment.

Vin has this special ability to describe the game, add stories and anecdotes, and weave them into a beautiful tapestry. Each game, game after game.

Many years ago, Bob Costas and I were joking about this rare talent of Vin's. We agreed that Vin's timing was so good, he had to be getting some cooperation from the players. In deference to the many years he had been broadcasting games, it was apparent to us that the players secretly had agreed not to hit a ball off the wall or do anything similarly exciting until Vin had finished his anecdote.

Now *that's* respect.

The truth is, though, Vin has a feel for the game, not only for what just happened but for the big things that are about to happen. There are a few techniques to developing this; for instance, you try not to start a story with two outs—obviously, the third out can come on any pitch, and then you have to go right to a commercial and you're not going to get that story in.

Similarly, when the big stars are coming up, that's not the time for some big story. The stars become stars by doing remarkable, game-changing things. At that point, stay with what's going on on the field, stay with the game itself.

Yes, over the years, I've picked up a few things from the Master, Vin Scully. To paraphrase Roy Hobbs, a pretty fair hitter in a pretty fair movie, *The Natural,* "There goes Vin Scully, the best there ever was at broadcasting this game."

It's the
GAME, STUPID

Sometimes, when I hear an owner or a player—anybody connected with baseball—being interviewed, I'll wonder: Why did he say that?

Did he really think about what he was saying? Did he consider how it would come across to Joe Fan?

Let me give you an example.

A few years ago, the Orioles were in Milwaukee for a late-September series. The Brewers were in the thick of the pennant race; the Orioles weren't.

Unfortunately, the Brewers didn't let the excitement level get too high at County Stadium. Instead of promoting the pennant race, the Brewers were very vocal in the newspapers whining about the fact that they were one of baseball's "small market, poor teams."

One article concerned three of the Brewers' top players and how they would be free agents at the end of the year. General manager Sal Bando was quoted as saying that there was no way the Brewers, as a small-market club with limited resources, would be able to pay the money to re-sign them. Bando didn't out-and-out say the players would be gone the following season, but he came pretty close.

The Brewers were on a roll; if they stayed hot, they had a chance to pull off a miracle reversal and take the division title

But the Brewers refused to capitalize on this bit of good fortune. (Talk about purists!) Rather than emphasize the excitement, the general manager, in the local newspaper, was warning of impending doom. The timing seemed, at the least, unfortunate. From my standpoint, Bando might as well have been announcing, "Listen, fans, don't bother coming to the ballpark. Even if we win the division, we'll be lousy next year."

I'm sure Sal didn't think his comments were out of line. But when I read them, I cringed.

In baseball, we've gotten into the habit of denigrating the game. Unintentionally. Unwittingly. Yet we do it.

In other businesses, employees and owners don't knock the product. When you order a burger at McDonald's, the server doesn't whine about the runaway price of pickles.

Baseball is different. In baseball, knocking the product is a tradition. It happens every day, and it happens in ways that are subtle and, well, not so subtle.

I worry about that. I worry about what happens when for years and years fans are forced to listen to a drumbeat of criticism, especially when that criticism comes from within the game. It can't help baseball's image.

We should know better. All of us: owners, players, managers, and broadcasters—especially broadcasters. But we don't seem to catch on.

Baseball forgets that fans are interested in one thing and one thing only: the game.

Forget about revenue sharing. Forget about big markets, small markets. Forget about free agency and budget balancing. Forget about even the most veiled reference to the internecine wars between owners and players. Never bring those subjects up again.

Fans want the game: news about the game, discussion about the game. They come to baseball for the box scores in the morning paper, a fifteen-minute vacation from the world with their cup of coffee. Maybe they check out the top ten hitters.

But they don't read salary lists, and they don't care who wins or loses in arbitration. So don't bother baseball fans with that nonsense. It annoys them. It angers them. Worst of all, *it's booooring.*

One of the most intriguing events prior to the start of the 1997 season was the major, major trade involving the Braves and Indians. Three bona fide stars switched uniforms in one blockbuster deal, Marquis Grissom and David Justice going to the Indians and Kenny Lofton joining the Braves.

This was one helluva trade! It was the kind of deal that turns people on, gets them talking baseball and arguing about baseball. Both teams gave up a lot, but each got value in return— and, at the time, you could very easily have made the case that both were actually better off.

Fans in Cleveland and Atlanta were really excited about the trade, which for them was exactly that: a trade, purely an exchange of exceptional baseball talent.

But the baseball executives who made the deal didn't see it that way, and they seemed determined to make sure that the fans didn't have any more fun than they were having. All John Schuerholz, Atlanta's general manager, and John Hart, GM of the Indians, had to say about the deal was how it had been driven by baseball's insane economics. The message to fans was that this wasn't a deal either wanted to make or was happy about making, but a deal both felt forced to make in order to balance their ledgers. As if the whole idea of the trade disgusted them. Incredible.

What about the players? What about the big-time talent being added to each ballclub? John Hart was picking up David Justice, a great slugger to replace the departed Albert Belle, and Marquis Grissom, an outstanding center fielder who's a fine leadoff man. Not in the class of Lofton, for sure, but a fine leadoff man in the NL for many years.

As for Schuerholz, one of the most respected GMs in the game, he had just engineered a deal for someone who has been one of the dominating players in the game, a player who can create havoc on the bases, who causes problems for the opposition the moment he leaves the dugout.

In May, I asked Schuerholz about the trade and got the same answer that he'd given publicly—that it had been economically driven.

"But was it a good baseball trade?" I asked.

"Hell of a deal for us!" he admitted.

Despite that, fans weren't hearing about the baseball, only the economics. On *SportsCenter,* they got Schuerholz explaining, grim-faced, that the best aspect of the deal was that it trimmed the Braves' payroll by six million bucks. And John Hart lamented that, with Lofton about to become a free agent, there was no other fiscally responsible choice for the Indians but to deal. (Then, of course, free-agent Lofton ended up back with the Indians for the 1998 season.)

My point is, quit whining. You've made the trade. Now talk about *the trade.* The *players.* Who you got. Who you gave up. *The baseball.* Save the economics for the boardroom, for the investors and your bankers; they're the only ones who care about your budget. Your customers—and the people you want to *make* your customers—are only interested in the wins and losses.

"If I were a fan, how would that sound?"

In baseball, that's a question people should be asking five times a day. Maybe ten times a day. It isn't being asked enough. From now on, management must be more aware of the messages it sends to fans. The same goes for players, too.

Not long ago, I was reading one of Peter Gammons's always informative baseball columns in the Sunday edition of *The Boston Globe* when I came across a quote from Devon White of the Arizona Diamondbacks. The sheer audacity of this comment—coming from someone who has made a handsome living from this game—lingers in my memory like the dull pain of a toothache.

A sportswriter asked White if he'd kept track of the major-league expansion draft a few days earlier—a draft that indirectly brought him to the Diamondbacks.

"To be honest, I didn't follow it," White replied, adding that he'd been attending a Phoenix Suns game. "Basketball is my game and always has been. I don't know why I got into this sport."

Reading this, I wondered about White's choice of professions, too. Maybe he should have followed his heart and become a basketball player. Hey, maybe it's not too late. If White wants out of baseball to find true career fulfillment, I'm sure Jerry Colangelo, the owner of the Diamondbacks, won't stand in his way.

But that's a separate topic.

The topic here is Devon White and the game of baseball, a game that predates Devon White by 100 years and will be thriving for years after anyone can remember that Devon White ever played.

Devon White has a responsibility to the people who pay his salary and to this game that provides him with a nice living. That responsibility is to promote the game and to nurture it. That's something players should take more seriously—not just Devon White, but all players. It's just not acceptable to be out in public making statements like "I don't know why I got into this sport."

To me, the answer is education. I suggest that each club launch an informational program for its players. The curriculum would play up the history of Major League Baseball and a history of that particular team. If it's the St. Louis Cardinals, then explain the significance of wearing the uniform of the Cardinals: the tradition of Stan Musial, Lou Brock, Bob Gibson. Same for the Boston Red Sox, the San Francisco Giants, whoever. Let's not take for granted that these guys already know the histories and know the great players; some do, others don't. Ideally, players would walk out of that class feeling proud to be associated with that organization. And players, for the amount of money being invested in you, you can invest a little time learning why a team's fans—who ultimately pay your salaries—care so much about the uniform you're wearing.

The keys are to create a connection and to instill a sense of responsibility. When a player is out in public, he should think about his responsibility as a public figure representing his team and baseball and that awareness should be reflected in his actions. He shouldn't always blow off fans seeking autographs. He shouldn't *ever* be rude to kids. And when that player is speaking to a member of the media, he shouldn't denigrate the game.

Such denigration comes in many forms and from many directions. As an industry, we keep saying that the game is too slow. It's ponderous. No one wants to sit through a nine-inning game anymore. And we say that at news conferences so the whole world can reflect on how baseball is too slow, too ponderous, and not worth anybody's time. Why? Why do we say that?

Bud Selig chose the 1997 World Series as a forum to get off a few cracks about the pace of games.

"The Unfinished Symphony had a better chance of finishing before that game last night," Mr. Selig quipped after Game Three.

This from the acting commissioner, the game's supposed number-one booster and goodwill ambassador. Why is any baseball official, much less Mr. Selig, making a statement like that during baseball's premier event? Those ill-timed remarks should have been reason enough for the other baseball owners to hurriedly dismiss him as commissioner.

Can you imagine a commissioner standing up the day after Carlton Fisk's legendary home run in the sixth game of the 1975 World Series and making jokes at baseball's expense about how long that game took? Although that game gets talked about often, and remains fresh in the memories of many as one of the greatest World Series games ever, have you ever heard anyone talk about what a really long game it was? No. that wasn't the point. And it has never been the point in baseball. (For the record, that game lasted four hours, two minutes.)

Six years ago, baseball declared war on slow play. That war continues today. Initially, the owners made a big splash about their efforts. They cited statistics, they formed a committee, headed by a highly respected former umpire, Steve Palermo, to study the problem. They turned it into a major deal.

At the time, Mr. Selig and some other baseball executives talked about this issue as if it was being aired for the first time. In fact, improving the pace of games has been a topic of discussion for people in and around baseball most of this century.

"I definitely believe slow, dull games are keeping people away from the parks."

That sounds familiar, doesn't it? It seems as if you hear something like that a couple of times every week. "The game today takes too damn long."

But this quote was taken from *The Sporting News* in 1956. The man speaking was Cubs business manager Jim Gallagher, who was also a member of baseball's rules committee. The quote was part of a front-page story forty-two years ago detailing ways that baseball could go about speeding up games. In fact, the American League had plans to institute a speed-up rule that year that would have limited each manager to one mound conference per pitcher per game.

Sure, baseball always should be looking for ways to improve the pace of play, to keep the games moving. But my point is, why did the owners make this so public? Why call attention to a problem? Why not quietly analyze the problem, know what they're talking about, then take action?

Today's owners didn't do that. Instead, they invited a lot of people to join the discussion, including some who saw an opportunity to take a few cheap shots.

A number of sports columnists got into the act. The ones I read knocked the very idea of a three-hour baseball game, and that was as far as the commentary went. In some cases, the writer didn't even see the game in question; if it took three hours, eight minutes, that was all that mattered. More proof baseball is going down the tubes.

Baloney!! Or, as Vin Scully says, "Farmer John's all-beef bologna!"

In baseball, there can be a game that lasts three hours, fifty minutes but was so exciting you were sorry to see it end. (Like the sixth game of the '75 series.) On the other hand, there could be a two-hour, ten-minute game that was so dull you spent most of it counting the discarded peanut shells in your row. The length of the game is not necessarily related to the quality of play—or your enjoyment of it.

Should baseball take steps to speed up the game? Sure. Of course. And we've already proposed some simple ideas. But before the owners get out the scalpel and start cutting, maybe they ought to examine their own contributions to slower games.

During every game, after each half-inning, there's a break of two minutes, five seconds. This was mandated by baseball sometime in the 1980s, and this time is slotted for the commercials that help pay the bills of radio and TV stations and, ultimately, the salaries of owners, players, and even broadcasters.

When I started in baseball in 1974, and right through the mid-1980s, a one-minute commercial break between innings was the norm. Naturally, things moved a little more quickly. In the eighties, the Orioles had a starting pitcher, Storm Davis, who worked particularly fast; when an Orioles inning ended, Storm would run out to the mound, throw three or four warmup pitches, a throw went down to second, and Storm was ready. That fast.

Our only commitment between innings was to run one

sixty-second commercial, but Storm was so fast that we were hard-pressed to get back from our commercial break in time for his first pitch.

Since 1982, the time of the average game has increased by seventeen minutes. If the owners want to reduce the length of games by that much, they know how to do it: Go back to the norm of the early 1980s and reduce commercial breaks between innings from two minutes back to one minute. If they're going to complain about the length of the games, then they should start by addressing what *they've* done to make them longer.

On the other hand, this would be an expensive change. Shorter breaks mean fewer commercials, and fewer commercials mean less revenue to the clubs from their radio and TV partners.

If there's anything to be said in public by the owners about shortening games, it should be an announcement that the time between innings is being reduced to the standards of fifteen and twenty years ago. Any other changes should be made quietly, without fanfare.

Of course, before the owners do anything more drastic than that, they might stop to reflect on whether there truly *is* a clamor to speed up the games. I mean the game itself: the home run swings, the outfielders racing into the gaps. The actual events the fans come to see.

The family that spends $120 to buy four box seats to a game—are those parents hoping it gets over quickly? Do they say, "Gee, I hope this baby is over in two hours ten"? Or do they hope that Roger Clemens pitches a no-hitter, or that Barry Bonds hits a couple of home runs and that it's a great game? I think we know the answer to that.

However, there *are* two groups of people at the ballpark who often want it over in a hurry: the baseball writers and columnists, and members of my very own fraternity, the baseball broadcasters.

Their opinions, I say with all due respect, shouldn't count on this issue. It's in each writer's interest for the game to be short, or shorter; that way, he can meet his deadlines and have a little time to actually write well and creatively. That's what's on the mind of the newspaperman. It's understandable, and it's interesting, but it has absolutely nothing to do with what the fans want to see or why they come to the ballpark. (Also, being at the game is the writer's job, and it's only natural, when you're paid by the task and not by the hour, to want that task to be finished as quickly as possible.)

The only opinions about slow play that I pay attention to come from fans—the people who pay to see the game, who are there because they want to be, not because they have to be. What can we do to make the game more enjoyable for them? Let's find out. And then let's do it.

If baseball had a commissioner, we might not be talking about commercial breaks. And we might not still be talking about speeding up the game, for whatever steps baseball was going to take would have been taken years ago. That's the way things work when someone—anyone—is in charge.

Baseball fans don't care who the commissioner is. I really believe that. They don't discuss it over a beer, they don't argue about it with their friends. It just doesn't come up. Ever heard of a heated debate over who was the better commissioner, Bowie Kuhn or Happy Chandler? I haven't.

What fans do want, I believe, is someone in charge of baseball. Someone to hold accountable. Someone who loves baseball as much as they do. They want someone to represent the interests of the game, someone who'll speak up for baseball as a whole, not just the owners.

Baseball hasn't had any commissioner since Fay Vincent resigned under pressure on September 7, 1992. And it has been even longer since the game had an all-powerful czar—one not beholden to anyone or anything but the best interests of baseball. The last commissioner fitting that description might have been the legendary Kenesaw Mountain Landis, five decades ago.

Red Barber, the late, great Dodger broadcaster, once wrote that Landis's power was so pervasive that announcers selected to broadcast the World Series had to have a private meeting with the iron-fisted commissioner. During the meeting, Landis laid down ground rules for broadcasting the games that he expected them to follow.

Hmm, maybe I should reconsider the phrase *all-powerful commissioner.*

The owners say they are searching for a permanent commissioner and I take them at their word. But they've been looking for six years. That's a long time. And when they do get around to filling the job, how independent will the new commissioner really be? The idea of appointing a true commissioner—one who would be in charge of owners as well as players and umpires—seems to hold little appeal for a majority of the people who own baseball teams.

Baseball's next commissioner should possess vision, a clear-eyed, far-reaching vision to take baseball into the next millennium. Someone with the power and charisma to turn baseball's disparate interests away from their petty grievances and self-interest and toward coming together for the common good. What Spock said to Captain Kirk is apt for baseball as well as the *Enterprise:* "The needs of the many outweigh the needs of the few."

Mr. Selig is not the person to do it. Mr. Selig hasn't contributed any great ideas. In fact, most of his initiatives haven't been baseball ideas but business ideas. Increased revenue sharing among the owners has been a favorite cause for him. That's important, and a good start has been made in that area, but it has nothing to do with the fans' enjoyment of the game.

Similarly, Mr. Selig has been the force behind radical realignment. The plan didn't address the pressing problems of the game; its only apparent plus was for the business side of the game, that it *might* create a small bump in revenues.

And, of course, there was Mr. Selig's other contribution: helping to galvanize the owners around the hard-line plan that induced the players' strike in 1994. That horrible event blew up not only that year's great pennant races, but also the hot pursuit of some of baseball's most cherished home-run and batting records—not to mention depriving baseball fans of a World Series for the first time in more than ninety years. Yes, this is quite a legacy!

By appointing one of their own to run baseball, the owners effectively abolished the office of the commissioner. Baseball is still paying for that mistake, because there's no central authority in the game. If you compared it to the federal government, it would be as if the presidency had been abolished, leaving the leadership of the country solely in the hands of the Congress—with Newt Gingrich and Trent Lott being the country's most visible spokesmen (we might call Newt the "acting president"). There would be this familiar person who knew his way around Washington—but he wouldn't be the president, the person who is supposed to lead the entire country.

Right now, baseball is a nation without a president. It's a free-for-all, a power grab among all its various quarreling constituencies. The players' union and the umpires' union have done exactly what unions do in a leadership vacuum: They've pushed for more and more. Likewise, it seems, each owner has pursued a course that will serve the best interests of his franchise and his franchise only. This, too, is only natural.

A true baseball commissioner would represent owners, players, and umpires, but also would look out for paying customers, the citizens of baseball. Fans are the reason baseball exists. A baseball commissioner's office should always be where the best interests of the fans reside.

At this point, the owners apparently have no interest in the concept of an independent commissioner—or in any kind of commissioner. What's more, most baseball executives seem satisfied with the way baseball operates now. They don't appear to be demanding a change.

Edward Bennett Williams, the late Orioles owner, used to say that a baseball franchise was a public trust. Williams's point was that owners were only stewards of what ultimately did not belong to them, but to the fans. If the fans went away, there would be nothing left to own. This is a point that today's owners would do well to remember.

Sometimes, I think baseball suffers when it strays too far from the game itself in its search for leaders. There's a virtue in knowing the history of the game, but that too often gets ignored.

I don't know Gene Budig, the American League president, very well. What I know of him as a person—his record as a college president, as a respected educator, and as a major general in the Air Force reserves—is impressive. By all accounts, Gene Budig is an honest and decent man.

As a baseball executive, though, I give him lower marks.

In 1996, Dr. Budig was judge and jury when Roberto Alomar raised the ire of the baseball world by spitting in the face of umpire John Hirschbeck. The same year, Budig handled a less notorious case in which Albert Belle was discovered using a corked bat.

Belle's actions earned him a ten-game suspension. Alomar, for one of the most deplorable acts ever committed against an umpire, received five games.

On the Alomar case, my opinion is that Budig's decision was wrong. That's also the opinion of every umpire I know, many ballplayers, and a majority of fans. A five-game suspension sends the message that abusing an umpire is wrong, but not *that* wrong. A more logical penalty would have been thirty games.

I have no idea who advised Dr. Budig on the Alomar matter, but his best counsel would have been the baseball history books. In the books, Dr. Budig would have found precedents for cases like the Alomar controversy. One such incident is very similar—Frank Crosetti's physical confrontation with umpire Bill Summers in the 1942 World Series. For that act, Crosetti was handed a thirty-day suspension from the commissioner, Kenesaw Mountain Landis. (Bart Giamatti, when he was National League president, showed that his reputation as a student of baseball history was well earned; when Pete Rose, then the Reds' manager, shoved umpire Dave Pallone in a much-publicized incident in 1988, Giamatti gave Rose the same thirty-day suspension that Landis had given Crosetti.)

Maybe Dr. Budig knew about the Crosetti case. Maybe he didn't. What I'm saying is, he should have known. And that knowledge should have been put to use in setting a more appropriate penalty for Alomar.

And that's the point of everything I'm talking about here. Baseball people should know better. Hey, let's get personal: Wayne Huizenga should know better.

Huizenga, the owner of the Florida Marlins as I write this, though maybe not as you read this, is a puzzle. I don't understand why he got into baseball. He's a brilliant businessman, without question, and an extremely wealthy man, I know. But during his five years as owner of the Marlins, he did nothing to improve the image of Major League Baseball or build a trust with the fans. In fact, I'd say Huizenga's five years as the Marlins' owner wrought an astounding amount of damage on the house of Major League Baseball.

It started off with lots of promise. In 1993, Year One for the expansion franchise, the Marlins drew more than three million people, the second-best attendance ever for a first-year team. It was the traditional honeymoon period for an expansion team; the fans didn't expect good baseball from their fledging club, and, as expected, the club delivered—but the fans turned out anyway.

In the summer of 1994—the middle of the second season of the honeymoon—Huizenga apparently decided that the baseball business, which he'd only recently bought into, was terribly broken. He became one of the lead instigators in a hard-line management strategy that brought about a players strike—which, in turn, ended the honeymoon between the Marlins and their fans.

When the owners hired replacement players with whom they intended to begin the 1995 season, Huizenga was at the forefront. Worse, he marketed the no-name players relentlessly.

One radio advertisement boosting the Marlins' replacement team sticks in my mind. It began with an announcer, saying, *"Joe Replacement, he loves this game."*

Then came the voice of a replacement player.

"Hi, I'm Joe Replacement and I'm with the Marlins now. My dad said, 'Joey, whenever you put on that uniform, you play hard because it's an honor to wear that uniform. Don't do anything to disgrace it.'

"So when I'm out there, I always think of my dear old dad. And I play hard."

Pause. Then the announcer comes back with,

"Joe Replacement and the new Marlins.

"They love this game."

The implication, of course, was that Jeff Conine and Gary Sheffield, the real Marlins, were overpaid slobs who didn't love the game and were charlatans stealing the fans' money.

This was an unfortunate message to send to the fans. When the replacements were sent home, which was inevitable, and the likes of Conine and Sheffield returned to Joe Robbie Stadium, what were the Marlins' marketing plans then? They had just spent six weeks hyping replacement players, and at the same time denigrating their real product. Marlins fans didn't come back in anywhere near their prestrike numbers. After all, for six weeks the Marlins had sold them on the notion of Joe Replacement. And where was he now?

For the next three years, Huizenga continued to toy with the emotions of Marlins fans.

In the winters of 1995 and 1996, he decided to plunge into the free-agent market and buy a championship team, collecting players such as Bobby Bonilla, Moises Alou, Kevin Brown, Al Leiter, Devon White, and Alex Fernandez, and hiring manager Jim Leyland.

Then in June 1997, with the team not playing up to preseason expectations, Huizenga announced he was putting the Marlins up for sale. Here he had spent all this money to put a top team on the field, he complained, and where were the fans?

"The other night we had Alex Fernandez pitching and there were twelve thousand people there. Here's a local player that we are paying a lot of money to and all we got were twelve thousand people," Huizenga told the *Fort Lauderdale Sun-Sentinel.*

In October 1997, Huizenga's spending spree paid the ultimate dividend as the Marlins defeated Cleveland in a memorable seven-game World Series. What's more, attendance had picked up late in the season, finishing at 2.5 million. (For a little historical perspective, the 1974 world champion Oakland A's had home attendance of 840,000.)

The 1998 season figured to be still better. Anyone who has been around baseball any length of time at all knows that when a team has a great year, the big payoff is always the next year. The Marlins, by following baseball's past example, no doubt would have had a huge presale of tickets and sponsorships for 1998, capitalizing on all the euphoria in South Florida surrounding the team's success. And with another strong team in place, the Marlins might well have come close to selling out every home game in the 1998 season.

Huizenga, however, didn't change his mind about selling. The morning after Game 7, America woke up to the owner of the world champion Marlins explaining that a World Series title isn't all it's cracked up to be. "It's a bittersweet victory," Huizenga said on NBC's *Today Show.* "We're pleased and excited that we won. But we lost $34 million."

When asked how soon he anticipated selling the team he said, "Well, as quickly as time would permit."

Two weeks later, on November 11, 1997, the dismantling of the world champion Marlins began when the club traded their RBI leader, Moises Alou, to Houston for three minor leaguers (read "inexpensive"). That move was followed on November 18 by deals that cost the Marlins two other key players, White and ace closer Robb Nen. It was also revealed that the Marlins' new plan was to reduce their $53 million player payroll to under $20 million in preparation for the team's sale. After all, Huizenga had already given Marlins fans almost a full night to celebrate their first world championship, something Red Sox fans have not celebrated in eighty years, Cubs fans in ninety years. What more could they expect?

This wholesale divestiture of talent was reminiscent of another of baseball's famous "going out of business" sales. In 1920, Red Sox owner Harry Frazee sold a young Babe Ruth to the Yankees for $125,000 and a loan of $300,000. The Red Sox haven't won a World Series since, a fact many New Englanders have long blamed on the "Curse of the Bambino."

In the year 2077, I wonder whether Marlins fans will be ruefully referring to the "Curse of Huizenga."

Wayne Huizenga wants to sell. Thank God. Maybe baseball will survive, after all.

PARTNERS

One of my best friends in the business is Ken Coleman, former voice extraordinaire of the Boston Red Sox. Ken and I were partners in Boston from 1980 to '82. We had wonderful rapport on the air, and we had fun off the air. It was two years of exciting baseball and a lot of laughs.

So I'm a little embarrassed to admit that I once wasn't all that fond of Ken.

In 1975, Ken and I were the final two candidates for the same job, working TV games for the Cincinnati Reds. Ken got the job.

This made perfect sense. Ken was an established broadcaster, with decades of experience in Cleveland and Boston. I was an ambitious but inexperienced twenty-three year old. I was also unemployed, as Charlie Finley had just fired me about two weeks before spring training began. I wasn't given a reason for the dismissal—but then, with Charlie, reasons seemed almost beside the point. I was hired in the seventh year after the A's had moved from Kansas City to Oakland. I was their sixth broadcaster.

My predecessor with the A's, Jim Woods—as good a broadcaster as there ever was—went from Oakland to Boston, where he teamed up with Ned Martin. That twosome became one of the most popular Red Sox broadcasting teams of all time. But, of course, Woods hadn't been the right broadcaster for Charlie; when he fired Jim, Charlie said in the papers that Jim "wasn't exciting enough when nothing was happening." It's hard to argue with logic like that.

Anyway, I went to Cincinnati to audition for the Reds job, an audition that consisted of doing two commercials for their primary beer sponsor: "Hudepohl. Remember the name. You'll never forget the taste!" The TV station said they liked my youth and were hoping to go with youth, but after a long tug-of-war between the station and the sponsor, the decision was made to go with experience instead.

I handled the news graciously: "Ken Coleman? I can't believe they took the old, washed-up guy!"

Flash ahead five years. Ken had moved back to Boston. I had been working as the lead radio/TV broadcaster for the Texas Rangers.

One day after the 1979 season ended, I got a phone call from Ken. It seemed that the radio station that carried the Red Sox games had decided not to bring back Ken's partner, former Sox infielder Rico Petrocelli. Ken had recommended me to the station honchos, and he was calling to encourage me to speak with them.

"You're the perfect guy," Ken said. "I really enjoy your work. I think we'd make a strong team; you're my number-one choice for the job."

Eventually I took the job and went to Boston to work with "the old, washed-up guy."

The reality was that Ken was a great professional, still at the top of his form. Also, working with Ken was like having my agent right there with me on the Red Sox broadcasts. He was always looking for ways for me to blossom, to show off my talents and establish myself in the market. The more bits I tried, the more Ken wanted me to try.

I have this unusual hobby with baseball voices. I collect them, and I perform them. Mostly, my voices are broadcasters.

I do Vin Scully of the Dodgers and Chuck Thompson of the Orioles—doing the same game, if you'd like. I also collect stadium public-address announcers, a genre I seem to have to myself.

For years, I did my voices around batting cages and in clubhouses. I never did them on the air. I never thought about doing them on the air—after all, I figured, you never hear Vin Scully doing it.

During my first spring training with the Red Sox, Ken and I were driving all over Florida, from Alligator Alley to Yee-Haw Junction, following the Red Sox as we broadcast almost daily from the Grapefruit League. On our journeys, we told each other our stories and had each other laughing away the hours.

After leaving Florida, we headed north to open the season. After three games in Milwaukee, we moved on to Boston for the eagerly anticipated home opener at Fenway Park. On a typical overcast, drizzly New England day, the Sox played the Tigers. Along about the seventh inning, it began raining heavily enough that the game was stopped and the grounds crew put the tarp on the field.

The audience for the broadcast was huge; Opening Day always draws top ratings. In addition to that, we were inching toward the afternoon rush hour. Soon, more than half of New England would be listening. In the event of a rain delay, the format on the Red Sox network was for Ken and me to just keep talking.

So . . . Ken just started talking. It was baseball talk: tales from spring training. A word or two about our endless drives across Florida. And then Ken, as if we were back in the rental car, just the two of us, started to lead me into a story involving a Vin Scully impression.

Until that moment, I'd never done the voices on the air. I'd never imagined doing them. I didn't *want* to do them on the air.

Now, to my total amazement, Ken is looking at me and saying with total nonchalance, "Jon, for our listeners out there, would you do that Vin Scully thing?"

Trusting Ken's instincts, I fastened my seat belt and took the plunge: for the eighty-eight stations along the Red Sox New England radio network, I did my Vin Scully schtick. I did some stories about life with Charlie Finley, including some in his voice. I did Bob Sheppard, the PA announcer at Yankee Stadium, and Sherm Feller, the PA man at Fenway.

I guess Ken had mentally filed away each story and each impersonation as we'd driven across Florida. He remembered which ones I could do, and on the air he carefully set me up to tell each story and deliver each impression. I was totally in his hands.

Eventually, the weather cleared and we finished the game. That night, when I got back to the hotel in town where I was staying, I had this six-inch stack of telegrams: people welcoming me to New England, people saying they'd really enjoyed the broadcast, and so on. It was gratifying.

Many had mentioned how we filled the rain delay. No one demanded that I be detained by state troopers and dumped in Rhode Island. People seemed to have liked what we had done. Thank heavens. Also, there were several calls from radio and TV stations in New England.

One was from a producer at a local TV station, asking me to be a live guest on their eleven o'clock news. They sent a chauffeured car to the hotel, and a half hour later I was on the set with the anchor guy. He welcomed me to Boston and said, "At about a quarter to five, I'm sitting in bumper-to-bumper traffic on the Southeast Expressway and all of a sudden you're doing Vin Scully. I laughed so hard, I almost caused a twenty-car pileup. Ha, ha, ha."

"Thank you," I said.

Then the anchor guy says, "Do your Vin Scully now, will you?"

I'm in Boston. I'm on the eleven o'clock news. And I'm doing Vin Scully. Crazy.

A month later, Jack Craig wrote a profile of me for *The Boston Globe* with the headline "JON MILLER, BOSTON'S NEW VOICE(S)." After a week with the Red Sox, I was now known for my impressions, for my comedy. I started getting invitations to speak at luncheons and banquets. All of a sudden I'm on the rubber-chicken circuit—and I didn't have an act. I needed one, and quick.

Those rides along Alligator Alley and through Yee-Haw Junction had created a monster.

Ken was one of my favorite partners. Now he's one of my favorite ex-partners, along with Monte Moore, Chuck Thompson, and two favorites with whom I worked on the occasions when I had a chance to do a few Games of the Week on NBC—Joe Garagiola and Tony Kubek.

You never forget your first partner. I'll never forget Monte Moore.

After the 1973 season, I tried to get a job broadcasting minor-league baseball, but I also applied for every opening I knew about with a major-league club, even though I didn't hold out much hope of getting a big-league job at age twenty-two and without any pro-baseball experience.

When I read that Charlie Finley had fired the veteran Jim Woods from the A's broadcast team, I thought myself so unlikely to be hired that I didn't even call anybody about the job. But I did send a tape to Finley in Chicago. Finley, in turn, sent all the tapes—there were more than 100 applicants—to Monte Moore. He asked Monte to find the best four or five and play them over the phone for him.

Monte had never heard of me. And, with so many tapes, it would have been understandable if he'd immediately thrown mine into the reject pile. But he did listen to my tape, and he liked my work. Charlie liked it, too. And I got the job.

I was in the majors! And at $24,000 a year—I was rich!

Charlie's reputation as a big-time meddler was legendary, so before I was hired, as politely as I could, I put the question to Monte. "Am I going to be miserable?" I asked. "Is he going to be telling me what to say on the air?"

"Absolutely not," Monte assured me. "He'll never tell you what to say on the air. He rarely sees the team play. He counts on our descriptions as an accurate gauge of what's going on; most of his player moves and whatnot are based on that."

At one point that summer, the A's were in Baltimore to play the Orioles at Memorial Stadium. It was the sixth inning, I think, and I was working on the TV side, my usual assignment for the middle three innings. The first three and last three I worked on the radio.

Mike Cuellar, the Orioles pitcher, uncorked a wild pitch with Reggie Jackson on third. Reggie made a dash for the plate, arriving at the same time as the throw. Cuellar applied the tag—a close play, but the umpire called Reggie safe. The A's were ahead, 1-0.

A huge argument ensued at home plate. Cuellar was outraged. He was sure Reggie should have been called out.

When we rolled our replay, it clearly showed that Cuellar was right. Jackson was six or seven inches from the plate when Cuellar applied the tag. The A's had gotten a break, I pointed out.

The next inning, I was back on the radio side. For the benefit of the radio audience, I described what we'd seen on the television side and what the replay had revealed—that Jackson was a half foot away from the plate when Cuellar slapped him with the glove. Based on the replay, the correct call would have been out, I said on the air.

Then I forgot about it—until the end of the inning, when

the A's traveling secretary, Jim Bank, came into the booth with a message.

"Charlie just called," Jim said. "He told me to tell you to quit arguing with the umpires."

I was steamed. Hadn't Monte told me that Charlie would never interfere with what I said on the air? That was the deal. Wasn't that the deal?

I stewed about Charlie's call for the rest of the game. Later, Monte and I were sitting together in the press parking lot, waiting to get on the team bus and head back to the hotel. I started to tell Monte about hearing from Charlie, but he stopped me.

"Charlie told me about it. He called me when the game was over," Monte said.

Monte was as angry about Charlie's antics as I was, I could tell. And, from what I could gather, so could Charlie after he'd spoken with Monte.

"What did Charlie say?" I asked.

"He was all defensive," Monte replied. "I told him, 'Look, Charlie, I promised Jon when he took this job that you would never tell him what to say on the air. That's what we agreed on.'"

"And Charlie?"

"Oh, you know Charlie," Monte said. "In that gruff voice, he said, 'I'm not telling Jon what to say. I don't mind him reporting what he saw. But he kept talking about it over and over. We're trying to sell the public on this hustling ballclub. We got a guy hustling home on a wild pitch. The umpire calls him safe. And my broadcaster is telling our fans it's a bad call, and telling them over and over.

"'If he's going to say it, tell Jon to say it just once.'"

"I see, just once," I said. "Not over and over."

"Yeah, just once," said Monte.

"Not over and over."

Monte cracked up.

. . .

My greatest teachers have been my partners, especially in my early years broadcasting baseball. Monte imparted his unique scorekeeping system—much of which I'm using twenty-five years later—and a great knowledge of the game. Ken was a great teacher. I learned something from Ken every broadcast.

Maybe the most important thing I picked up from Ken was to describe what was happening on the field. People care about the game; they tune in to hear the game. It's fine to be armed with statistics—it's even advisable. But the broadcast isn't about statistics. No one is listening to hear so-and-so's slugging percentage from July 8 to September 9. They're listening for the game.

Back in 1980, I had my awakening. The Red Sox were in Detroit, and pitching for the Tigers was Mark "The Bird" Fidrych, one of the kookiest but totally lovable characters ever to wear a baseball uniform.

Fidrych had been the talk of baseball during his rookie year, 1976, when he went 19-9. Arm troubles eventually knocked him out of baseball prematurely, at the age of twenty-six, but for several years, he was perennially attempting to come back, always trying to recapture the magic.

And Fidrych still had the magic—at least, with the fans. The game drew a huge crowd at Tiger Stadium, and, from what we gathered, a big audience for our broadcast back in New England. Fidrych is from Massachusetts, a New Englander himself.

Before the game, I asked our radio engineer if he'd dub a tape of the broadcast for me; with all the excitement, I thought it would be a neat souvenir. I also wanted to critique my performance. I think it's a good idea to listen periodically to a broadcast to make sure you're doing the job properly and haven't fallen prey to any bad habits.

I was ready for this game. I'd prepared long and hard. I knew everything there was to know about Fidrych. I knew all of his great moments and about all of his various arm injuries. I knew what Sparky Anderson, his manager, was saying about him. I knew what Roger Craig, his pitching coach, was saying about him. I knew what Fidrych himself had said the day before.

And I knew even more: my first wife and The Bird were distant relatives, so I knew family stories that weren't even public knowledge.

This is the way I thought you were supposed to prepare. You gathered up every scrap of background information, then you scraped together even more.

It turned out to be a great game. Fifty thousand fans jammed ancient Tiger Stadium. Fidrych pitched seven strong innings, leaving with the lead. But Fidrych's pitching was beside the point; he'd put on a show, and the fans loved it. Maybe this time his arm would hold up. For Tiger fans, the evening was about excitement, about hope.

Fidrych talked to the baseball. Fidrych got on his hands and knees and groomed the mound. Between pitches, he'd assume his trademark, storklike stance on the pitcher's slab, glove held away from his body, hunched over slightly at the waist.

The next day, I listened to the broadcast on tape. Ken's innings were stunning. I couldn't get over the job he'd done making the whole thing come alive so vividly for the unseeing radio audience. Every eccentricity, the smallest detail. Ken had found an adjective for every move. He'd painted a rich picture of an unusual game and the unique pitcher.

Then I listened to my innings.

I had all the stats. Career winning percentage. Number of victories against teams with leadoff batters named Leo. That type of thing.

And I had my anecdotes. The story behind his first arm injury. The story behind the second arm injury. The third, the fourth . . .

But I'd lost the feel of the game. It's great to have stories, and it's fine to have numbers—but Mark Fidrych was live, right in front of me. There he was, the guy on the mound. It's radio. So let's tell the people what he's doing! If he's down on his hands and knees, talk about it. If he's talking to the baseball, talk about it. When he's applauding a good play behind him, say that. If he's sprinting off the mound after a third out, say that, too.

Call it an epiphany, if you will, but as I listened to Ken do that game, something clicked. I'd learned something very valuable from one of the very best teachers.

Thanks, Ken.

I'm including Chuck Thompson in this chapter, even though he only qualifies on a technicality.

Chuck and I have never officially been partners. Not full-time anyway; by the time I arrived in Baltimore in 1983, Chuck had retired from the grind of everyday radio work.

In 1990, Chuck returned to Orioles radio, working a couple of dozen games a year, filling in when I was off doing ESPN work, or when my partner or I were taking time off. If there's ever been a better substitute, I don't know him.

When you think of Chuck, the number-one thing—and the number-two, number-three, and number-four things—you think of is the voice. Chuck Thompson has the greatest voice of any broadcaster I've ever heard. Personally, I'd rather listen to Chuck than to Pavarotti, especially explaining the infield-fly rule.

This isn't only my opinion—it's the opinion of a lot of people who know baseball and know voices.

About ten years ago, I bumped into Jim McKay and Jim's wife Margaret at the Miami airport. Jim, a Maryland resident, is the wonderful ABC sportscaster of so many years and a small investor in the Orioles. Jim was marveling at Chuck, the pristine sound of his voice.

"He sounds exactly the same today as he sounded in 1950," he said.

I wanted to agree, but couldn't—I was born in '51. But I do

agree with anybody who says that Chuck has a classic baseball voice. It's big. It's distinctive. And it's full of life.

One of the greatest kicks for me has been just being with Chuck and listening to him. He literally sounds exactly the same way in person as he does doing a game. There's absolutely nothing put-on about his style. He doesn't go into the "Chuck Thompson, broadcaster" mode. He's just Chuck Thompson, on or off the air.

One of the qualities that shines through is Chuck's niceness. Chuck is the kind of guy who wants to buy you a soda or a beer, who always asks about your kids—and remembers their names! He drives the speed limit. He even says "please" and "thank you."

The only place I've ever seen Chuck become impatient is at a crowded restaurant. Chuck refuses to stand in line for a meal.

Chuck is so gracious, he has a terrible time uttering a mean thing about anybody, even on the broadcast. Even if somebody has screwed up. If you listen carefully, you pick up that Chuck is perturbed—but he always couches it. He apologizes in advance for perhaps sounding a little critical.

For all the reasons just stated, Chuck is good company away from the ballpark. Several years ago, Chuck and I were with the Orioles in Oakland, and we had an off day. In passing, Chuck mentioned that in all the years he'd been coming to the Bay Area with the Orioles and when he was broadcasting Colts football games, he'd never done any sightseeing. He'd been around San Francisco, to restaurants and whatnot, but he'd never seen the real sights. Never actually seen a giant redwood.

I had no intention of turning him over to Grayline. So I rented a car and the two of us drove up to Muir Woods in Marin County, to the spectacular forest of old-growth coastal redwoods. We parked the car in the small lot, and then Chuck and I made the short walk into the redwood grove.

As we strolled in, Chuck stopped and gazed up into the giant cathedral of trees, stretching hundreds of feet into the sky. I don't think Chuck had seen anything so impressive since Brooks Robinson in the 1970 World Series.

"Holy guacamole! Will you look at that," he said. "I can't believe what I'm seeing here. This is truly a remarkable, remarkable sight."

There might have been an "Ain't the beer cold" thrown in there, too.

That's Chuck. To hear him is to know him. To like him, too.

In 1986, NBC hired me for a few Games of the Week. I was subbing for Bob Costas, who was off doing NBC's football pregame show.

This was the pinnacle. The Game of the Week. The telecast I'd grown up with. And my partner? Only Tony Kubek, the Yankee shortstop turned broadcaster I'd watched for eighteen years. For many years, Tony and Curt Gowdy (and later Joe Garagiola) had done all of baseball's biggest games for NBC.

I was excited. My agent told me the exposure would be a boost for my career. I guess; mostly, I wanted to ask Tony about the ball that Bobby Richardson snared off the bat of Willie McCovey to seal the '62 World Series, sending me into such a deep depression that I missed the next three episodes of *The Donna Reed Show*.

Our game was at the Astrodome. The night before, we were at the ballpark. I was sitting next to Tony. He leaned over and said, "I guess we ought to talk about working together.

"You're the play-by-play man. You're in charge. My job is to work around you, to take my cues from you. It's my job never to step on you. If I step on your lines, that's my fault. Don't worry about it."

I didn't want to be giving orders to Tony Kubek. I couldn't give orders to Tony Kubek; I hear Tony Kubek's voice and I flash back to Converse sneakers and chocolate milk with lunch.

"I appreciate what you're saying," I said. "But don't be telling me I'm in charge. You be in charge. Just do whatever you want."

"No, that's our format," Tony insisted. "The play-by-play man is in charge."

OK, I was in charge.

Actually, the person who truly was in charge of the telecast was Harry Coyle, the legendary director, the father of televised sports. Harry just about invented how sports are covered on TV. He had directed World Series telecasts since 1947.

By 1986, Harry wasn't doing every Game of the Week, but I was lucky: Houston appeared headed for the postseason, and Harry was in town to prepare for the playoffs, checking on camera positions and such. He was going to be in town, so he said, "What the hell, I'll direct the game."

Working for Harry was one of the memorable experiences of my life. Before the game, we had a meeting. Harry spoke briefly.

"There are two rules never to forget," he advised. "Number one, if you say, 'There's activity in the bullpen,' that's a cue to me that you know the name of the pitcher warming up. I'll have a shot of that guy warming up within two or three seconds. If you don't know who it is, it could be embarrassing."

Harry paused.

"The second rule is, never swear on the air."

I tried to observe these rules. I don't recall breaking either one. Anyway, that telecast was one of the easiest I can remember. Harry never spoke to me during the inning, only between innings, and he always seemed to have camera shots of whatever we were talking about.

Working with Tony was as exciting as I had imagined. He has great knowledge of the game, and he has a good sense of humor. He was fun.

I went on to work with Tony again a few times that year and over the next couple years. Then, in 1988, NBC asked me to sub for Vin Scully. Since 1982, Vin and Joe Garagiola had been the lead voices for the Game of the Week. But one of Vin's children was getting married that particular Saturday and he took the day off. They wanted me to fill in.

This was a thrill. As I've said elsewhere in this book, Vin is the best there has ever been. To sit in his chair, even for one day, was special.

And I got a kick out of working with Joe Garagiola, someone I'd long admired. We're talking legend—a man who sat on the *Today* show set with Frank Blair and Gene Shalit all those years. A man who wrote *Baseball Is a Funny Game,* one of the best-selling baseball books of all time.

As I had with Tony, I got a chance to sit with Joe at the ballgame the night before our telecast. And as with Tony, I got a lesson in humility—Joe's.

"You're the play-by-play man," Joe said. "You're the boss."

This must have been in the NBC Game of the Week handbook; both Tony and Joe said almost exactly the same thing to me.

"There's only one thing I'll ask of you," Joe said. "Listen to me. Listen to what I say. My style doesn't work unless you listen to what I say—and respond.

"For instance, I might say to you, 'Jon, every bone in my body tells me that guy is going to be running on the next pitch.' I'm asking you, make a note of that. Because now the next pitch comes in and the guy doesn't run. Nothing happens.

"Well, go ahead and zing me. Zing me good. 'Thank God you're not managing.' Or, 'Thank God you're not catching.' Whatever. Just drill me. We'll have a good laugh over it. And then I'll proceed to make my point.

"It's only a problem for me if I make a comment, a prediction, and you ignore me. If I say, 'Every bone in my body tells me this guy is running,' and he doesn't go, and you just start talking about something else—then I look like an idiot."

I thought this was most interesting. Joe is a very funny guy. That's the style he brought to the broadcast. Yet as Joe's partner, you became an integral part of his style.

I've never worked with Harry Caray. I'm kind of sorry about that.

I think it would be fun teaming up with Harry, just as I think it probably would be fun costarring in a movie with Robin Williams. Different personalities, but the same presence. I mean, Harry is a force of nature. He's a show all by himself.

The way Harry broadcasts a game, it's obvious he's a fan. That's his calling card: he's the fan who got a chance to go up in the booth and be a broadcaster. Harry reacts to a situation as a fan would. That's his style, and it's worked for him for fifty-two major-league seasons.

If Sammy Sosa—the big star making the big money—pops out with the bases loaded, well, Harry's disappointed, just like the fans. If a Cubs batter comes up in a crucial spot and swings at a couple of bad pitches, Harry will be down on the guy, just like the fans. There's a complete and total identification between Harry and the fans.

As a baseball fan, I'm a Harry Caray fan. And as a broadcaster, I'm a Harry Caray fan, too. One thing I really admire about Harry's style is the way he frames each pitch. By that, I mean the way he sets apart the play-by-play from the rest of his dialogue, as if it were in a frame, hanging by itself.

It doesn't matter how fascinating the anecdote might be— when it's time for the pitch, Harry pauses and says, "Here's the pitch," or maybe, "Pitch on the way." Doesn't matter whether it's radio or television. Harry frames every pitch.

Of course, the greatest thing about Harry is Harry, the voice, the mannerisms, the style. Harry leaning out of the Wrigley Field press box to lead the crowd in a chorus of "Take Me

Out to the Ballgame"; Harry's famed home-run call: "It could be, it might be, it IS . . ."

And of course, Harry's all purpose exclamation: "Hoe-lee Cowww!"

When I speak at banquets, I'll often do a little of my Harry material, exaggerating Harry's amazing voice and putting him into everyday situations. For instance, Harry at home when the alarm on the clock radio comes on: "It could be, it might be, it IS . . . time to get up! Holy cow!"

A couple of years ago, *ESPN Sunday Night Baseball* was at Wrigley Field for the Cubs and Phillies. And who should stop by the booth during the third inning but Harry himself. Joe Morgan, Harry, and I chitchatted for a while on the air about the Cubs.

Then Harry steered the conversation to me. "Jon, I've heard your takeoff on me," he said. "I thoroughly enjoy it. But I ask you: Do I look inebriated?"

I thought Joe was going to fall out of the booth he was laughing so hard.

"Now, Harry," I stated, "you know I just do a caricature of you. It's not the real you. I do you the way comedians always did John Wayne and Kirk Douglas. Because you're so famous, so recognizable. Harry, you're big. You are very big."

Harry just looked at me with a big grin. "You know, Jon," he remarked. "You're a helluva politician."

Harry's reaction to my Harry impersonation is typical of the feedback I've received through the years. I haven't spoken about the mimicry with the rightful owners of all my voices—for instance, Vin Scully and I have never spoken about my occasional Vinny riffs, though I've been told by others he enjoys them. But those I have had a chance to speak with—Chuck Thompson, Harry Kalas, Phil Rizzuto, among others—have told me how much they enjoy them. And that's nice.

Or as Chuck might put it, "Good golly, that just gives me a very, very warm feeling inside this grand old body of mine."

Fear Never
STRIKES OUT

No matter who they are or where they play, baseball players fall into two categories: Those who have been hit in the head, and those who fear they will someday.

It's a hard way to live, but once you've seen the damage that a speeding baseball can do, you understand, and you empathize.

Over the years, I've seen some nasty accidents. Back in 1980, I was broadcasting for the Red Sox. The Orioles had come to Fenway Park, and early in the game, Ken Singleton, their hard-hitting designated hitter, was batting against Mike Torrez.

Singleton was one of the best DHs of his era—a switch-hitter with a pure swing from both sides of the plate. In his prime, everything off his bat was a line drive.

Singleton scorched a rope back through the middle. The ball took off like a rocket and nailed Torrez right in the forehead. It was on top of Torrez so quickly that he didn't even have time to get his hands up. The ball ricocheted all the way to left field; Jim Rice picked it up and flipped it in to second to hold Singleton to one base.

Other than Rice, I doubt anybody noticed what happened to the ball—all eyes in the ballpark were on Torrez. The guy had absorbed a terrific blow. Somehow, he'd stayed on his feet, but the shot had staggered him. And the Boston trainer was immediately out on the field to see if Torrez was OK.

The trainer went through all the tests: How many fingers do I have up? Who was the first president? All the questions you ask when trying to assess whether the brain is functioning. Then, after a few pats on the behind—this was the most amazing part—Torrez stayed in the game! Five minutes after he'd almost been killed on the pitcher's mound at Fenway Park!

Torrez pitched to one more batter, Eddie Murray, who bounced into a double play to end the inning. When Torrez got back to dugout, he apparently mentioned to someone, "Geez, all of a sudden I have this splitting headache." They rushed him off to the hospital, and we didn't see any more of Mike Torrez that afternoon.

There's a part of this story that I couldn't figure out that day, and almost twenty years later, it still doesn't compute. If there's a neurologist out there, maybe you could write in and explain.

Torrez was walloped with a line drive zipping along at 100 miles an hour. Trained medical personnel had examined him, and pronounced him fit to continue. Then, two outs and ten minutes later, he's in the back of an ambulance. I'm not a doctor, but it seemed odd.

I knew pitchers feared being nailed, but I hadn't realized how deep those feelings ran until I talked to a number of pitchers about it. Obviously, not everyone is affected the same way, but there isn't a major leaguer who hasn't at least contemplated the dangers of standing out on that mound, alone, utterly vulnerable.

In 1986, my wife, Janine, and I were invited to join six or seven Orioles players, their wives, and about 150 baseball fans on the annual Orioles Caribbean cruise. It was a great time, and I spent a good part of the trip hanging out with Don Aase, then the Orioles' closer, and Don's wife, Judy. They're nice people. We had a great time in the tropics.

One day, sitting at Grand Anse Beach in Grenada, I mentioned to Don and Judy that during the season I had a recurring dream with a baseball theme, though it was not strictly about baseball. This dream was troubling me.

It was a sexual dream. I'm in my bedroom, it's a tender moment. All of a sudden, Ralph Houk, one of my managerial idols, walks in and kicks off the sheets.

"Sorry, Miller, but you've had it for the night," the Major says. "I'm making a call to the bullpen."

Then, in my dream, Ralph Houk actually brings in somebody *to finish the sexual act.*

I swear I've had this dream. What a psychiatrist or a psychologist would make of it, I have no idea, and I don't care to find out.

When Don Aase heard this, he told me about a dream he'd had several times. It had a baseball context, but unlike mine, there was nothing cryptic about it.

In Don's dream, he was on the mound when a scorching line drive was hit right at his head. Just then, he would invariably sit bolt upright in bed, throw his arms in front of his face, and let out a bloodcurdling shriek.

"The first couple times I had the dream," Don told me, "Judy would wake up in a panic, yelling: 'What is it, Don? What's happening?'

"I'd say something like, 'It's a line drive right at my face.'"

After the scene repeated itself several times, Judy knew exactly how to handle Don. At the first indication he was having this terrifying dream, she'd wrap her arms around him and comfort him, whispering, "Don, Don, you're in bed. There was no line drive. You're OK now. Go back to sleep."

It's no different for hitters. For many, the fear of being beaned never leaves them. It can be repressed, pushed deep into the subconscious, but it's always there.

Dwight Evans, one of my favorite Red Sox, was badly beaned in 1978. That was the year the Sox had a fourteen-game lead and blew it. As their advantage slipped away, Dwight hurried his recuperation and possibly came back too soon. He was never the same that year. I remember him saying that, for the rest of that season, each time he lifted his head to catch a fly ball, he got very dizzy.

Once, Dwight and I were talking about some of the injuries he'd been through. Suddenly, he stopped and leaned in.

"Don't tell this to anyone," he said, "but the one guy who frightens me is Goose Gossage."

That was understandable—Gossage scared a lot of hitters. He was this big, mean-looking guy straight out of one of those fifties Wild West movies. He had the big mustache. He had a big, sweeping motion; the arms went this way, the legs went the other way. He was out there for one reason only: to throw the ball as hard as humanly possible. Once it left Goose's hand, well, his philosophy seemed to be, "It's somebody else's problem now."

Gossage had one habit that totally unnerved Evans: in mid-windup, Goose looked away. Not on every pitch, but often enough to notice. Instead of locking in on the catcher's mitt like most pitchers did, Goose would shoot a glance at the pitching rubber, or into the dugout—everywhere but where the ball was going.

Dwight couldn't handle that. When Gossage looked away, it was over for him. Gossage could have thrown underhand, but Dwight would've been halfway to the dugout.

Every ballplayer deals with anxieties differently. Evans spoke about being beaned—to me, at least. It seemed to be his way of dealing with the bad memories.

Mike Devereaux, a fine outfielder for several years with the Orioles, was the opposite. In 1994, Devereaux was hit in the side of the face. It was a Sunday—I was off doing *Sunday Night Baseball.*

When I saw him the next night, I could tell it had been a horrible shot. Half of Mike's face was swollen. He looked terrible. I went up to him in the clubhouse and commiserated with him. Then I asked him about the pitch that had hit him, just to get a little information for the broadcast.

Mike sort of recoiled. "Jon, I really don't want to talk about it," he stated firmly.

"You don't want to talk about the beaning?" I asked, a bit surprised.

"You can understand that," Mike said. "I just don't want to talk about it anymore."

That was Mike's way of handling the situation. The whole episode had been traumatic, I'm sure, and not just for him—around the Orioles clubhouse, there were a lot of concerned faces. A lot of those guys, I sensed, were trying to avoid thinking, "Tonight, it could be me. I could be the one with the concussion, or the fractured skull." It's a natural reaction, and a hitter has to keep such thoughts in the dark recesses of his subconscious.

If hitters only had to concern themselves with fastballs, life would be easy. They would move away from pitches on the inside, knowing that a pitch that appeared out of the strike zone would stay out of the strike zone.

Of course, life isn't easy—not since the discovery of the curveball, the darting sinker, the cutter, and the slider. Now, with each inside pitch, a hitter has a decision: Is this pitch headed for my head a fastball, in which case I should duck—now? Or is it a curveball, which, well thrown, will veer over the plate for a strike? It's never an easy call, especially when, as major leaguers do, you have a millisecond to decide.

Cal Ripken had some great stories about prolific curveballs and curveballers. Cal says the best curveball pitcher he has ever faced was Bert Blyleven; the first few times he saw Blyleven's curve, Cal said, his front foot was nearly in the dugout when the ball bent back over the plate for a strike.

After being embarrassed this way a few times, Cal came up with a formula, one he used each time he batted against

Blyleven. When Blyleven threw a pitch that looked like it was about to nail him in the ribs, Cal swung. That curve always ended up being a strike. If Blyleven's pitch looked as though it was going to go behind him, Cal didn't swing—that pitch would usually end up an inch or two off the inside corner for a ball, Cal explained.

With this approach, you'd figure Cal would be in constant danger of being plunked by an inside fastball—a pitch that starts inside and stays inside. But that never happened. Cal's sharp eyes give him an advantage over many hitters: he's able to pick up the seams on the ball as it hurtles plateward and, depending on the spin, quickly determine whether it's a fastball or some kind of breaking pitch. In other words, he knows when to duck.

One day in 1995, I mentioned to Cal something that Ted Williams once said. Like Cal, Williams maintained that he could see the seams on pitched balls. When he detected a curveball, Williams intentionally swung in the plane where he figured the ball would end up, not the plane on which the ball was traveling that moment. Cal said he did the same thing. But Brady Anderson, who was at the next locker, said he never saw seams on the ball—he just swung at the ball and tried to hit it.

By the way, for this book, we checked with the Elias Sports Bureau and found that Cal truly did have Blyleven figured out for a while. As Cal told me, his first at-bats against Blyleven had been painful (0 for 5 in 1982, Cal's rookie season). But from 1983 until 1986, the year Cal and I got into our discussion about the best curveball pitchers, Cal was 15 for 37 (.405) with three home runs against Blyleven. There aren't many who had that kind of success against that master of the breaking pitch.

When I think back to Devereaux, I realize he probably was going through the same thing Cal had described. He knew he'd be back in the batter's box. He knew he'd be seeing more pitches on the inside—some of them way on the inside—and he had to regain the mental edge. As a hitter, if you're not able to beat that fear, you lose to the pitcher every time.

As fans and as broadcasters, we don't understand how frightening it is to bat in the major leagues; we think we do, but we don't. Just once, we should have to step into the batter's box and experience a Randy Johnson fastball. Just once. I'm guessing we'd have more sympathy and better understand the dangers.

Even bunting is dangerous. I've never seen anybody get hit in the head, but I have seen hitters square to bunt—only to end up in a cast.

Campy Campaneris, the veteran A's and Rangers shortstop of the sixties and seventies, was a very good bunter. He moved runners over with the bunt; he'd push one past the pitcher for a base hit. Occasionally, he'd be called on to drop the most difficult bunt—the suicide squeeze.

In late 1978, with Texas at the Kingdome in Seattle, I remember Campaneris in the middle of a squeeze play gone haywire. Campy was at bat with a runner on third. In a squeeze, it's critical that the base runner not break for home too soon—a sure way to tip the pitcher, who'll respond by throwing the pitch somewhere hard to bunt, like at the hitter's body or head.

The runner broke too soon, and the pitch was two feet off the plate headed for Campy's sixth rib. Campaneris didn't have a chance. Thinking quickly, he held the bat out as a shield, and the ball didn't hit him in the chest—though it did break one of his fingers, landing him on the disabled list for a month.

You don't have to be a player to get injured at a ballpark. In fact, you don't even have to be on the field.

One year in spring training, Don Zimmer fell off a stationary bike (!) and landed on his head. They were concerned about his mental status, since not only does Zimmer have a plate in his head after several beanings during his playing career, but he also managed Bill Lee, the Spaceman, for a couple of years. One of the questions they asked him was, "Who was president before Reagan?" Zimmer's answer was, "I didn't know before I fell, and I don't know now."

You can't even escape peril in the broadcast booth. I learned that late in the 1986 season, when the Orioles were in Milwaukee for a game of little consequence to everyone involved except one man—the Brewers' starting pitcher of the day, Ted Higuera.

Higuera, a fine left-hander, was bidding for his twentieth victory, a notable achievement for any big leaguer, but particularly significant for Higuera. If he did it, he would become only the second Mexican-born player to reach that plateau in the big leagues. Fernando Valenzuela, a sensation with the Dodgers, had become the first just a few days earlier.

With little else to work with, I tried to build the drama of Higuera's quest for twenty wins, talking about the international significance of this event and trying to hold my audience.

Now, in the visiting radio booth at County Stadium in Milwaukee, there are two windows separated by a narrow metal strip. The windows slide open, letting in the cool breezes of a September night in Wisconsin. And, on this night, a screaming foul ball.

In the ninth inning, with two out and the Brewers ahead 9-3, John Shelby came to bat for the Orioles, took a big cut, and sent a ball rocketing back at our booth. Another day, I might have gone for the catch, but I was too busy doing justice to Higuera's dramatic bid for No. 20. I stayed on mike and ducked to my right, at which point the ball ricocheted off the metal strip and coldcocked me in the forehead. I felt as if I'd been pounded with Mike Tyson's strongest right hand.

The blow staggered me. Am I all right? Am I hurt seriously? Am I about to pass out? Am I about to pass out ON THE AIR?

It took me half a minute to collect my wits and figure out that I was bruised but otherwise fine. I didn't even mention that I'd been nailed on the broadcast.

Shelby hit the next pitch back to Higuera, who threw to first to earn his much-anticipated twentieth win. It was the moment I'd been building toward throughout the broadcast—but when it came, I was still too zonked out to notice.

My call, as best I can remember, sounded something like this:

"Back to Higuera . . .

"He throws Shelby out at first . . .

"And that's the ballgame."

So much for my big buildup.

Some booths can be veritable war zones, and there's no place more exciting—or frightening—for a broadcaster to work than Tiger Stadium.

In Detroit, the booth sits in the backstop, by far the best vantage point of any booth in the big leagues. But because of the closeness to the action, you're also at constant risk of getting nailed with a foul ball coming at you at ninety-five miles per hour.

Ernie Harwell, the Tigers' Hall of Fame broadcaster, protects himself by draping a net in front of the booth. I sympathize with Ernie; if I'd worked thirty-eight seasons at Tiger Stadium as Ernie has, I'd have asked for a net, too, and probably barbed wire. But as a visiting broadcaster, I'm always so pumped up by the incredible view that I can't bear to obstruct it with a big net.

On my visits to Tiger Stadium, if I ever start feeling complacent, I just think of Larry Osterman. One thought of Larry Osterman never fails to snap me to attention.

For several years, Larry was the broadcaster on the Tigers' cable-TV games. His partner for some of that time was one-time Tigers outfielder Jim Northrup. A few years ago, Larry and Jim were working a game at Tiger Stadium when a foul ball zipped into the booth and caught Larry flush on the forehead. No bounce, no ricochet—flush on the forehead.

The force of the blow was like a cannon shot, knocking Larry off his chair and sending his headset flying. Northrup was in shock; one minute, he's bantering with his partner, and the next, Osterman is lying spread-eagled on the floor.

Northrup reached over to help Larry, but as he did, he heard the director barking instructions through the headsets.

"Jim, you've got to stay on the air. You're the only one on the air. You *cannot* go off-mike."

It was a difficult situation for Jim. He handled it as best he could, continuing to call the game and, at the same time, trying to comfort his fallen comrade.

This went on for several pitches. Then, Northrup noticed a hand rising from under the table. Then another hand. Groggily, Osterman climbed back into his chair. There was a big welt on his forehead. Decorating the welt was the imprint of baseball stitches. Otherwise, Northrup could tell that Osterman seemed OK—bruised, but OK.

Northrup wasn't sure what to say.

"Larry, it looked like you might have been hit with that foul ball."

Osterman managed a smile.

He looked at Northrup and said, drolly, "Who are you?"

Some broadcasters love it when a foul ball heads for the booth. They're very aggressive, jumping out of their seats and giving it the Gold Glove effort. Others are more timid: if there's a table, they're under it; if there's a door, they're behind it.

Former ballplayers are all over the map. Joe Morgan, for instance, has a very strong desire to hit the deck. When a baseball is in the vicinity of the booth, Joe clears the area in a hurry.

On the other hand, Ken Harrelson, the former American League slugger who now works White Sox games, always tries hard to make the catch. Ken's thing is to catch the ball, then toss it down to the fans below.

One of the best I've seen at catching foul balls is my former partner in Baltimore, Joe Angel, who is now the lead broadcaster for the Florida Marlins. Joe has all the tools to be a superb foul-ball snagger. He has the great hands—very soft. Never drops one. And just as important, Joe is fearless. He rarely shrinks away from a ball headed for the booth.

In spring training one year, Joe and I were doing a game at Bobby Maduro Stadium in Miami. The broadcast booth there is right on the roof, and foul balls occasionally come in. This night, a foul ball came back at us. Joe was on the air, using a stand mike, which means that the microphone was on a table in front of him. He wasn't connected to the microphone as he would be with a headset mike.

So, this ball came back at Joe. And he reached out with his left hand and snared it, all the while staying on-mike giving a full description of this foul ball. What made it great was the fact that Joe never even left his seat or turned his head. The ultimate in cool!

In the mid-70s, when I worked in Texas, my partner was a quiet, pipe-smoking gentleman, Bill Merrill. Bill had a unique approach to foul balls: when a ball came into the booth, he'd never try to catch it, but when the ball began pinging around the booth, he was all over it, with the quickness of a Deion Sanders.

Once he'd picked up the ball, Bill rushed to the window of the booth and held it up as if he caught it. He'd get a nice crowd reaction and then he'd do the Ken Harrelson thing, tossing it down to someone in the seats.

I always thought that was pretty smart of Bill. And he never got hit in the head.

The
OWNERS MANUAL

In all the years Charlie Finley owned the A's, he never lived in Oakland; Chicago was his home. This meant that he didn't have to see too many A's games, which was probably just as well, because he really didn't seem to care much for the game—he thought it was too dull. Still, I never met anybody who enjoyed owning a baseball team more than Charlie did.

This story may help to explain why.

One night back in the mid-1970s, the A's were in Oakland and, as usual, Charlie wasn't. In Chicago, he'd invited several friends to an elegant restaurant. As his guests arrived for dinner, Charlie arranged for a telephone and a speakerphone to be set up at his table, so that his party could listen to the broadcast of the A's game.

Charlie listened to the games on the radio a lot, and we knew it. Monte Moore and I had this running gag about the A's affiliate station in Chicago. Monte Moore called it WCOF—for Charles O. Finley.

Thanks to Charlie, we had a record audience in Chicago that night, even though all our listeners were in that restaurant. All enjoying their appetizers as, 2,000 miles to the west, A's shortstop Campy Campaneris came to bat at the Oakland Coliseum.

Charlie ordered another telephone and dialed Oakland

again—this time calling the guy who ran the scoreboard at the Coliseum.

"If Campy gets on base, you start flashing 'GO' on the scoreboard," he ordered.

A few seconds later, Campaneris singled, just as Charlie had hoped. And then, over the speakerphone, Charlie and his guests heard a rhythmic cheer going up at the Oakland Coliseum.

"Go!"

"Go!"

"Go!"

"Do you hear that? Do you hear that?" Charlie was exultant. "I'm two thousand miles away having dinner in Chicago, and I just made fifteen thousand people at the Oakland Coliseum all start shouting 'Go!'"

Charlie loved pulling strings. He loved to manipulate people.

Working for Charlie was an experience, but not one that filled me with admiration for my boss. Some people have the mistaken impression that Charlie was a great innovator and maybe one of the best promoters that baseball ever had. When he passed away last year, Charlie's reputation as a master showman only seemed to grow.

As a former employee of Charlie's, I couldn't agree less. To me, his legacy is just the opposite. I look at Charlie as someone who built a fabulous ballclub and did everything *but* promote it well.

I'd pick Charlie as the most overrated owner I've been around. And I'd single out Edward Bennett Williams, the late Baltimore Orioles owner, as the most underrated. But I'll come back to him shortly.

It sounds harsh to say Charlie Finley nearly killed the A's. Killed the A's? Wasn't Charlie the guy who put together an incredible roster of players—Reggie, Catfish, Rollie Fingers, Joe Rudi? The guy who built the A's of the 1970s into one of baseball's great dynasties, a team that dominated the sport on the way to winning five straight division titles and three consecutive World Series?

Yes, Charlie achieved all of that. But if we give him credit for the marvelous records of those A's teams, as we should, Charlie also should be pilloried for the inept way he ran the business of the A's franchise.

How inept was Charlie, the baseball businessman? All those years the A's were establishing themselves as one of the great teams in baseball history, their average attendance was less than a million fans a year. In 1974, their third of three straight world-championship seasons, they didn't even reach 900,000!

That's particularly astounding when you consider that a winning team's success really doesn't kick in at the gate until the following year, when the excitement of the previous season translates into off-season ticket sales. With anticipation high for another good, exciting team, attendance is guaranteed to be higher.

That scenario has been repeated over and over in baseball. In 1997, the Yankees easily eclipsed what they drew in their world-championship year. In 1983, the Orioles drew 2 million for the first time on their way to a World Series; the next year, they were never in the pennant race—three weeks into the season they were already twelve games behind—and still beat their World Series–year attendance by a couple of thousand.

Not the A's.

To be sure, Charlie had some farsighted ideas. He pushed for night World Series games. He was virtually the inventor of the designated hitter. And if it had been up to him, the baseballs that Ken Griffey Jr. is crushing these days would be of the bright-orange variety. (I said farsighted, not good.)

But when it came to selling his own product, Charlie was a total flop. A bust. A joke. This was his idea of a promotion: During the 1974 season, in May, he announced that at every Monday-night home game for the rest of the year, every seat in the house would be half-price. He called it "Family Night."

They should have called it "Undercut Your Product Night." On one Monday night, the Boston Red Sox, a pretty attractive draw even then, came into the Coliseum for a three-game series. The opener was hardly a marquee pitching matchup, with young lefty Dave Hamilton going for the A's against Dick Drago for the Sox. It was a half-price family night, though, so the crowd was 37,095.

The Tuesday and Wednesday games, with much better matchups, drew miserably. The paid attendance Tuesday, to see Boston's Roger Moret pitch against Kenny Holtzman of the A's, was an anemic 3,033. And on Wednesday night, with the same two teams, there was a classic duel featuring Vida Blue (who won nineteen games that year) versus Luis Tiant, "El Tiante," two outstanding big-name pitchers, one of the best pitching showdowns of the season. But it wasn't a Monday night at half-price, so the crowd—and I use the word loosely—was 7,281!

And who could blame the fans? The laws of economics had taken over. Charlie had not followed his own advice, which he repeated many times in staff meetings: "People will line up for s—— if you tell them you're giving it away free."

Charlie was his own general manager, and he had a very able guy, John Claiborne (later a GM with St. Louis and Boston), who ran the farm system and carried out other front office duties. But Charlie was the one on the phone chatting up general managers and scouts from other teams. They might have thought they were angling for jobs with the A's, but in reality Charlie was digging for information from them about players.

And it worked. He fleeced a lot of people that way, picking up an opinion about this or that prospect. Maybe baseball people should have been wise to Charlie, but baseball was different then—it wasn't a corporate, big-business thing yet. Today, with the amount of money involved in buying a franchise, it's become much more a cutthroat business.

As I mentioned, Charlie didn't really like baseball. He thought it was boring. So, he was always looking for ways to jazz things up. The DH made perfect sense to him: Why let pitchers bat? That was so unexciting. Another thing that intrigued Charlie was the concept of designated runners; he always carried a very fast runner who could do very little else.

One of Charlie's speedsters was a guy from Panama named Allan Lewis. Allan could play the outfield, but he was a weak hitter who was on the club for one reason only—to run. His job was to go in the game in a key spot as a pinch runner, steal a base, and maybe help score a big run.

Charlie was a master at dreaming up nicknames. As an owner, that might have been his biggest talent. He came up with "Catfish" for Jim Hunter. He tried to pressure Vida Blue into legally changing his name to Vida "True" Blue. Charlie's nickname for Allan Lewis was "the Panamanian Express." It fit for awhile, but as the years went on, Allan became more of a local than an express. So in 1974, Charlie replaced him with the world-record holder in the sixty-yard dash, Herb Washington. ("Hurricane Herb" was Charlie's nickname for him.)

Herb was a blur, maybe the fastest guy I've ever seen in a major-league uniform. (I'd like to have seen him race Deion Sanders and Bo Jackson when they were all in their primes.) He lasted two seasons with the A's and, in his first year, racked up a respectable twenty-nine steals. These days, Herb is an accomplished businessman—he owns five McDonald's restaurants in Rochester, New York. He's been far more successful in the fast-food business than he ever was in the base-stealing business.

When Charlie signed him, Herb knew as much about baserunning as Ronald McDonald does. Charlie hired Maury Wills to come to spring training for a week to teach Herb how to run the bases. Maury did a great job, imparting everything he could, but it was going to take a lot longer than a week to turn Herb Washington into a savvy base runner.

When the regular season began, Herb was still with the

club—and he still had no clue. The A's began the year in Texas. Late in the opening-night game, with the A's ahead 7-2, manager Alvin Dark brought in Herb as a pinch runner at first base with two out.

The next A's batter hit a fly ball. Any kid in Little League can tell you that, with two out, the base runner's job is to break with the crack of the bat in the hope of advancing if the ball isn't caught.

My theory is that Herb didn't play Little League.

As the ball arched toward the outfield, Herb turned on his heels and went back to first, standing on top of the base with two feet.

"Run, Herb, run," screamed the first-base coach, Jerry Adair.

"He's going to catch it," noted Herb.

"HERB, DAMMIT," shouted Adair, "THERE ARE TWO OUTS! RUN!"

"Oh," said Herb.

Poor Herb didn't know what was going on.

Herb's signing had created a furor at the A's spring-training camp in Mesa, Arizona. Sal Bando, the A's captain, told me that Herb's signing had taken a job from a legitimate player who had worked hard for it. And for what? Just for Charlie to get some publicity for himself. You know, "That Charlie Finley, what an innovator!"

Charlie's managers loathed dealing with him. He'd call them in the middle of the night with an idea about the lineup. He'd be in his office in Chicago at six A.M., four in the morning Pacific time. It didn't matter if there'd been a game the night before; Charlie would get on the phone with Dick Williams, Alvin Dark, or whomever was his manager of the moment and start grilling him. The poor guy hadn't brushed his teeth yet and Charlie would want to know about things that happened the night before. Or he'd insist on chatting about a trade he was working on. An hour later, he'd be back on the phone demanding to have the same conversation all over again. Eight or nine calls a day to his manager wasn't unusual for Charlie.

One time, Alvin Dark had a serious problem. He'd just come in the year before and inherited the coaches from Dick Williams's regime. At least one of them really resented Alvin because he had been hoping to get the job himself, and now he had to coach for Alvin.

A couple of weeks into the season, Alvin had an awkward situation. He'd sit in the dugout, relaying signs, and this one coach—the third-base coach—was occasionally missing signs. Not in just one game, either; in critical situations Alvin's instructions weren't always getting through to his players. Batters he wanted to bunt weren't bunting, runners he wanted to steal weren't stealing, all because this coach was missing Alvin's signs.

Things weren't getting better, and Alvin feared they'd get worse. So, reluctantly, he spoke to Charlie. Reluctantly was the only way A's managers I knew ever spoke to Charlie.

"We've got a problem. Our third-base coach is missing some of the signs. It's really hurting us," Alvin said.

"Maybe your signs are too complicated," Charlie replied. "Show them to me."

It wasn't that simple, Alvin tried to explain. "First you have to know the indicator. Then you've got to know the key. Then I give the sign."

"Don't worry about that," Charlie said. "Give me the indicator. Give me the key. Give me the sign."

So Alvin went through the whole routine—the shirt wiping, chin stroking, earlobe wiggling. A veteran third-base coach would have caught on immediately.

"Alvin," Charlie exclaimed, "no wonder he misses signs. Your signs are too complicated. Make it simple. Touch your hat for a bunt. Touch your earlobe for a steal."

If Alvin had gone along, Charlie would have known the signs. So would every team in the American League.

Charlie blustered for a while. But eventually, the coach was fired.

As I said, Charlie was very shrewd—but like any fan, there were things he knew about baseball and things he didn't. One night, we were televising a home game, and Charlie went on the TV broadcast with Monte Moore. Later, he came by the radio booth, where I was working.

The next thing I knew, Charlie was sitting next to me and we were on the air together. The A's had the bases loaded and catcher Larry Haney at bat. The first pitch to Haney was a wild pitch, plating a run for the A's.

"Jon, let me ask you this," Charlie began.

This is trouble, I'm thinking.

"Does Larry Haney get credit for an RBI on that?"

This guy is supposed to be a baseball genius, right? The architect of all these great clubs? One of the game's great minds? And on the air, he's asking if Larry Haney gets an RBI on a wild pitch?

Now, he was the boss and I certainly didn't want to insult him on the air. "Well, as any ten-year-old could tell you Mr. Finley, that's no RBI" probably wouldn't have done much for my job security. So I tried to get a laugh out of it.

"Well, Mr. Finley, I don't think they're going to give him an RBI on that. But, you know, as owner of the ballclub, you could show your appreciation for Larry's efforts and give him a bonus."

Charlie sort of cackled and said, "Yeah, yeah, I'll give him a bonus—and take it out of your salary!"

Ladies and gentlemen, the one and only owner of your Oakland A's—Charles Oscar Finley!

Have I mentioned that Charlie was cheap?

There are lean operations. There are shoestring operations. And then there was the A's front office during the Finley years, when a dollar spent was assumed to be a dollar wasted.

The year I worked for Charlie, the front-office staff consisted of eight people. Not eighty—as in the number of front-office workers employed by teams like the Yankees and Dodgers. *Eight*—as in Cal Ripken's number. Eight people were responsible for everything from running the ticket office to editing the media guide to arranging for the team's travel.

And still Charlie was searching for ways to economize.

He was particularly touchy about long-distance phone calls. Almost any long-distance call made by an A's employee was considered by Charlie to be an unwarranted expense. Even a call to Charlie himself.

If you needed to reach Charlie, you'd never simply pick up the phone and dial his office in Chicago. What an extravagance!

Instead, you followed the careful instructions set out by the owner—meaning, you placed an operator-assisted, person-to-person, collect phone call.

Invariably, Charlie answered.

"Person-to-person call for Mr. Finley."

"Charlie's not in," Charlie would say.

He'd get the name of the party calling, and a few minutes later he'd return the call on his WATS line, from which he could make unlimited long-distance calls at a flat rate.

We're talking about THE OWNER OF THE WORLD CHAMPIONS OF BASEBALL!

We were a major-league club and our monthly phone bill was $28.34.

Charlie might have been frugal, but he was never shy. His appetite for publicity was enormous. And he'd come up with some wild schemes to focus attention on himself, including many involving his players. In 1974, the A's promoted a nineteen-year-old outfielder to the big leagues from Birmingham, the A's class-AA farm team. His name was Claudell Washington.

Claudell wasn't a talkative person. Upon his arrival from the minors, I interviewed him and found most of his answers were "Yes" and "No."

Trying to sound impressive, I said, "Claudell, you're not only making the jump all the way from double-A to the major leagues, but the jump to the world champions of baseball. Any trepidation about the move?"

"I had the flu in spring training," Claudell shrugged. "But I'm fine now."

Right away, Claudell made a contribution to the A's. In his fourth game, he delivered a game-winning, tenth-inning hit—memorable because it deprived Gaylord Perry of his fifteenth consecutive victory.

Then, on August 30, a day before his twentieth birthday, Claudell turned in his best effort of the season—five for five, three singles, a double, and a triple against the Tigers at Tiger Stadium. A five-hit game by a nineteen year old about to turn twenty. Heady stuff.

Charlie must have been mightily impressed as he listened in on WCOF. During the ninth inning, he phoned Monte in the booth from Chicago with what, even for Charlie, was a bizarre order.

"You have to get Claudell on the postgame show," Charlie announced. "And, listen now, you have to tell him that Charlie Finley was so pleased with his five-hit game that to celebrate his twentieth birthday tomorrow, he's giving him . . . a five-thousand-dollar raise!"

Charlie wasn't finished.

"Now, Monte," he continued, "if you don't have Claudell on the postgame show—and announce what I just told you, just the way I told you—*I'm not giving him the money!*"

Monte didn't want to be the cause of Claudell missing out on $5,000. Nor did I. So we did our damnedest to make sure that Charlie would be forced to make good on this typically twisted pledge.

Still, we almost failed Claudell.

On the road, I was responsible for handling the postgame interview, usually conducted in the visiting-team dugout. But that night, we had a problem with our remote hookup. From the A's dugout, I couldn't communicate with Monte or be heard on the air.

To do the show that night, I had to bring the star of the game a few rows into the lower stands—directly below the visiting team's radio booth—where our engineer could drop us a cable with a microphone attached.

When Monte gave me my cue, I said, "We're here with Claudell Washington. What a night, Claudell!"

Then, trying to sound like the late Johnny Olson, the "Come on DOWN" man on *The Price Is Right,* I added, "Charlie Finley is very excited for you. In honor of your five-hit game, and your twentieth birthday, the owner of the A's is giving you a five-thousand-dollar raise." At which point, thirty or forty fans who'd crowded around to listen to my interview with Claudell let out this rousing cheer, as if we had a studio audience.

I smiled at Claudell, and then pointed the microphone at Claudell for his comments.

"Thanks," he said.

Thanks?

That's it?

No "I'm the luckiest man on the face of the earth"?

Claudell was showing wisdom beyond his years. In effect, he was saying, "How lucky can I be? I still work for Charles Oscar Finley."

Ed Williams owned a baseball team, but that's about all he and Charlie Finley had in common. Williams was a fascinatingly complex and driven person; when he died in 1988, he was among the most brilliant and distinguished trial lawyers in American history—in a league with the legendary Clarence Darrow. His clients ranged from the wrongly accused to the probably guilty to the publicly disgraced—mobsters, union bosses, tainted politicians. They sought out Ed Williams for one reason only: If anybody could get them off, they knew he could.

The courtroom was the stage for which Williams saved his greatest performances, but there were other stages and other roles for him too. Williams was counselor to U.S. presidents; he held a high post in the Democratic National Committee. Late in his life, Williams, it is said, even turned down a chance to become CIA director.

At the ballpark, we saw yet another side of Williams, that of an intense, almost obsessed sports fan. Williams was crazed about sports. He once was a financial backer for a boxer, Irish Mike Baker, who lost a fight for the middleweight championship. He was president of the Washington Redskins and owned 13 percent of the team, which he sold after buying the Orioles.

Of Williams's many sporting passions, the Orioles ranked at the top. It's hard to imagine an owner more emotionally invested in the fortunes of his team than Ed Williams was. When the Orioles were at Memorial Stadium, and Williams's schedule permitted, he'd sit up in his box, agonizingly animated. With each pitch, you could see this man really suffering. He'd pace around. At times, he'd look away in disgust. Games were tougher on Williams than on most of his players; at the end of nine innings, the owner looked as if he'd been through a six-month murder trial.

In 1983, the Orioles gave Williams probably the most important gift of his life, his one and only World Series title. Even that year, there were some rough spots, as the team stumbled through two seven-game losing streaks. Manager Joe Altobelli and the Orioles players handled the adversity well, but the owner was despondent. I remember sitting in the pressroom at Memorial Stadium one night in August during one of those depressing losing streaks, when Williams came in, looking fatigued.

"I have never in my life been so depressed as I am about this losing streak," he moaned.

I sat there amazed. I mean, I'm just a broadcaster working baseball games on the radio, and the guy eating crab cakes across the table is a close friend and confidant of presidents and prime ministers—and he was so down in the dumps he couldn't bring himself to eat.

"This losing streak is killing me," he said. "It seems like we have a good ballclub and here we are in August, the big days of the season. We should be running into shape, and instead we're in this long losing streak. I don't know what to do about it. I'm down on the manager. I'm down on the general manager. I'm down on the players. And it feels like we're never going to get this thing turned around."

"You're never as bad as you look when you're losing," I said, tossing out Earl Weaver's time-tested bromide. And I added, "This is a veteran team that knows how to win. It's a club that usually finishes strong."

But I couldn't console the owner when he got in one of those mind sets, and neither could anyone else. He stayed in his funk until the Orioles snapped out of their losing streak that night (and, by the way, went 34-10 over the next forty-four games to clinch the AL East title).

But I'll always remember that scene and how this great lawyer and powerful person could be so down about a ballclub. I wasn't down about it, and I was there every day. The players weren't down about it; they assumed they'd shake out of it soon. But Ed Williams, he was real down about it.

"In my business, even one loss makes you a failure," he once told me. "It's real hard to get used to sixty-two losses being a great year." But such is the nature of baseball, regardless of who the owner is.

Williams was filled with opinions, often expressed in a cutting manner. He once referred to Altobelli, by then his ex-manager, as "Cement Head." Wayne Gross, a power-hitting third baseman not noted for his range, was "the cigar-store Indian." Utility infielder Juan Bonilla was an ice-cream flavor to Williams, who joked in a singsong tone that he couldn't pick among "strawberry . . . chocolate . . . Bonilla."

During spring training in 1986, Williams suggested that infielder Jackie Gutierrez, an accomplished whistler who was beset by many personal problems, change his tune to "Nobody Knows the Trouble I've Seen."

People on the receiving end of Williams's barbs may not have always seen the humor, but Williams meant no serious harm. He didn't discriminate: everyone—including Williams himself—was a potential target. Even during the most trying times, and often about the most depressing subjects.

Cancer, for instance. Williams battled the disease for the last twelve years of his life. The word is *battle;* he battled every step of the way. By all accounts, he should have been dead a year or two after his initial diagnosis.

Williams refused to dwell on his health publicly, and he never lost his droll sense of humor about the disease, even when it was plainly overtaking him. But over dinner one night with Larry King at Duke Zeibert's, the renowned gathering place for the rich and powerful in Washington, D.C., Williams made an exception.

At the time, Williams and King had both endured physical problems. Williams's health concerns were old news; Larry, though today in excellent health, had suffered a heart attack and recently had undergone bypass surgery.

As they dined, Larry recounted for Ed the horror of his cardiac event—an unexpected chest pain while dining out, the frightening ride to the hospital, the grim confirmation that he'd suffered a heart attack.

Williams sat glumly, listening to Larry's medical history. When it was his turn, he was out to do Larry one better with tales of his lengthy illness—the multiple operations, radiation treatments, and experimental therapies.

After a few minutes, Larry couldn't listen anymore.

"Ed," he said. "My heart attack was awful. I wouldn't wish one on anybody. But if I had to be sick, I'd much rather be sick like me than be sick like you."

Williams's back stiffened. Nobody was going to insult his illness and get away with it.

"A heart attack is much worse than cancer," Williams replied coolly. "There's no comparison. A heart attack is embarrassing. When you have a heart attack in a restaurant, you fall backwards in your chair. Maybe you have a mouthful of food. Everybody stares."

It became a full-fledged debate, Ed Williams and Larry King parrying over who had the more desirable illness. Too bad they didn't save it for Larry's CNN colleague, Pat Buchanan, on *Crossfire*. That show could use a little comic relief.

When he bought the Orioles in 1979, Williams wasn't embraced by the fans, to put it mildly. Many worried whether he secretly planned to move the team to Washington. Since Williams's law practice and his circle of high-powered friends were in the nation's capital, those worries probably were justified. Williams tried to address those concerns his very first day as owner, saying that the team would stay in Baltimore "as long as Baltimore supports them."

That didn't calm any fears. It was an uncertain time, and even the players seemed to have their bags packed. "I know Mr. Williams is from Washington and he might want to move the team there," said Rick Dempsey, then the Orioles' catcher. "But if they're going to move it, they should go far away, like Denver." Later, there even was talk that the Orioles would play thirteen games a year at RFK Stadium in Washington.

None of the speculation ever panned out: During the nine years Williams owned the team, the Orioles played every one of their home games at Memorial Stadium. And it was on Williams's watch that the plans for the building of Camden

Yards got under way, a project that cemented the team's roots in the heart of Baltimore.

Though his critics conveniently forget, Williams was deeply—and publicly—committed to keeping the Orioles in Baltimore for most of the years he owned the team. In 1983, a few days after the Orioles finished off the Phillies to become world champions, Williams pledged to keep the team at home:

"Once I made the promise the Orioles would remain in Baltimore as long as Baltimore supported them," he said at a luncheon with local business leaders, and repeated later at a sports banquet. "Now I am telling you the Orioles will stay in Baltimore as long as I am alive."

Baltimoreans loved the message, and they began to warm to the messenger. At both events, Williams was embraced as if he were a native son. Both times, wild applause; both times, standing ovations. I know—I was among those applauding and standing.

Ed Williams didn't live to see Camden Yards, but make no mistake: He would have been very proud of the Orioles' magnificent ballpark. With its classic architecture and modern fan conveniences, Camden Yards combines the best of the old and new in baseball. And the fans simply cannot get enough—when summer arrives in Baltimore, it's a rare night when all 48,000 seats aren't spoken for.

The driving force behind the building of Camden Yards was not, however, Ed Williams. Williams wanted the ballpark; better than anyone, he understood how a modern stadium would transform his ballclub, turning it into one of the most prosperous and profitable in baseball. But he was not the person who willed Camden Yards into being.

William Donald Schaefer was.

Schaefer, Baltimore's colorful four-term mayor and later governor of Maryland, knew too well the importance of professional sports to his community. While he was mayor, the city suffered the devastating loss of the Baltimore Colts, its beloved football team, which defected to Indianapolis on a wintry night in 1984. He'd witnessed a city in mourning, and he'd mourned, too.

As governor, Schaefer in 1987 fretted about the Orioles. Williams had refused to sign a lease of more than one year at Memorial Stadium, on the grounds that he couldn't operate profitably at the old concrete horseshoe. Without a long-term lease, the Orioles were alarmingly portable. Should Williams die, the team easily could be picked up and moved—to Denver, Phoenix, any of the cities then yearning for a big-league ballclub.

Schaefer wasn't alone in seeing the possibilities. George Will, a diehard Orioles fan and member of the team's board of directors, was also deeply concerned. The potential buyer who most worried George was Marvin Davis, a Colorado oil scion and one of Ed Williams's leading law clients. Davis was on record as seeking a team he could buy and move to Denver.

"Imagine EBW has died," I recall George saying. "At the funeral, here comes Marvin Davis, dressed in a dark suit and genuinely in mourning for his lost friend. After offering his condolences to the widow Williams, Davis takes her arm and says, 'I know there's a lot pressing on your mind now, Agnes. I'm prepared to ease your burden—permit me to take the ballclub off your hands.' "

At this point in George's nightmare, Davis reaches into his coat pocket and pulls out $90 million. Cash.

"Take it," says Davis to Mrs. Williams. "Take it and never worry about the ballclub again."

To prevent such a scenario from ever playing out, Schaefer devised a two-pronged strategy: build a state-financed, baseball-only ballpark for the Orioles and get Williams's signature on a long-term lease.

Schaefer spearheaded the effort, schmoozing and arm-twisting to garner the votes required to pass stadium-funding bills in the Maryland General Assembly. When the future of the project was in doubt, Schaefer asked Williams to speak to the legislators himself.

On March 4, 1987, appearing before an overflow crowd of spectators and a bank of cameras in Maryland's statehouse, Williams turned the tide of opinion. "I see that we're going into a loss situation at Memorial Stadium, and much quicker than I had projected," he told the packed house of legislators and press. "I'm not rich enough to operate a major-league team in the red. I'm not rich enough to build a stadium."

Fourteen months later, then in the final stages of his disease, Williams finally signed the stadium deal. Not that he had to— and from a purely business perspective, not that he should have.

He was a dying man putting his financial affairs in order. To a buyer ready to pull the team out of town, the value of the Orioles would have been astronomical. On his deathbed, why did he care whether the Orioles stayed in Baltimore?

My answer is simple: because Ed Williams cared about Baltimore. And, in the end, Baltimore had begun to appreciate Ed Williams.

Just ask anyone who was present on the night when the agreement for the new ballpark was announced. The date was May 2, 1988. The hapless Orioles were the biggest story in baseball; they'd started the season with a record twenty-one consecutive losses and were returning to Baltimore from a lengthy road trip humming along at 1-23.

In other cities, 1-23 gets you hanged in effigy. In Baltimore in 1988, it got the Orioles a sellout crowd of 50,402.

Unbeknownst to the throng, the biggest event of the evening would happen before the game, when Schaefer and Herbert Belgrad, chairman of the Maryland Stadium Authority, announced from the field that the new stadium would become reality.

"It is Mr. Williams's night," a triumphant Schaefer declared.

Ed Williams was too ill to join the festivities on the field that night. Frail and painfully thin, he watched the ceremonies from the privacy of the owner's box. It was the last time he ever attended an Orioles game.

On August 13, Williams died. Three days later, when the Orioles next played in Baltimore, I was called in to the executive offices at Memorial Stadium for a meeting with Larry Lucchino, the club president, and Calvin Hill, a team vice president. They were drafting a tribute to Williams that I would be delivering over the public-address system before the ballgame with Oakland that night.

Larry and Calvin asked for my input. One of the themes, they said, should be Williams's devotion to Baltimore and his commitment to Orioles fans. The three of us collaborated on the text. Later that night, I read these words:

"During his years, the Orioles experienced unprecedented explosions of enthusiasm, loyalty, and love. He saw it. He nurtured it. In the good years . . . and in the bad years.

"He admired the mettle of the fans, and he fell in love with the city. And he gave the fans his word, his promise, and then he gave the fans what no one before had given them—a formal commitment, keeping his word. And as a result, the Orioles will be ours for a long, long time.

"For that, Edward Bennett Williams, we are forever grateful. We thank you."

Baseball suffers when it loses an Ed Williams. Just as it loses when the O'Malley family takes its leave.

An O'Malley has held a seat of power in the Dodgers front office for the last five decades and through a number of baseball's most important mileposts. (And, in effect, Peter O'Malley still may be running the Dodgers, even if the sale of the club to Fox goes through; it's been said that Fox has offered him the team presidency under the prospective new ownership.)

Walter O'Malley, Peter's ironfisted and infamous dad, changed—Brooklynites would say destroyed—the geography of the big leagues when he moved the Dodgers to Los Angeles, setting off baseball's West Coast gold rush.

For me, the Dodgers under the O'Malleys were a model franchise. Like no other owners I know, they did the big things right and the small things right.

It all starts with stability, and no franchise matches the Dodgers in that regard. Many teams strike out in a new direction every two or three years, but not the Dodgers under the O'Malleys. Dodger managers weren't fired—they retired with gold watches. General managers stayed for years and years. Even Dodger players developed strong ties with the club. After the advent of free agency, it was still common for Dodger line-ups to be heavily laden with players scouted by the Dodgers, signed by the Dodgers, developed by the Dodgers, and forever the property of the Dodgers.

I also like and admire the way the Dodgers treat their fans. The Dodgers pamper their fans. They nurture those relationships. If you're a Dodger season-ticket holder, you're a celebrity to the Dodgers. You're a cherished person. The Dodgers want to know: What can we do for you? And nothing you could ask would be considered unreasonable.

Nobody has more promotions in the ballpark than the Dodgers. Something is going on every game, everything from a Dodger pin giveaway to some sort of interactive contest. At Dodger Stadium, you just never know—with a little luck, you might spend the evening as a member of the grounds crew or find yourself suiting up for batting practice.

The Dodgers must have been doing something right: under Peter O'Malley's stewardship, they were the first franchise to crack 3 million in attendance. And they were first to hit 3.6 million. For the other owners, there must be a lesson in there someplace.

Hieroglyphics
I HAVE KNOWN

If you look in the corner of my office, under a big stack of newspaper clippings and a couple of last year's press guides, you'll find about twenty of the most important books I never look at. That's the best way I know to describe my baseball scorebooks.

During the season, my scorebook is indispensable. Just thinking about losing one, I get a chill. But once the season ends, so does my attachment. I rarely have use for an old score book again. If a friend comes over and we start reminiscing about a game several years back, maybe I'll pull it out, but otherwise the scorebook stays on the shelf, permanently.

Some people keep score for archival purposes—ten years from now, they want to be able to turn to the page that tells the story of a particular pitch in a particular inning in a particular game. I've never had reason to do that.

As a broadcaster, I need my book to offer up basic information quickly and accurately. Where did Barry hit his single in the third inning? How many strikeouts tonight for Hershiser? I need to know now—before the next commercial break.

One of the nice things about scorekeeping is that anybody can do it—and down through the years, almost everybody has. Grandfathers. Grandkids. Official scorers. The girlfriend of the star pitcher on the high-school team.

Keeping score is a link. It links the players on the field and the fans in the bleachers.

It's a link between fans, even those with different scoring languages. My strikeout symbol is "K." Yours might be "SO." The neat thing about scoring is that we're both right.

Scorekeeping links the generations. Fathers and mothers pass down scoring habits to their children. I know a guy who always insists his son record the game-time temperature. He won't tell me why.

There's something elegant about scorekeeping. At least, that's what some of our finest writers say. Thomas Boswell, the excellent sports columnist of *The Washington Post,* once wrote, "No other American sport has anything that genuinely approximates the scorecard—that single piece of paper, simple enough for a child—that preserves the game both chronologically and in toto with almost no significant loss of detail."

Scoring is for everyone. Fans keep score. Baseball writers and broadcasters keep score. Even baseball legends have kept score: Connie Mack, whose tenure in the major leagues spanned seven decades, rarely set foot in the dugout without a scorecard and a sharpened pencil. In *The Joy of Keeping Score,* author Paul Dickson's definitive book on the subject, Mack is quoted. "Over the years I have found that keeping my own score has given much added interest to every baseball game I have watched—and I have lost count of the number." Which is understandable, considering that Mack managed in 7,755 big-league games.

I learned to keep score from my dad, Jerry. I was ten years old, a fifth grader, and he took me to my first major-league game at Candlestick Park—a Giants-Dodgers game. He bought me a scorecard (complete with pencil) and then taught me his system. My dad's scoring method could best be described as no frills, perfect for an apprentice scorekeeper like myself at the time: "K" for strikeout, "BB" for base on balls, "8" for a flyout to center. When you perused his scoresheet, you knew who made the plays and who got the hits. That was plenty. And to this day, I use basically the same scoring method he taught me on that April night at Candlestick so many years ago. Keep it simple.

Just as every scorer has his or her own system, every scorer has his or her priorities. Red Sox broadcaster Joe Castiglione is a pitch-count guy; Joe puts a high priority on counting pitches. If you see Joe, ask him to show you his counters. He always carries two little hand-held counters (one for each team's pitcher), and every time a pitch is thrown, Joe clicks.

I don't keep my own pitch count. If I need to know how many pitches Mike Mussina threw, I ask. The club PR directors usually have that information at hand. Keeping it myself, I find, is a distraction. Hey, I'm too busy.

There are a lot of decisions to make when you're keeping score: what to write down, what to trust to memory, which types of information are pertinent and which will probably be beside the point.

I'm always careful about recording a runner's trip around the bases. If I need to, I want to be able to reconstruct the entire itinerary—how he reached, where he stopped, how he scored. That's important stuff. I need to know whether Cora scored from second on the Griffey single or from third, and the only way to be sure is by writing it down.

My scoring system isn't fancy and it isn't complicated. I use the diamond method: If a guy hits a single, I make a line, sort of representing the foul line from home plate to first base. To the side, I'll make a slash denoting a single. If he subsequently advances on a ground ball to second, I'll extend the line from first to second and, above the line, jot down a 4-3, indicating that was the play that advanced him. In that way, I follow each runner around the bases, and when they score, I complete the whole diamond and color it in.

Fly balls are easy; there's not a lot you can do with fly balls. When a ball is caught on the fly, I simply jot the number of the field in which it fell into a fielder's glove: for a fly ball to left, "7"; centerfield, "8"; and so on. If the ball is hit on a line, that's worth noting. Line drive to left, "L7." Same for a ball that carries to the warning track in left: in my book, that's "D7" for "deep left." If it's deep to left-center, that makes it "D78."

I do keep a multicolor score book—it's black and blue. And if the game is memorable, there's a lot of red there, too.

My old A's partner, Monte Moore, introduced me to multicolor scorekeeping. For a broadcaster, Monte explained, the key to effective scorekeeping was being able to refer back to just the play you wanted, just when you needed it. What good was a thoroughly accurate, richly detailed scorecard if it took you thirty seconds to find the strikeout with the bases loaded in the fifth?

Monte was right, and he'd developed a color-coded system that enabled him to do just that. I borrowed liberally from it, though over the years I've adapted it to my own purposes. I don't say it's the only way to do it or even the best way, but here's what I do:

The black pen is for recording the starting lineups. Once I've jotted them into the book before the game, that's it for the black pen.

The blue pen is for recording each at-bat, the nitty-gritty of scorekeeping. Homers, doubles, infield bouncers. Anything that belongs in the little boxes is written in blue.

The red pen is the special-occasions pen. If there's a stellar defensive play or an unusual play (an ejection, an injury, or the like), I'll mark the box with a red star. When I check my book for the inning of that great play, I'm looking for a big red star, which is easy to spot. RBIs, stolen bases, hit batsmen—all get a symbol in red for ready reference.

I also use red and blue to jot down replacements. Blue ink is for pinch hitters, red ink is for a pinch runner (with a "PR" beside his name) or a defensive replacement. The color differences are extremely helpful here: at a glance, I know why and how a guy came into the game.

As I said, I'm not a pitch-count guy. But there are situations when it's important to stay on top of the numbers—for example, when a pitcher is coming back from an injury, or anytime the manager tells you a pitcher is on a pitch count.

Some pitchers are automatic pitch-count situations. Gregg Olson was like that. In the late eighties and early nineties, Olson was one of the dominant closers in baseball, a hard thrower with a devastating curveball. When Olson threw strikes, he might be out of an inning in nine pitches. When he didn't, he might still be out there after thirty-five. With Olson on the mound, the pitch count often was the story, as it could determine his availability for the next day's game.

There are broadcasters who could teach college-level score-keeping, and there are others who, if such a course existed, would be wise to register for it. The range of abilities is very broad.

Ex-ballplayers generally are not polished scorers. There's a reason for that: Many never learned how. While my father was teaching me to score, these guys were doing heroic things on the field, like setting the California state record for consecutive no-hitters. Something like that.

Brooks Robinson, who broadcast Orioles games on TV for many years, eventually came up with some kind of system. Jim Palmer, the great Hall of Fame pitcher, is another one who wasn't that familiar with scoring when he made the switch to broadcasting.

The Scooter, ex-Yankee ballplayer and now broadcaster Phil Rizzuto, uses one of the simplest systems for scoring I've seen. We were at Yankee Stadium with the Orioles one night, and Phil showed up late. In the bottom of the second, he stopped by our booth to get caught up on what he'd missed. Phil didn't have a scorebook; in his hand, he had the mimeographed paper they hand out in the press box, with the Orioles lineup listed on the left side, the Yankees lineup on the right side, and the umpires' names at the bottom.

Next to each name, Phil put a slash for an at-bat. On the other side of the guy's name, he put a slash for a hit. If a guy had two slashes to the left of his name and one to the right, Phil knew he was one for two. And presumably, the fact that every hitter was zero for two, one for two, or two for two, with no information on how or why, was all Phil needed to know.

Bill White, the Scooter's partner on Yankee broadcasts for many years, often tells the story of leaving the booth for several minutes to get a cup of coffee or run to the bathroom. When he returned, he asked Phil if he could glance at his score book.

For the first batter, as Bill tells it, Scooter listed a six to three, a ground ball to short. For the second batter, a single to left. Bill dutifully copied the information into his book, no problem.

But then Scooter lapsed into a scoring shorthand totally unfamiliar to White. For the third batter, Phil had jotted in "WW." Same for the next.

"I understand the ground ball to short and the single to left," White said. "But, Scooter, what's 'WW'?"

"Oh, that," Phil replied, matter of factly. "That means I wasn't watching."

As I said, there is no right or wrong. But when I see some scoring systems, my reaction is that they leave a lot out.

"What if you need to know how Bichette got to third?" I'll ask the scorer.

"Oh," he'll say, "I just remember." And that's great. That's the best system of all. If you can keep it in your head, that's even better.

Bob Costas, one of the best in our business, records very little on his scorecard. In 1989, the Orioles and the Toronto Blue Jays were in a furious pennant race that wasn't decided until the last weekend of the season. Bob and Tony Kubek were in Toronto on a Friday night to prepare for Saturday's Game of the Week on NBC. Not only was it the last Game of the Week that season, it was the last Game of the Week on NBC ever; the TV rights changed with the next contract.

I asked Bob to join us on the Orioles broadcast for an inning. When he arrived, he didn't have a scoresheet. I offered him mine.

Bob thanked me, but declined. "I don't keep score like you," he said.

He was right. A guy doubled, and Bob just wrote "2B." He didn't track runners around the bases, counting on his ability to remember how the runner advanced or where the double was hit. It wasn't an elaborate system, but it served Bob's purpose. To do a national telecast, he said, he didn't need an elaborate scoring system because he only needed the scoresheet for that game; he didn't have to keep track of a season's worth of events like I do when I'm travelling with a team.

After my dad, the most influential scorekeeper in my life has been Monte Moore. Monte was the first guy I ever saw who used a big scorebook.

Monte's scorebook had at least two-hundred pages in it. You could put the whole season in that one book, from the first Cactus League game to the seventh game of the World Series. It had a great cover—kelly green, with the A's insignia printed on it in gold. Monte had the books custom printed. The year we worked together, he gave me one. What a great scorebook.

Monte had a rule about scorebooks and beverage consumption: Never put down a soft drink next to your scorebook. Ninety-nine times out of a hundred, it won't spill, Monte reasoned, but that hundredth time you might ruin your scorebook, the most valuable reference book you've got. The way the players feel about their favorite bat—their "gamer"—we broadcasters feel about our scorebooks.

Thus, Monte's admonition impressed me. Over the years, I've always tried to be very cautious when drinking and scoring; rather than keep my cup beside my scorebook, I'd find a place a couple feet away, even on the floor. If the broadcaster with whom I was working wasn't familiar with Monte's Cup Rule, I'd tell him. I had this missionary zeal about keeping my scorebook dry.

But one night at Memorial Stadium, I strayed from Brother Monte's teachings. I put a cup of diet Coke down right next to my scorebook.

You know the rest. I knocked over the cup, sending a flood of carbonated chemicals onto my open scorebook.

Great. Just great. I was so ticked I wanted to pick up my chair and throw it out the window, but that hardly seemed fair to the fans sitting in the box seats below us. So I grabbed a towel and dried off each soggy page as best I could, which wasn't that well. The damp pages clumped together; I opened the book accordion style trying to achieve maximum drying power.

The next night, the pages were dry, and I hadn't lost any of my score sheets. Thank heaven for ballpoint pen. I used that scorebook the rest of the season. When I opened it each night, I heard a minor fizz.

Only slightly less irritating than drowning your scorebook is leaving it home.

In 1985, the Orioles' radio station asked me to speak at a function in Annapolis, Maryland, as a favor to an important sponsor. The timing was such that I'd be making the appearance just before a game I was working that night—always a bad idea, but the station impressed on me the importance of this particular sponsor to our future and mutual good fortune, so I agreed.

When I left Annapolis for the ballpark, I realized I had forgotten my briefcase. "What an idiot," I hollered at myself.

It was close enough to gametime that I had no time to go home and retrieve it. There was no way to replace the things I'd left home. I carry a lot of stuff in my briefcase: my files, my tools, my everything. Press guides, newspapers, tape recorder, microphone, binoculars, stopwatch (used for timing pregame interviews), pens and pencils, notes about both teams, and my trusty hourglass egg timer. My egg timer! Now I was really steamed. I rely on that egg timer.

I've used an egg timer in the booth for more than twenty years, ever since I'd learned about its usefulness from Red Barber in his excellent book, *Rhubarb in the Catbird's Seat.* Red's point was that the score is the most important piece of information in any broadcast. Nothing else you say has any relevance until the listener knows the score. Red used a three-minute hourglass to remind himself to give the score. Every so often, he'd glance at the glass to see if the sand had run through; if it had, he'd give the score and turn over the timer.

Ernie Harwell, whose first major-league job was as Red Barber's partner, saw my hourglass egg timer one time and asked, "Is that a three-minute egg timer?"

"You're close, Ernie," I said. "It's two and a half minutes."

Ernie said something very interesting. "I think the nature of the listener to baseball games is so transient today, popping in and out of the broadcasts, that in our job, you really should give the score every sixty seconds." As Ernie says, it's impossible to give the score too often.

Well, that night back in 1985, I had nothing to fall back on. I grabbed a scorecard from the press box. I borrowed a pen. I did the game naked. The experience taught me how valuable my scorebook is; several times in mid-inning I needed to check something from the previous night's game, the pitcher's previous start, or the last series between the teams two months prior, and I couldn't do it. And each time I thought, "What an idiot!"

The only thing worse was the time I lost my scorebook.

In 1990, the first year of *ESPN Sunday Night Baseball,* we were in Milwaukee to do a Brewers-Rangers game. An hour before the first pitch, I sat down in the booth and opened my briefcase. I rooted around for my scorebook. My scorebook was . . . LOST!

I wasn't worried about losing my record of the Sunday night games—one game in New York, the next game in San Diego, losing them didn't matter. But every Orioles game of the 1990 season up to that date was recorded in that book. The answers to all my questions about the Orioles season were in that book. Hitting streaks. Hitting slumps. And those beautiful red stars.

My "gamer"!

Where was it?

The game was starting. My book was nowhere in sight. In the pressroom, I picked up a scorecard, then quickly jotted in the lineups.

I've never been reunited with a lost dog, but I can't believe it feels any better than when they found my scorebook. During a commercial break, our director, Marc Payton, told me to check out the monitor.

And there was Bobby Valentine, the Rangers' manager, smiling into our camera looking like a used-scorebook salesman, proudly displaying a beat-up '73 "classic scorebook" that still "runs like new."

My scorebook!!

I had left it sitting on the bench in the visitors' dugout at County Stadium in Milwaukee.

All I could think was, one more time:

What an idiot!

A Few Good
(BASEBALL) MEN

One of my favorite managers of all time is Ralph Houk. You remember Ralph Houk: He managed for twenty years in the majors, starting out with the great Yankee team of 1961, the Mantle, Maris, Elston Howard Yankees, and later managed in Detroit and finally in Boston.

Ralph's nickname was "the Major," and it was a good fit. He was a World War II veteran, big, strong, and tough, and he had this no-nonsense style of speaking. Ralph was the kind of guy that, when you looked at him, you had this uncontrollable urge to salute.

Ralph took that military mindset into the dugout with him. Every game, it was like Ralph and his players were headed into battle. He was their supreme commander, their comrade to the end, and would always be there to support them. If somebody screwed up, as often happens in baseball—one guys screws up and costs a team the game—Houk would always stand up for that guy.

It was really ingenious, the way Ralph operated. After a game, the press would be all over him, asking questions that invited him to point the finger of blame at one of his players. But Ralph would never do it; he'd shade the story to shift the blame for blowing the game onto himself.

I remember a classic example involving Gary Allenson, a

catcher for the Sox in the early eighties. We were at Fenway, in the ninth inning of a tie game. The bases were loaded and the Red Sox were laboring to keep the go-ahead run from scoring.

The Sox had a pickoff play on. The first baseman broke in behind the runner, but Allenson's throw was wild, down the right-field line. The winning run scored.

Ralph's explanation was, "I don't know what I was doing out there. I ought to be fired for even thinking about calling that play. I owe my guy an apology. I'm the one who told him to do it and it didn't work out. I ought to be horse-whipped."

Only it was Allenson who called the play. Houk took the heat because—well, because that was Houk. The players appreciated it and played all the harder for him as a result.

Ralph's approach was very simple: Me and my players against the world. One for all and all for one.

I loved that about Ralph. He was a real character, different from any manager I'd known before or since. In this chapter, I've picked out a few more people who fit into the same category as Ralph. They're my favorites, people I think left baseball a better place than it was when they found it. They've made their contributions between the foul lines, in the clubhouse, and in the front office. Some are household names; others you probably don't know. Without any one of them, baseball would be a duller place.

REGGIE JACKSON

During the 1997 National League Division Series, my partner on several ESPN telecasts was Reggie Jackson. With Reggie in the booth, you get commentary on the ballgame and, as a bonus, commentary on Reggie.

During Game Three of the Braves-Astros series, we cut to an interview Reggie had done with Braves starter John Smoltz. The audio portion of the interview was screwed up through no fault of Reggie's, so we left it and threw it back to Reggie and me in the booth.

"A lot of echo in that room you guys were sitting in," I needled, which got the banter going.

"I haven't figured out if you have a great sense of humor or you're a wise guy," Reggie said. "I always thought I had a great sense of humor. But they said I was arrogant."

"Oh, I'm arrogant," I said. "I patterned myself after you."

I would only say that to someone I know well or someone I didn't like. I've known Reggie a long time—twenty-four years. Reggie and I have been through a lot together.

I love listening to Reggie talk. Reggie defies all the stereotypes about ballplayers being minimally intelligent people who haven't a clue what's going on in the world. Reggie is the opposite; he's well read and well spoken, and Reggie knows what he knows.

In intellectual pursuits, Reggie isn't always a patient man. I recall a story about a conversation Reggie had with a Yankee teammate, Mickey Rivers. Reggie was trying to persuade Mickey to see something Reggie's way, and Mickey wasn't budging. Reggie tried again. He tried a third time. No luck. Now, Reggie was disgusted.

"You know, Mick," Reggie finally said. "You're a fool not to agree with me. I have an IQ of one-eighty."

Mickey shrugged.

"Out of what?" he asked. "A thousand?"

In his way, Mickey was a genius, too.

Reggie and I met in 1974, when he was in the prime of his Hall-of-Fame career, swatting forty-plus home runs a year for the Oakland A's. I, on the other hand, was a lowly rookie broadcaster, learning the nuances of ordering off the room-service menu.

Reggie noticed me immediately. There were times I wished he hadn't been quite so observant. I was just twenty-two years old when I was hired in Oakland, a kid in every way but one: my receding hairline. As we traveled around the league the first time, Reggie decided he could make some money off that hairline.

Here's how it worked: Our first trip into a city, Reggie would corral a big star on the opposing team. He'd parade me in front of the player, then he'd make a bet that the guy could not come within eight years of guessing my age.

This went on, city after city, wherever we traveled. Reggie was very particular about who he let play the game. You had to be a star. You also had to be a pretty bad guesser. I recall being sized up by Alex Johnson in Texas, Dick Allen in Chicago, John Mayberry in Kansas City, and, on our first trip to Milwaukee, by George Scott, the legendary "Boomer."

Reggie's game produced a lot of laughs. What it did not produce were winning guesses. Guys would look at me and say, "I don't think he looks that old . . . I guess thirty-five." Thirty-two was the closest anybody came. Reggie would have a big laugh and collect his money. As for me, I was happy a virtually destitute superstar ballplayer was able to supplement his income this way—though, at age twenty-two, I was not thrilled that the youngest anyone thought I looked was thirty-two.

(My hair, or, better said, lack of hair, was undoubtedly a factor in Reggie's little guessing game, but it has never been a major issue for me. Still, there was a time back in the 1970s when I did briefly wear a hairpiece.

I didn't actually go out in search of a new head of hair; in 1976, a new head of hair came searching for me. At the time, I was the voice of San José's professional soccer team, the Earthquakes. After our initial telecast, I got a phone call from a lawyer.

"I saw your first telecast," he began. "It was excellent."

"Thank you very much," I said.

"And I think I can help," he continued.

"Help with what?" I asked.

"I think I can help with your hair-deficiency problem."

"I see."

"I have a client who can take care of that."

The guy explained that he represented a hair-replacement company that wanted to feature me in an ad campaign. If I agreed to appear in the company's newspaper advertisements, I'd receive a $1,200 toupee.

I thought it over for a day, then called back and accepted. A week later, I had my state-of-the-art hairpiece. The hair was average length, chestnut brown with a slight curl. When I had it on, I thought I looked just like Frank Gifford.

Next came the photo shoot. The photographer informed me we'd be taking two pictures—a Dismayed Jon [without hair] and a Joyful Jon [with my hairpiece]. He took me over to Spartan Stadium in San Jose to shoot Dismayed Jon. The idea was to slump and look mopey. Then we went over to the hair studio for Joyful Jon, for which I wore my hairpiece and managed *a gigantic smile.*

It was quite literally a new me—a tousled me—and early results were encouraging. About a month after getting my hair, CBS-TV hired me as the play-by-play man on the North American Soccer League's championship game, Soccer Bowl '76.

"This hair is really paying off, Giffer," I congratulated myself.

A few months later, all my plans unraveled in a sink in Santa Monica. I was preparing to televise a college-basketball game, and noticed that the hairpiece had become a tad greasy. I slipped it in the sink and started washing it with a specially formulated "hairpiece shampoo."

When I took it out of the sink, the polyurethane base, which had been molded to the shape of my scalp, was pulled up around the edges, almost inside out. The hair itself was a tangled mess, and when I tried to work the knots out with my fingers, big wads came loose from the base. Like an idiot, I kept trying, which only made things worse. Before I stopped,

I'd taken out four big clumps. My once-handsome hairpiece now looked like a dead rat you'd find in the gutter.

After taking my sad hairpiece to a hairstylist the next morning to see if it could be salvaged, I wore it on the telecast that night. But it wasn't quite the same. I was now wearing a hairpiece with a receding hairline! I became the only man in America wearing a hairpiece to whom people would walk up and say, "Have you thought of wearing a hairpiece?"

During the 1978 season, the year I moved to Texas to broadcast Rangers baseball, I finally said the hell with it. I wasn't going to bother anymore.)

Reggie has always been a great interview. He seems to have an intuitive sense of what a reporter's needs are in putting together a story. He speaks his mind and he has good insights.

In 1980, I was in my first year of broadcasting the Boston Red Sox. Reggie was with the Yankees. They came into Fenway Park in September and, in an exciting game, Reggie had a big night that included hitting a home run, and the Yanks beat the Sox.

I went down to the Yankees clubhouse to try to get Reggie on my postgame interview show. I set up my microphone in the visitors' dugout, on the third-base side. Then I went looking for Reggie.

He was nowhere to be found in the clubhouse. Time was short; we'd be on the air in a few minutes. Somebody said they'd seen Reggie in the trainer's room. I poked my head in and there was Reggie, stretched out, with a huge bag of ice tied around the inner part of his right thigh. Even for a radio interview, he was scantily dressed, wearing his Yankees shirt, an undershirt, and a towel around his waist.

"Are you all right?" I asked him.

What do you say to someone in that condition?

Reggie explained he'd aggravated a groin injury.

"I just came by to see if you'd do the postgame interview. It doesn't look good."

Reggie smiled. He lifted himself off the trainer's table and, to my surprise, he began hobbling down the runway toward the dugout at Fenway. I hurried ahead to alert the crew upstairs that Reggie was coming.

A couple of minutes later, he limped over to the microphone. I interviewed Reggie about the game and then, when we were about finished, I set the scene for our listeners: the ice bags, the limp, the whole thing.

"Ladies and gentlemen, Reggie has this huge bag of ice wrapped around his thigh. He's limping. He's partially dressed. And yet . . . he's here."

"Jon, I had decided not to do any interviews tonight because of my injury and the pain," Reggie said. "But I made an exception for you. I wouldn't have done an interview with anybody else tonight, but because of my friendship with you and my respect for you as a broadcaster, I came down."

For a first-year Red Sox broadcaster, receiving an endorsement like that from Reggie Jackson on our eighty-eight-station New England network was priceless—which Reggie, of course, knew.

And I was very grateful.

Which, of course, he also knew.

KIRBY PUCKETT

A few years ago, Kirby wrote a book about his life, titled *I Love This Game*. Talk about four words that sum up a man's life.

I've never met anyone who loves baseball more than Kirby. I've never met anybody who loves life more than Kirby. He's just an upbeat, happy, contented person—someone I admire tremendously.

When Kirby was playing for the Twins and I'd run into him at the ballpark, we'd trade smiles, shake hands, and invariably would begin a conversation that went something like this:

Me: "Kirby, how're you doing, man?"

Kirby: "Fantastic, Mill."

(Kirby calls me "Mill." Kirby was the only person in the world who called me Mill, until lately, when he changed that to "Mills.")

Me: "Fantastic again? You were fantastic last month. You were fantastic last year. Kirby, how can you always be fantastic?"

Kirby: "C'mon Mill, you know that every day I put on this uniform is a fantastic day!"

Every time. And every time, I knew that Kirby meant it.

Kirby grew up in circumstances that don't lend themselves to unbridled optimism. He was raised in the projects of Chicago's South Side; they were mean streets, filled with danger and despair. A lot of kids didn't make it out, but Kirby was special, with a great love and great talent for baseball, the game he played all day long.

Kirby began playing baseball in area youth clubs, worked hard on his game, and won a college scholarship. Before long, he was playing every day in the big leagues. A few years from now, we'll all be in Cooperstown for Kirby's induction into the Hall of Fame. That will be a fantastic day, too.

Kirby might still be playing if not for the eye problem that forced him to quit. Two years ago, he noticed his vision wasn't what it should be. Ron Shapiro, Kirby's longtime agent, and mine as well, arranged for him to go to Baltimore to be checked out by a team of world-renowned eye doctors. The tests confirmed everyone's fears: Kirby was suffering from glaucoma. His vision might stabilize, but it wasn't likely to improve enough for him to return to baseball.

Since his retirement, Kirby has been working in the Twins' front office. He's also dabbled in broadcasting. In 1996, Kirby and I even got to work as partners for ESPN.

Kirby's broadcasting debut came in the heat of fire—ESPN's first-ever telecast of playoff games. My regular partner, Joe

Morgan, had a deal with NBC to work postseason games for them, a commitment he had made before he could have known there might be a conflict with ESPN coverage. Here we were preparing to do our biggest games of the year, and Joe was off working with Bob Costas at NBC, leaving me partnerless.

A few days before the first game, I got a call from Steve Bornstein, the longtime president of ESPN who also runs ABC Sports. Steve wanted to talk about Kirby working with me on the games when Joe wasn't around.

Steve was calling personally, he said, because he wanted to gauge my reaction to working with someone of Kirby's scant experience. He reminded me that Kirby hadn't done a ballgame before and could hardly be considered a professional broadcaster. Would I mind working with a novice?

I thought it was an inspired idea, and that Kirby would be a great addition. People love Kirby, and not just in Minnesota. I believed that Kirby's infectious enthusiasm—that upbeat demeanor that people throughout baseball respond to so positively—would serve him and ESPN well in the booth. Just let Kirby be Kirby.

But to get the real Kirby Puckett, I told Steve, Kirby and I should work as a twosome in the booth. I know how unselfish a person Kirby is, and I feared that if he were the third man, his instincts would be to hang back so as not to get in the way of the other broadcasters. I felt that with three in the booth, we'd practically have to interview Kirby to get him to contribute.

But Bornstein felt it wouldn't be fair to Kirby or ESPN to put him in there in such a big game with absolutely no experience whatsoever. I could certainly understand that point as well, and the decision was made to add a veteran analyst, Dave Campbell—like Kirby, a former player.

Our first game as a threesome was Cleveland at Baltimore, ESPN's first postseason Major League Baseball game. Kirby spent most of that telecast being very polite, sitting politely and not commenting.

Periodically, I would ask him a question about things happening in the game. When Kirby did comment, good things happened; we heard the warm, genuine Kirby Puckett, the person loved by everyone.

Joe Morgan and I were together for Game Two of the Cleveland-Baltimore series, and then we went to St. Louis for Game Two of the NL series between the Cardinals and the Padres. But on Friday, Joe had to go off to Texas for NBC. I went on to Cleveland for Game Three of the Indians and Orioles, and as in the Game One telecast, I hooked up with Kirby and Dave.

Before this second telecast, ESPN asked Kirby whether he'd be willing to spend time with Andrea Kirby, a broadcast consultant who helps athletes improve their performance on television.

So here's Kirby Puckett. The guy's a multimillionaire, a huge baseball star. He has very little interest in pursuing television as a career; he's only doing the games because he was asked to help out. Yet, when they ask if he can spare a couple of hours to work with Andrea—early in the morning on a day when we'll be working a game—his reaction is, "OK, bring her on."

Kirby was funny about it. At our pregame production meeting, he poked me and said, "I'm trained. I'm trained, Mill. I'm ready."

For the last two games we were together, Kirby did a great job. He had enthusiasm for the job, his comments about particular game situations were insightful, and he certainly brought star quality to the booth. If I had a criticism to make, it simply would be that Kirby sometimes was quick to excuse a ballplayer's bad play. He'd dismissed an error, saying, "Anybody can make a mistake . . ."

No surprise there. For a former ballplayer new to the booth, it's natural to identify with the player and, perhaps, to offer a pat excuse. But the baseball fan in our audience doesn't need a former superstar in the booth telling him that mistakes happen. He already knows that. What he wants to know is what the player should have done and why.

Kirby was very capable of making those points. Case in point: A critical play in Game One of the Orioles-Indians series. In the sixth inning, Baltimore loaded the bases. With one out, Roberto Alomar lifted a fly to medium right, where Manny Ramirez made the catch and fired to third.

It was a glaring mistake, and a costly one.

We'd been anticipating a close play at the plate, but there was none. Chris Hoiles lumbered across with an important run, making it 5-3 Orioles. Next, Rafael Palmeiro was hit with a pitch, reloading the bases. Then Bobby Bonilla parked a grand slam to make it 9-3, paving the way to a 10-4 Oriole victory.

Of course, it hadn't all been Ramirez's fault, but he had failed to make the proper throw—to the middle of the diamond where the cutoff man could either let it go to the plate or cut and fire to third for a play there.

Kirby, with honesty and insight, quickly pointed out what went wrong. But then he added, "Hey, Manny's only human."

Nevertheless, this is a minor criticism of Kirby. If he sets his mind to it, he can be a very good broadcaster. But Kirby's dream is to open a full-service car wash in Minneapolis. They have good ones in Chicago, he says, but not in Minneapolis. He knows he'd be good at it and he'd be with people every day.

And for Kirby, every day he'd be at the car wash would surely be a fantastic day.

JOE CARTER

Here's what I think of Joe Carter: If I were managing a ballclub, I'd call a team meeting, bring my players together, and I'd tell them, "Watch Joe Carter. Be like Joe Carter." Then I'd call for adjournment.

I love Joe Carter. He's the total package—one of the great RBI men of his era and one of the great gentlemen of the game.

Often, my conversations with Joe have taken place during batting practice. Being around the batting cage as the players take BP is one of my favorite pregame rituals. For a broadcaster, it's an excellent place to gather information about that night's game, in conversation with managers and coaches or by watching hitters as they take their hacks.

But the batting cage also is a place of business, and it's important to keep that in mind. Some guys will chat as they stand around, watching other hitters and awaiting their turn in the cage. Others don't want to be bothered—they're concentrating on getting ready for the game.

When I find Joe at the batting cage, he always wants to shake my hand and tell me about his winter. He's just a special person, always upbeat, always confident, and always friendly.

Oh, and he loves to play the game.

Joe's a star, no doubt about that. This guy is just one of the all-time masters at knocking in runs. There's more to driving in runs than simply getting lots of RBI opportunities; you also have to know how to bring them in.

There's a certain approach, a certain mind-set to RBI situations. Frank Robinson used to tell me it had taken him three or four years to learn how to hit in RBI situations. Joe Carter is another guy who knows what it takes.

Joe is also a thinking man's player. And for that reason, he's a perpetual headache for opposing teams.

In 1988, Joe was with Cleveland. On a sultry August night, the Indians were in Baltimore to play the Orioles at Memorial Stadium. The Tribe was threatening against Orioles starter Jeff Ballard, with Joe at first, Julio Franco at third, and one out. The next Indians batter, Ron Kittle, lifted a pop-up in foul territory that was caught by first baseman Jim Traber beside the Cleveland dugout.

Traber spun and immediately checked Franco at third. He had no idea that thirty feet away, Carter had tagged up at first and was on his way to second base.

Traber's teammates pointed and shouted, finally getting his attention—just in time for the O's first baseman to make a hurried, off-balance throw that sailed into left field and allowed Franco to score from third.

The beauty of the play was that even if Traber had made a good throw to second, Franco would have headed home the moment the throw was made and would have scored easily as Carter got himself into a rundown.

It was the only time I've ever seen that play executed, and it spoke volumes about Carter's approach to the game.

Joe plays hard. But I've also seen a playful side of his personality.

In June 1992, Joe, then a Blue Jay, was the victim of the most spectacular catch ever made at Camden Yards. He was facing Rick Sutcliffe with two runners on in a scoreless game. An inning before, Baltimore right fielder David Segui had reached over the wall to pull back a home run off the bat of Joe's teammate Candy Maldonado. This time, Carter hit one deep into left-center.

Mike Devereaux never gave up on the ball, snaring it on the dead run as he reached his glove above the wall—an incredible grab. And, as it turned out, a game-saving catch; the Orioles won the game, 1-0, on Cal Ripken's RBI single in the eighth.

After that game, I saw Joe in the Toronto clubhouse and, despite the day's injustices, he was in very good spirits.

"Call a cop! We've been robbed!" Joe said, jovial as ever. No long face. No deep depression.

As I said, if I were a manager, I'd tell my players, "Be like Joe Carter."

EDDIE MURRAY

When Eddie Murray homered in what proved to be his last at-bat as an Oriole in the 1996 American League Championship Series, I thought, "What a perfect ending to a great career," hoping Eddie would retire with that last, legendary home run.

But Eddie didn't seem to care about being a legend, or about being treated like a superstar. For years, he literally wore a sign that implored people *not* to treat him like a superstar: on a gold chain around his neck, in glittering script, hung the words "JUST REGULAR."

For Eddie, baseball isn't about legends or perfect endings. Eddie just loves the game. And so, in 1997, at age forty-one, Eddie returned to the big leagues for one final year, to see limited playing time with the Anaheim Angels and, later, the Dodgers.

I put Eddie on my list of special people because I know what a good friend and decent human being he is. I know the Eddie Murray who is admired by the guys he plays with. I know the Eddie Murray who knows the name of every secretary and every intern in every front office he has ever been associated with.

There's another Eddie, though, and I can't pretend he doesn't exist. That's the Eddie who has kept up a twenty-plus-year feud with the media.

Eddie has his reasons for having kept reporters at arm's length. Sometimes he's trying to make a point. Sometimes there's a principle involved.

In Baltimore many years back, a TV reporter was stopped for drunk driving. Eddie wouldn't do interviews with him or with anyone from his station because he believed the guy needed help before he killed someone, maybe a kid.

Over the years, there have been many occasions when Eddie refused to speak to a writer because he believed the writer had been unfair to one of Eddie's teammates. Eddie is a great teammate, the consummate teammate; if someone was unfair to one of his teammates, then Eddie was going to stand up for that teammate and show solidarity with him.

For Eddie, being a teammate means every guy in the clubhouse pulling together and looking out for one another. That's the way it was when Eddie was growing up as one of twelve children, with his mother, Carrie Murray, making the rules and governing with an iron—but also very loving—hand.

Starting in 1983 when I came to Baltimore, Eddie and I had a very friendly relationship. I rarely interviewed him on the air, but I tried to stop by and speak with him off the air before every game. We'd talk about the opposing pitcher, or perhaps Eddie's views of how the infield at a particular ballpark was playing that day. Talking to Eddie was always great preparation, I found. He always gave me some insight that I could use in the broadcast.

You had to love Eddie Murray as a player. I don't think there has ever been a better RBI man in the history of the game. He was the guy you want at the plate with the game on the line and the bases full.

How many times did Eddie deliver in the clutch? How many pages do we have? We're talking about someone who put up nineteen career grand slams (second only to Lou Gehrig's twenty-three); batted in 1,917 runs, seventh on the all-time list; and with the bases loaded had a batting average of .406 over a twenty-one-year period. We're talking about the third man in history to record 3,000 hits and 500 home runs, the others being Willie Mays and Hank Aaron.

For me, a few of Eddie's games—and a few dramatic swings—stand above the rest. His memorable home run in Game Three of the AL Championship Series against the White Sox in 1983 turned that series around.

The Orioles and Sox had split the first two games of that best-of-five series, setting up the pivotal third game for the Orioles, who were playing in front of a hostile crowd at Comiskey Park and facing one of the Sox' toughest starters, twenty-two-game-winner Richard Dotson.

Murray took charge. In the first inning, he launched a spectacular three-run homer off Dotson into the right-field upper deck, and the Orioles never looked back, winning 11-1, on their way to wrapping up the series in four games.

Murray's home run in Game Three proved to be a turning point—and a flash point. In the fifth inning of that game, Dotson hit Cal Ripken with a pitch, and then threw the next two pitches *way* inside to Eddie.

Things quickly got out of hand. Both benches emptied. Both bullpens emptied. Jim Palmer ended up on the mound with Dotson, lecturing him on what a stupid move it had been to put Ripken on and fall behind 2-0 to Murray with John Lowenstein due to bat next.

"Lowenstein kills you," Palmer scoffed. "Now you're going to have to walk Murray. Then Lowenstein hits a double and you're out of the game. What were you thinking?"

Sure enough, when order was restored, Murray walked and Lowenstein hit a two-run double to make it 5-1, and Dotson was finished for the night.

The '83 World Series against the Phillies wasn't particularly productive for Eddie. Pitching was the key in that series, which the Orioles put away in five games. But in Game Five—the clincher—Eddie delivered the decisive blows, slamming home runs in his first two at-bats.

Murray's bases-empty homer in the second inning staked the Orioles to an early 1-0 lead. Then, in the fourth inning, he hit the crusher—a two-run shot far over the right-field wall that ricocheted off "MURRAY," the spot on the big electronic scoreboard at Veterans Stadium where his name was displayed.

Now that's clutch.

Eddie once told me there are certain hitters and certain pitchers you don't want out there when the heat is really on. They don't hold up under the pressure, he said. You know it before they swing the bat or throw the pitch.

How could you tell, I asked.

"You can see it in their eyes," Eddie said.

This was very interesting to me, because it reminded me of a story I'd heard about the great Japanese slugger, Sadaharu Oh. To make himself into a great hitter, Oh had gone to a samurai dojo to study the discipline of the ancient Japanese warriors. Oh had focused on swordsmanship and the mental aspects of being a samurai. He'd learned that when confronted with a foe, before he drew his sword, the samurai would look right into the eyes of his enemy. The idea is to look so deeply that, in effect, the samurai is able to see through the eyes and into the head. That way, the samurai knows his enemy's moves before he makes them.

Oh took that philosophy into every at-bat. Every time he stepped into the batter's box, he looked directly into the eyes of the pitcher and tried to get into his head, in essence, to anticipate how the pitcher planned to attack.

It sounds far out, but whatever Oh was doing, it worked. He hit 850 home runs in his career, the world record.

Years later, Eddie Murray was telling me a story with pretty much the same punch line: You can see it in their eyes.

In a past life, Eddie might have been a great warrior. Eddie's that kind of person.

Eddie not only is a clutch man at the plate, he's also a clutch man in the clubhouse. When I came over to the Orioles in 1983, it didn't take long to realize Eddie was the central figure. It was his clubhouse.

That's a pretty bold statement, considering some of the veterans on that club. Jim Palmer was still an Oriole in 1983. Cal Ripken was an Oriole. There were some strong personalities and veteran leaders on the club: Ken Singleton, Al Bumbry, Rick Dempsey. But none of those guys were leaders the way Eddie was.

Eddie kept tabs on struggling teammates. He counseled players with personal problems. When a new player was traded to the Orioles or brought up from the minor leagues, Eddie would offer to help find him a place to live, often inviting him to stay in his house until he did. While he was there, Eddie might show him around town, introduce him to people, even help him get a car. (The Orioles obviously noticed and appreciated these leadership qualities, because Eddie is returning to Baltimore in 1998 in a new role—as an Orioles coach.)

Some players take it upon themselves to learn about the media, how it works and how they can make it work for them, to burnish their public images. Eddie wasn't interested; playing to win and being a good teammate are the only things in the game that were important to him. During his playing days, he took the attitude that it was less than honest even to concern himself with how he might be portrayed in newspapers.

More often than not, I've found Eddie to be very cooperative; when I was broadcasting in Boston and the Red Sox and Orioles were playing, Eddie always accepted our invitations for interviews on the postgame show. Never a problem.

Later, when I became a broadcaster for the Orioles, I settled into a routine of having Eddie as the pregame guest on Opening Day every season. Since he was the big star, the heart and soul of the Orioles, it was appropriate that Eddie be the one to offer what amounted to a "State of the Orioles" interview.

Eddie and I did our Opening Day thing three years running, from 1983 through 1985, until, in 1986, I asked for an interview and he refused. No explanation; he just said no and headed off for the clubhouse, with me following.

"Eddie, why not?"

"It has nothing to do with you," he said.

The reason he wasn't talking, he told me, was because of a comment made by my partner on the radio broadcasts. Eddie complained that the remark, about one of his teammates, had been very unfair. He was plainly angry about it.

I agreed with Eddie that the statement probably was inappropriate. But what did that have to do with my request? "I didn't make the comment," I reasoned. "Why not do the interview with me?"

That wasn't going to fly with Eddie. And I knew it.

"Don't take it personally, because I don't mean it that way," Eddie said. "I'm just not going to do interviews with anybody from your station."

Once Eddie's mind was made up, that was it. There was no point in talking about it.

Over the next couple of years, Eddie and I continued to have a good relationship and many good conversations—as long as the microphone and the reporter's notebook were put away.

But in the mid-eighties, as the Orioles slipped from being a contending ballclub to one that was barely competitive, Eddie became increasingly disillusioned—not just with the losses (though losing bothered him—a lot), but with changes in philosophy at the top of the organization. For years, the Orioles had grown their own talent, relying on their strong farm system. By the time young players made it to the big leagues, a certain way of playing baseball, the Oriole Way, had been instilled.

Over the years, Eddie had seen that system deteriorate. Players were reaching the majors not knowing how to play fundamentally sound baseball—the Oriole Way or any way.

Just as distressing to Eddie was the pitiful state of the Orioles' farm system. The talent just wasn't there. So the Orioles signed a couple of high-profile free agents and filled in the holes with suspect ballplayers discarded by other organizations.

That pained Eddie.

In 1988, near the end of spring training, the Orioles checked into a hotel in Bradenton, Florida. I quickly set off for the hot tub. By the time I arrived, Eddie was already there, having a warm soak.

I joined him. We talked about the club for quite a while, and the more Eddie said, the clearer it became that he didn't have good vibes about the '88 Orioles.

"Today, I saw a guy walking through the clubhouse. He looked like a clubhouse guy, so I threw my dirty socks to him," he told me. "Turned out he's my teammate. We just traded for him." Eddie shook his head.

He said he'd apologized to the guy, and after he got his socks back, they'd both had a laugh about the mistake. But there was a point to the story, and it was no laughing matter to Eddie: For a team a few days away from the regular season, he said, the Orioles lacked a lot.

As it turned out, of course, Eddie was right. Distressingly right. The year before, the Orioles had lost ninety-five games, and 1988 turned out to be worse—worse as in disaster beyond Eddie's or my wildest dreams. After twenty-one games, the Orioles were 0-21. At season's end, they had stumbled to 107 losses, earning themselves the distinction of the most wretched team in Orioles history.

But as Eddie and I had our hot-tub chat that spring evening, we didn't know that. I tried to get him to see the bright side, the possibilities, even on a team as bad as we both feared the Orioles of 1988 might be.

"Listen, Eddie, if the team is really bad, why not concentrate on *your* numbers?" I suggested. "Hit your thirty-five or forty home runs. Drive in your hundred runs. Even if it's a lousy year for the Orioles, you'll still be on the road to the Hall of Fame."

Eddie looked at me like I was crazy. He was incredulous.

"*My* numbers?" he said. "What's the fun in just putting up numbers? The fun is in winning ballgames, in twenty-five guys coming together and doing whatever it takes to win a pennant. Who cares about *my* numbers?"

That's the way Eddie had been raised, and that's the way he'd been taught to play baseball, to think about baseball, as a kid on the sandlots of Los Angeles.

Soon after Eddie came back to the Orioles in 1996, the club was twelve games behind the first-place Yankees, below .500 and going nowhere. Eddie made an immediate difference.

In his first game, on July 22, Eddie faced Minnesota's Rich Robertson and blasted a home run into the left-field seats at

Camden Yards. It was like old times. The fans went wild; many stood and chanted "Ed-die, Ed-die," just like in the old Memorial Stadium days.

When the fans refused to stop, Murray finally, reluctantly, appeared on the top step of the dugout and doffed his cap. "I just knew they'd stay up there until I acknowledged them," he said.

For Murray, it was home run No. 492, and he knew it. "I've gotten close enough that it's something I think about," Eddie told reporters. "Charles Steinberg [Padre VP and former Oriole stat man—but more on him later] beat it into my brain for about seven years: 'Man, you're really close . . . it's so close.' "

With Eddie in the clubhouse, many of the problems the Orioles were experiencing on and off the field melted away. Lingering disputes—between Bobby Bonilla and Davey Johnson, between Cal Ripken and Davey—also seemed to be forgotten.

For Cal, Eddie's return meant an old friend was coming home; Cal's hero was back. For Bonilla, Eddie meant something else entirely. All year, Bobby Bo had resisted Johnson's plans to make him the semipermanent DH; with Eddie on the club as the DH, any and all talk of Bonilla in that position ended.

On his return to the Orioles, there was something else about Eddie, something different from his earlier days in an Orioles uniform: He was now an elder statesman. Many players sought his advice and counsel.

Manny Alexander was a backup shortstop on a team that hadn't needed one in fourteen years. He was also somewhat of a pariah in the clubhouse. One of Eddie's first orders of business was to reach out to Alexander, helping him to relax and be—for the first time—a real part of the team.

And, sure enough, for the first time all year, the Orioles became a team, and even started to win. Teamwork and winning, it has always been what Eddie is about.

And, oh, he also became accessible to the media.

Now, I thought, if he could just hit his five hundredth home run in an Orioles uniform—while at the same time helping to bring them back from the dead and into the playoffs—this could be the stuff of which legends are made.

It was a lot to ask. But then, we're talking about Eddie Murray.

On September 6—the one-year anniversary of his pal Cal breaking Lou Gehrig's consecutive-games record—Eddie reached the seats and the record books. At 11:47 P.M., facing Detroit's Felipe Lira in the seventh inning, he pumped home run No. 500 into the right-field bleachers at Camden Yards.

The sellout crowd at Camden Yards had come in hopes of witnessing the event. The fans who waited out a two-hour-and-twenty-minute rain delay before the game got their just reward. Two dozen Orioles met Eddie at home plate; clouds of confetti descended on the ballpark. On a wall behind the fence in center a banner was unfurled. It read, simply, "CONGRATULATIONS, EDDIE—500."

Once the party began, the celebrants didn't want it to end. It took eight and a half minutes to restart the game.

It was an historic home run. And—no surprise here—a clutch home run: Eddie's blast had tied the game.

Five days later, Murray again was the key to an Oriole victory. On a late-season roll, the Orioles had a half-game lead over the White Sox in the wild-card race. Now, facing the Sox in a game critical to their postseason chances, the Orioles led early, 6-3, before Chicago rallied for three runs in the eighth to tie the game.

It was one of the season's best, most tension-filled games. And the drama mounted in the eighth inning when the White Sox brought in hard-thrower Roberto Hernandez. From the moment he entered the game, Hernandez seemed untouchable, throwing 98- to 100-mile-per-hour fastballs. The first five outs he recorded were strikeouts. Then, with one out in the tenth, with Rafael Palmeiro at third and Mike Devereaux at first, up stepped Murray.

It was a classic confrontation, the aging slugger versus the hard-throwing closer. And Eddie battled gamely, fouling off several of the reliever's best offerings. Finally, he delivered a clutch sacrifice fly, gaining the Orioles a victory that moved them a game and a half ahead in the wild-card race and two and a half in back of the first-place Yankees—the club they'd once trailed by twelve.

A month later, on October 13, Eddie stood at the plate against Yankee ace Andy Pettitte in Game Five of the ALCS. The Orioles trailed 6-1 in the eighth inning. Only six outs stood between them and the long off-season that would begin with their elimination from postseason play.

It was Eddie's final at-bat as an Oriole, and he made it count, launching one last home run into the left-field grandstand.

Although it didn't actually end up in storybook fashion, being the classic final swing of a great ballplayer—he did play another season—it was the last home run I ever saw Eddie hit. And it's the way I'll remember him.

CHARLES STEINBERG

One of my favorite people in baseball—and it sounds funny to say—is a dentist.

Charles Steinberg graduated from dental school, and he even had a thriving practice in Baltimore for a while. But these days, Charles isn't treating patients—not unless a member of the Padres' grounds crew needs an emergency root canal. His No. 1 job is spreading the gospel of baseball.

Charles is senior vice president of the Padres, the guy who thinks up some of the most creative marketing ideas in baseball. He was the inspiration behind the Padres' "Frequent Friar" ticket plan, a discount deal for fans who buy tickets to a number of games. He has spearheaded the Padres' marketing ventures into Mexico, including the opening of the team's first ticket office south of the border.

Charles was a shoo-in for my list of good people in baseball because of what, and who, he represents: the countless people around baseball who love the game and have made great personal sacrifices to be around it. They may not be as well known as the Griffeys and the Cansecos. And they're certainly underappreciated, but thank goodness for them.

Charles's story is part Walter Mitty, part Walter Alston. He is someone who basically willed and worked himself into a high-level job in major-league baseball.

Charles attended the Gilman School, a prestigious prep school in Baltimore where students wear sport coats and ties and profess a deep love of sports. Like all the other Gilman seniors, Charles participated in a senior-year project in which students are encouraged to spend a month pursuing an internship in a field of particular interest.

Charles chose the Orioles, and he landed an unpaid, decidedly unglamorous position in the team's public-relations department. That was 1977, several years before Charles and I met. But I've heard him speak nostalgically of those years. I've even read published accounts of them in a book called *Baseball Lives,* by Mike Bryan.

"I was doing menial work—pasting articles in scrapbooks, stamping names on slides—but I was thrilled. In the eyes of those who were watching me, this was unusual. They had previously experienced people who wanted instant glory, not someone who was willing to sit all day in the closet pasting articles. I was in every morning and every afternoon, and stayed for the games. Well, when the internship was over they asked whether they could call on me during the summer for part-time help and I said, 'Sure.'"

During Charles's early years with the Orioles, one of his chief responsibilities was compiling the famed Earl Weaver stats.

Earl was one of the first managers to rely on statistical information about how certain hitters fared against particular pitchers, and vice versa. He'd have an 8½ x 11 sheet of paper for each pitcher and hitter on his team, and the same for each player on the opposing team. In a situation that might call for a pinch hitter, Weaver reviewed the paperwork to see if the statistics revealed an obvious choice.

Charles did the job for several years, and he did it well. But he often tells the story of one major stats screwup that took a few years off his life. In the first game of the 1979 AL playoffs, the Orioles were playing the Angels at Memorial Stadium. In the eighth inning of a tie game, Nolan Ryan came out and in came a reliever, righty John Montague.

Charles was very careful to prepare statistics on every opposing player, even those who'd joined the team in recent days. But in this case, he'd goofed. He'd forgotten to include one of the Angels' late-season acquisitions—this same John Montague—who now happened to be *in the game.*

Charles didn't realize the omission until he received a phone call from the dugout. It was the Orioles' pitching coach, Ray Miller, calmly advising him of the oversight.

Charles quickly located Montague's numbers against the Orioles that year as a member of the Mariners. Those numbers for the first three series in which the teams met were on file in a big binder in the Orioles' PR office.

But there had been *four* series. The stats from that final meeting were never entered in the book. Why bother, Charles figured. There was no chance the Orioles and Mariners would meet again that season.

The Montague stats had to be delivered to Weaver—and fast. So Charles had the sheet with the less-than-current statistics brought over to Earl right away. Then he began furiously flipping through his scorebook searching for a Montague pitching line in any of the games in that last set with the Mariners.

It turned out that Montague had pitched in three of the games—and had been shelled in one, retiring no one while yielding six hits, including a home run to John Lowenstein.

Charles quickly compiled this little addendum to his stats package and had it rushed down to Weaver. By this time, it was the bottom of the tenth inning, and Montague was still in there. Armed with the latest stats, Weaver brought Lowenstein in to pinch-hit.

You probably can guess the rest: Lowenstein cracked a three-run homer to win the game.

The part of the story Charles enjoys telling most is the classy way Weaver handled the situation—calling Charles into his office, offering him a beer, and telling him to forget the whole thing ever happened.

In 1985, the giant video boards were just being adopted for use in major-league ballparks. The Orioles got one—a Mitsubishi Diamond Vision board—and put Charles in charge. Within a year, he'd turned Diamond Vision into a real source of entertainment for Orioles fans—and a money maker for the front office, through advertising, highlight films, and other videos.

All the while, Charles still had his dental practice. One night, the Washington Bullets' big man of the time Jeff Ruland— all 6-11, 290 pounds of him—came to spend a night out at Memorial Stadium in Baltimore. Ruland may have arrived as a fan, but before the night was over, he was also Charles's patient.

Around about ten o'clock, Ruland got a terrible toothache. Charles heard about it, drove Ruland over to his dental office, and ended up pulling the painful tooth.

In a move overlooked by many baseball scribes, the Orioles lost their in-house dentist a few years ago. Charles moved on to the Padres, rejoining his mentor, Padres president Larry Lucchino, who had worked for the Orioles for more than a decade.

Charles has a better tan than he used to, but nothing else has changed. He believes in the game, still has a burning passion for it. And he's still out there spreading the good word about baseball. Baseball can't have too many people like that.

ALVIN DARK

If I were drawing up a list of important people in my career, at the top would be Alvin Dark. Alvin was my teacher, my mentor, my friend—sometimes my chaperone. He's a wonderful guy.

In 1974, I was a rookie broadcaster with the world-champion A's. When I say rookie, I mean rookie: at age twenty-two, I'd never broadcast a major- or minor-league game, and I hadn't been east of Wichita, Kansas, since I was an infant.

In '74, Alvin was the A's manager, entering his fourth decade in a major-league uniform. He'd been in baseball at many levels, and he'd been a success at whatever he'd done. He'd been in four World Series, one as a manager (of the '62 Giants) and three as a steady-fielding shortstop with the Boston Braves and the New York Giants.

Alvin and I were quite a pair.

For most of the '74 season, I listened to Alvin Dark. I thought I knew something about baseball, but the first thing I learned from Alvin was how little that was. Before games, we'd sit in the dugout and I'd listen to his comments on the pitching matchup or his take on a player in a slump. Something of significance that day. After the game, I'd listen to him dissect the game, pitch by pitch.

Alvin's recall amazed me. He was always comparing what he'd seen on the field that day to a situation that had come up six weeks earlier. A pitcher who'd thrown a slider when he should have thrown a fastball. What the count was. How many runners were on base. How did he remember, I wondered? I assumed all managers had that gift. But I've never met another who could recall the little things that happen in a game as clearly as Alvin Dark did.

Among Alvin's many assets was his high tolerance for stupid questions. In those days, I was a veritable geyser of them. The Old Faithful of stupid questions. But Alvin never balked or complained; he always had time for me, even on the days when A's owner Charlie Finley had called him four times and was ringing his phone for a fifth.

In so many ways, my baseball education began that year with Alvin. I saw a lot; I learned a lot. The only time I was ever in a dugout during a major-league game was during that season—and it was purely accidental.

We were in Baltimore on a Friday night in April—my first trip to Baltimore and first visit to old Memorial Stadium. That night, as every night, I handled the postgame interview. With a couple of outs left in the game, I'd leave the booth and take up a position near the field; then, when the game ended, I was expected to be in position to do my job, which meant quickly grabbing the outstanding player and posing the requisite postgame questions, such as "Big win tonight, eh, slugger?"

Never having been to Baltimore, I wasn't sure where to wait out those final pitches. A security guard posted at the visiting clubhouse noticed me wandering the halls and directed me down a narrow corridor. I thanked him and walked about thirty yards until I ended up . . . *in the A's dugout.*

With the game very much in progress.

I took a step back into the hall, trying to stay out of everybody's way. And then I watched. And listened. And marveled. To everyone else there, it was probably just another unexceptional evening in the A's dugout, but to my untrained eyes and ears, the scene was utter chaos. With each pitch, the crowd roared. Bugle calls blared over the sound system. Over the PA system, Rex Barney's amplified voice boomed as he announced the hitters.

I was impressed and surprised by the seeming disorganization in the A's dugout. At one point, Baltimore sent up a pinch hitter, a rookie outfielder named Mike Reinbach. Alvin, holding his lineup card, hollered down the bench, "Anybody know this guy? Anybody faced this guy? What do we know about this guy?"

I was taken aback. The A's were in a tight ballgame, the outcome was on the line, and Alvin was asking if anybody ever heard of the pinch hitter. I hadn't realized that, in certain situations, things could become so seat-of-the-pants.

When we were on the road, Alvin was my personal Fodor's guide. He knew the best restaurants, the best stores, the best everything. New York was Alvin's town. He'd been a great player with the Giants back in the fifties, and he'd been a key man on one of the most fabled Giants teams—the '51 "Miracle of Coogan's Bluff" club that went to the World Series on Bobby Thomson's "Shot Heard 'Round the World."

As a twenty-two-year-old on my first trip to Manhattan, I stopped in for lunch at the famed Stage Deli. Right out front at the most visible table in the joint were Alvin and his wife. Alvin motioned for me to come sit with them—me, the kid, sitting with Alvin Dark, manager of the A's, former manager of my all-time favorite team as a kid, the '62 Giants.

I knew that Alvin Dark was big, but I didn't realize how big he was in New York. As we noshed on our hot pastrami, he was besieged. The waiters wanted his autograph. Customers came by to pose for photos. New York was Alvin's town. I remember being taken aback; the Alvin Dark I knew with the A's was a soft-spoken, quiet, Christian, family man. This Alvin Dark was the toast of Broadway.

In 1974, Charlie Finley threw Alvin into an almost impossible situation. I can't remember a manager walking into a more chaotic scene.

Dick Williams, who'd managed the A's to three straight division titles and two World Series championships from 1971–73, walked out after the season, announcing his retirement. Shortly afterward, though, he agreed to manage the Yankees.

Not so fast! said Finley. Because Williams was under contract to the A's for '74, Charlie argued that Williams shouldn't be allowed to manage another club. And, in court, Charlie won, preventing Williams from taking the Yankees job.

Meanwhile, Charlie took his time selecting a replacement for Williams. On February 20, the reporting date for pitchers and catchers to go to spring training, Charlie called a news conference in Oakland to announce Alvin as his new manager.

For Alvin, arriving at the A's training camp was like confronting the enemy, except the enemy was his own new team.

Sal Bando and Reggie Jackson, two veterans on the club, both greeted the new manager with indifference. I remember them saying, basically, "Who cares who the manager is, this team manages itself." Such was their loyalty to Williams, who had taken a young, unproven team and taught it how to win.

It's traditional for managers to hire their own coaches, or at least some of their coaches. Alvin had no such authority. His coaches had worked for Dick Williams—all of them. To make matters worse, one was very disappointed he hadn't been the one hired to replace Williams.

The trouble figured to start early, and it did. It was the third game of the year, and the A's were in Arlington, Texas. The A's starter was Vida Blue, who'd sailed through the first four innings and, heading into the fifth, led 5-1.

The first two Texas batters singled, and then, to the surprise of everyone—and the horror of Vida Blue—Alvin marched out to the mound and made a pitching change. In came Rollie Fingers, the A's closer who was seldom used until the final three innings. Out came Vida, who never in his career had been pulled that early with a 5-1 lead. Vida's disappointment at that snub was exceeded only by his anger at being removed before having pitched the five innings needed to qualify for the victory.

Fingers went the rest of the way—the last five innings—and Oakland won the game, 8-4. In the ninth, Reggie hit a three-run homer off Jim Merritt, just to make things a little easier.

After the game, no one even mentioned Reggie's homer. Rollie was angry. Vida was beyond angry. And back in Chicago, Charlie, listening on WCOF, was fuming that his ace reliever was being worked to death.

For his part, Alvin calmly explained the move. "Fingers hadn't pitched yet this season. And he's certainly our best reliever," he said. "So why not use him?" To Alvin, it was that simple—but he never did it again.

After six weeks under Alvin, the A's were floundering. Their record was under .500. They were stumbling around, hardly looking like world champions. Catfish Hunter wasn't pitching well. Fingers was giving it up more than he had in the past. And Alvin was getting a lot of flak.

At the Oakland Coliseum one night, after the A's had blown a lead in the ninth to lose again, Ron Bergman, a very fine veteran sportswriter who was the only reporter to cover the A's both at home and on the road, sensed a story. He hurried into the press elevator and down to the tunnel leading from the dugout to the A's clubhouse. As the players made their way up the tunnel, Ron stood quietly in a corner, watching and listening.

Bando, the A's fiery captain, gave Bergman what he was looking for. In a fit of anger, Bando tipped over a garbage can and snorted, "Alvin Dark! He couldn't manage a [bleep]ing meat market!"

The next day, Bando's quote was the headline in the newspaper, as if Sal had called a press conference to make this announcement. Soon after, Bergman made a survey of A's players and claimed that most felt Alvin inadequate as manager. No surprise there.

By mid-July, the A's were still playing mediocre baseball. On a Saturday afternoon at Shea, the temporary home of the Yankees, the A's staked Blue to a 3-1 lead only to lose when the Yanks posted a five-run fifth inning.

Vida didn't make it out of the big inning. Alvin went out to the mound to get him, and as he reached for the baseball, Vida showed his distaste for the manager by flipping the ball into the air and stalking off.

That was enough for Alvin. The next day, before a double-header, Alvin called his first team meeting of the season.

Standing in front of Reggie, Joe Rudi, and Catfish, Alvin did all the talking. He laid out the rules for conduct on the field and when traveling. Vida, he announced, was being fined for his actions the previous day. That behavior, Alvin announced, was to stop. It would no longer be tolerated. He laid out a whole schedule of fines for various offenses. And, finally, he made an irrefutable point.

"You guys said you didn't need a manager, that the best thing I could do was not get in your way. Well, I've stayed out of your way. I let you manage yourselves. And you haven't shown me anything. You're a sorry, third-place ballclub."

It was the defining moment of the season, the moment Alvin took control. The message—and the timing—couldn't have been better; in the first game that afternoon, the A's fell behind 3-0 with Catfish on the mound, but came back to win, 7-3. Then they took the second game, 6-1, to complete a sweep.

For the rest of the season, the world-champion A's played like world champions, winning their division, whipping the Orioles in the AL playoffs, and taking the World Series in five games. In doing so, the A's became only the third team in history to win three straight World Series—and maybe the last.

Looking back, I realized that Alvin had a plan, an ingenious plan. He realized he'd get nowhere if he walked in the first day and forced himself on the A's. He waited for his moment, and he made the most of it.

A year later, the A's won their fifth straight AL West division title. And they won without Catfish, who'd signed with the

Yankees as one of baseball's first free agents. Finley—who else?—had made that disastrous development possible by breaching his contract with the A's pitching ace, failing to make a payment that was due.

In the playoffs, the A's were knocked off by the Red Sox, but that's not what got Alvin fired a few months later. What ultimately did Alvin in was a newspaper article that came out during the playoffs, recounting a speech Alvin had made to a church group, in which he'd said that despite all of Charlie's success in worldly matters, if he didn't embrace the Lord he was going to hell.

I'll never forget the headline: DARK SAYS FINLEY IS GOING TO HELL.

Apparently, Charlie didn't like that. It wasn't the first time it was suggested, but it was probably the first time it seemed so literal.

Sunday in the Park
WITH JOE

One of my proudest moments as a broadcaster came a few years ago when *ESPN Sunday Night Baseball* was nominated for an Emmy for the first time. Our peers in the industry had just named us one of the best sports telecasts on the air.

The nominees that year included the World Series, Super Bowl, Olympic Games, Final Four—and *Sunday Night Baseball!*

When we started Major League Baseball coverage on ESPN in 1990, I remember executive producer Jed Drake talking about how ESPN intended to cover baseball better than it had ever been covered before.

Privately, I had my doubts about this. NBC had always been the standard for baseball, and no other network had ever been able to equal it. How were we, totally new to baseball, going to live up to that lofty goal?

That's why the Emmy nomination was so special. We'd done it!

In April 1996, ESPN enjoyed an even prouder moment—an Emmy victory for our baseball coverage. It was a victory shared by our producer Phil Orlins, director Marc Payton, and Drake. (I, however, didn't win—Al Michaels made me a two-time Emmy loser.)

Our telecast was not just recognized as the best baseball telecast, but as one of the premier sports telecasts in the business.

Fittingly, on *Sunday Night Baseball*, we have *the* premier baseball analyst, my partner, Joe Morgan. I've never known anyone who consistently offers as many good insights on a baseball telecast as Joe. When Joe is on the telecast, there's always a moment when you say, "You know, that's a really good point . . ."

It's not only me; more and more serious baseball fans are taking note of Joe's talents in the booth. Recently, Joe received a glowing review from no less an authority than Roger Angell, the distinguished sports essayist of *The New Yorker*. Angell praised Joe as "an eminence—perhaps the eminence—in his new field" of broadcasting. "He talks less than his comperes, I notice, and instinctively avoids the . . . bonhomie that so afflicts the trade."

Well, yes. My thoughts exactly.

In 1997, Joe and I did a Yankees-Brewers game in Milwaukee, a big game because the Yankees' starter was Hideki Irabu, the much-heralded Japanese pitcher. We hadn't seen Irabu pitch, but we'd been warned to look out for his temper.

Nice scouting report.

Little things irked Irabu. Balls he thought should have been strikes. Hitters repeatedly stepping out of the box. For five innings, Irabu kept his emotions mostly in check. In the sixth, though, the Brewers erupted—and, not coincidentally, so did Irabu.

The Brewers scored six times, breaking open a close game. Irabu stomped around the mound. He fired the resin bag into the dirt. He was visibly upset, mostly with himself.

"It's difficult to pitch well in that frame of mind," Joe noted, referring to Irabu's smoldering emotions. "When you're upset, you channel it in a positive fashion or you lose concentration. Most tend to lose concentration."

Later, I read that Joe Torre had called Irabu—and his interpreter—into the manager's office at Yankee Stadium to counsel him about his composure. Torre's point to Irabu was Joe Morgan's point—only, Joe had made his a few days earlier to millions of viewers on *Sunday Night Baseball.*

That's the beauty of Joe: he puts you in the dugout without the mess of sunflower seeds and tobacco juice.

In 1996, we had a game in Anaheim that came down to a key at-bat—Albert Belle, then the Indians' premier slugger, leading off the top of the ninth inning against Troy Percival of the Angels, one of the top closers in the American League, in a 2-2 ballgame. Power hitting against power pitching.

Percival blew his first pitch, a ninety-five-mile-per-hour fastball, right past Belle for a swinging strike one. The next pitch was another fastball that Belle managed to foul back to the screen. Now Belle was behind in the count, 0-2, and looking very much like Percival's next strikeout victim. Except to Joe.

"Albert Belle makes adjustments, Jon," he observed. "It doesn't matter whether you throw ninety-plus miles an hour. Albert adjusts."

Albert adjusted to Percival's next pitch, another fastball, smashing it over the center-field wall for a game-winning home run.

Right, Joe. Albert adjusts.

Often, a point Joe makes early in a game looms very large in the eighth and ninth innings.

In 1995, we were at the Kingdome for the one-game playoff between the Angels and Mariners that would determine the AL West champion. Randy Johnson was pitching for the Mariners and had an overpowering day, totally dominating an Angels lineup loaded mostly with right-handed hitters.

Everyone knows that Johnson is death on left-handed hitters. Very few left-handed hitters have the nerve even to be in the lineup when he's pitching. Larry Walker of the Rockies, in an infamous decision, announced days in advance of a much-anticipated 1997 interleague game that he would not avail himself of an opportunity to bat against the Big Unit.

Rafael Palmeiro of the Orioles generally takes the same approach. Even in the 1997 AL Division Series between Seattle and Baltimore, Raffy, the Orioles' leading RBI man, wasn't in the starting lineup in either of the games Johnson started. Orioles manager Davey Johnson instead went with Jerome Walton, a right-handed hitter.

Early in our game, Joe made the point that as tough as Johnson is on left-handed hitters, he's equally tough on right-handed hitters.

Johnson gets the lefties out with the great power, that exploding fastball everyone associates with him, Joe said. But then Joe pointed out something few people realize: Johnson's real strikeout pitch is his slider, a devastating pitch, in part because he's so effective at keeping it down.

Joe explained how Johnson throws the slider in two different spots to a right-handed hitter—one on the outside starts off looking like a ball but breaks in over the plate after the hitter has given up. The other comes in right over the plate at the knees, and breaks down around the ankles and to the inside, under the hitter's hands.

The Angels had a potent lineup of right-handed hitters, including Tim Salmon, Chili Davis, and J.T. Snow. All three went hitless, and Salmon not only went 0 for 4, he struck out all four times. Snow was the only one of the three to hit a ball to the outfield, a harmless fly ball to center. Johnson dominated the three of them all day long—which had been Joe's point from the beginning.

Now in its ninth season, *Sunday Night Baseball* is big, bigger than I'd ever imagined it would be when Joe and I started in 1990. Our games go coast to coast, and all over the Western Hemisphere. We get mail from Puerto Rico, Mexico, and from countries throughout Central America.

Even though I know the games are seen around the globe, I'm always surprised when I'm recognized in a faraway place. A few winters ago, Janine and I were on a cruise ship poking around Central America, and we stopped at San Andres, a tiny island off the coast of Nicaragua. It's an interesting place, because, though it's near Nicaragua, it belongs to Colombia. I'm told it's the island of choice for Colombians who want a Caribbean vacation.

During our visit to San Andres, Janine and I were in a taxicab. In this exotic setting, a continent removed from the nearest major-league ballpark, the taxi driver turned around and said, "Are you Jon Meeel-ar?"

It turned out that he was a big fan of *Sunday Night Baseball* and an especially big fan of my *Sunday Night Baseball* partner.

"Joe eez the best," he said.

He wanted to know everything about Joe. When we told him that Joe hadn't accompanied us, he was sorely disappointed.

"I don't see leetle Joe," he said, searching the back of the cab. "Where is leetle Joe? How could you come to San Andres without leetle Joe?"

The great thing about Joe is that he's just a totally natural, up-front person. If he likes you, he likes you; if he doesn't, he doesn't pretend he does. I guess you'd call him blunt. On the air, Joe is the same. He doesn't try to emulate anybody. He's not creating a Joe Morgan television persona—he's just Joe Morgan on the air, which is part of what I think makes him so good.

The other part, of course, is that Joe knows baseball. We're starting our ninth year together, and even after all that time, his understanding of the game blows me away. It shouldn't, though: Joe played twenty-two seasons in the big leagues, played on two world champions, won consecutive MVP awards, and has a plaque hanging in the Hall of Fame. Joe Morgan brings instant credibility to any telecast. When he speaks, people listen, which isn't a bad thing in this business.

I run into Joe's fans everywhere.

A few years ago, the Orioles were in Seattle. The same week, the Senior PGA Tour was holding a tournament in the Seattle area. Before one game, a number of the golfers came out to the Kingdome to promote their event. During their visit, I ran into one of the tour's biggest stars, Chi Chi Rodriguez.

What a nice man. We talked for twenty minutes, a good part of the time about *Sunday Night Baseball.* Chi Chi said many of the senior golfers were regular viewers. After the final round of a tournament on Sunday, he said, they'd all get together over a few beers and watch the game.

"We really like Joe," Chi Chi said. "He doesn't give you all the showbiz bull—the cute stuff of some of the other analysts. He tells it straight. I learn a lot about the game from Joe."

See, I told you that.

If you watch *Sunday Night Baseball,* you know our telecasts have changed the way baseball looks on television. And I don't mean my neckties.

I credit our crack technical staff for that. The *Sunday Night Baseball* crew, from Phil Orlins to Marc Payton to all the camera operators, is something special.

The best picture we've ever had on *Sunday Night Baseball* was from Camden Yards in June 1992. I'll never forget that picture—and neither, I'm guessing, will Tim Leary.

Leary, a right-hander, was the starter for the Yankees that night. Early in the game, Orioles players complained to manager Johnny Oates about scuff marks on baseballs Leary had thrown. It seemed many of the balls had unusual scrapes, all in the same place, as if they'd been scraped with the same object.

In the fifth inning, a Leary pitch sailed inside on catcher Chris Hoiles and broke Hoiles's right wrist. In a rage, Oates stormed out of the dugout carrying several of the scuffed balls.

On ESPN, we showed the action—Oates and the umpires jawing at home plate. But I noticed Leary doing something strange on the mound.

On the air, I shouted out something about Leary's actions on the mound. In a second, we'd switched to that shot—Leary with his glove up, totally hiding his face as the umpires made their way to the mound.

A few moments later, on replay, producer Orlins called up a close-up shot (from the field-level third-base camera) of Leary apparently putting something in his mouth. The obvious conclusion was that he was trying to hide a bit of sandpaper— though it couldn't be seen in the shot—as the umpires headed to the mound for a possible inspection for "illegal scuffing" implements.

In New York the next day, a frame of that camera shot was plastered across the back pages of the *Daily News* and the *Post. The New York Times* ran three of our pictures in sequence.

In *The Baltimore Sun,* the headline read: "ESPN'S CAMERA WORK GIVES US A TASTY BITE."

The credit for that memorable shot belongs to Scott Maynard, the crack camera operator who caught Leary in the act. But Scott was able to get it because, on *Sunday Night Baseball,* he was allowed to. If he'd been working for another network, it might not have been possible.

Our camera operators have certain responsibilities during the game: certain bases, certain fielders or runners, certain parts of the field. Together, the cameras cover all the things that could happen to every player in any given game. We hope.

But on *Sunday Night Baseball,* director Marc Payton encourages his camera operators to freelance. If they see a good picture, go for it. Don't wait for permission. Do it. We'll deal with the protocols later.

That night in Baltimore, Scott Maynard's responsibility was not Tim Leary, but when he heard me shouting about Leary on the mound he swung his camera to get a close-up shot of Leary. Two seconds after focusing, Maynard had the shot of Leary putting something in his mouth. We had our classic picture. And they say *baseball* is a game of inches!

Later, Scott and I were talking. When he'd worked on post-season telecasts for other networks, Scott said, he'd freelanced just the way he had in getting the pictures of Leary, and he'd been chewed out for it—for straying from his assigned coverage.

Working on *Sunday Night Baseball*, Scott told me, was a lot more fun because it was such a team effort, top people in the business working together to put on a first-class live telecast. It's gratifying when that effort is recognized, as it was in November 1997, when *Sunday Night Baseball* snared a Cable Ace award as best sports-event series.

There is no better example of ESPN's commitment to excellence than the telecast in April 1997 of the Jackie Robinson Night tribute game at Shea Stadium, the game marking the fiftieth anniversary of Robinson breaking baseball's racial barrier.

The game was played on a Tuesday night early in the season, hardly a prime opportunity for big ratings. But when ESPN was offered the chance to televise the game, the network didn't just accept—it jumped in, sparing no expense. ESPN even went so far as to clear satellite time so that during the game we could interview Pee Wee Reese live from Florida, where he'd been undergoing treatment for cancer. In addition, there were countless hours of research and labor committed to digging up old film and video so that Joe could provide a contemporary-sounding analysis of Jackie Robinson, the player.

ESPN was not required contractually to do this game—yet not only did the network carry the game, but it did so in a way that created a great new awareness in young people about who Jackie Robinson was—both as a ballplayer and a man. I was proud when this effort also was rewarded with a Cable Ace award.

Sometimes, Joe and I will sit down with the technical crew. As we talk, ideas emerge for new camera angles. One of Joe's recommendations led to a shot we now use frequently.

We call it a "relationship shot." It's shot from a camera placed high above third base to show both the pitcher and a runner at first base. The point is not only to see them, but to see them reacting to each other's movements in base-stealing situations.

Joe believes the key to any stolen base is the runner's jump against the pitcher. To truly see that on television, both the pitcher and the runner have to be in the camera shot. It was Joe's idea, and now it's a *Sunday Night Baseball* innovation.

On our second telecast in 1990, we developed another key element of our broadcasts, one we've used ever since. Every game, we pick two or three stars from each team, and when those players come up, we clear the decks. We don't play sound bites. We don't flash graphics.

The first time, I think we chose Kevin Mitchell and Will Clark from the Giants, and Tony Gwynn and Joe Carter from the Padres. Eight years later, we're still choosing: Ken Griffey Jr. whenever we have the Mariners; Frank Thomas and Albert Belle when we're doing the White Sox. The old rule takes effect: When the superstars are on stage, we give them the stage. In effect, we're telling the viewer, "Say, you might want to give that clicker a rest for a while. Here's the slugger, here's the reason you tuned in."

Another wrinkle is swing comparisons. For instance, we'll show Ken Griffey Jr. taking a big swing on one side. Then, using a split screen, we'll show a vintage film of perhaps Babe Ruth or Mickey Mantle taking a cut. Side by side. Same time. Then Joe will discuss how the swings are alike and how they're different.

In 1993, we used the split screen to pair John Olerud of the Blue Jays and Ted Williams—a modern-day player threatening to hit .400 and the last man to actually hit .400.

We've even used a split screen to compare a hitter with himself. One such comparison showed the Will Clark of the last couple of years versus the Will Clark of eight years ago, when he was much more of a home-run threat.

With Clark, Joe was able to point out differences in his stance, swing, and timing, illustrating why Clark doesn't pull the inside pitch or hit with much power anymore.

I'm constantly learning from Joe. I like to think that I know baseball rules, even obscure ones. But Joe had me beat there, too.

One night we were at Wrigley Field for a rare night game. Andre Dawson, then the Cubs' big gun, stroked a base hit to right-center and took a big turn as the center fielder very deliberately gathered up the baseball.

The outfielder didn't throw the ball in right away. He stopped to see what Dawson had in mind. Then he faked a throw and Dawson faked going to second base, taking the opportunity to get a few more feet from first. The outfielder then zipped a throw to first base, behind Dawson, not realizing he'd been lured into a trap. Dawson broke for second and made it easily.

"That's a single for Dawson," I said on the air. "He takes second on the throw."

"I don't think so, Jon," Joe broke in. "Dawson has to get credit for a double because he made the whole thing happen."

Joe had reason to be confident; as a player, he'd made the same play happen several times. He'd always received credit for a double.

I, on the other hand, had never seen the play called that way and was just as sure Dawson would get credit only for a single. A few seconds later, the official scorer ruled, "Single, second on the throw."

I felt confident now of how smart I was and was planning some patronizing remarks to Joe. "He is, after all, usually right," or "I don't think they'll revoke your Hall of Fame status over this, Joe." You know, helpful stuff like that.

When the inning was over I pulled out my rule book. The very situation that had played out in front of us was described in detail. According to the rule book, the proper scoring was to award the hitter with . . . a double!

Joe and I sent a copy of the rule book—opened to the appropriate page—to the press box for the scorer to have a look. A few minutes later, the ruling was changed and Dawson had his double.

The next day when I rejoined the Orioles, this play was the topic of much discussion around the batting cage. Many of the players had seen the game, and all the ones I spoke to said that when they saw the play their first reaction was to agree with me—a single. They were impressed that Joe knew differently. So was I.

When people ask me to pick the strangest play I've seen on *Sunday Night Baseball,* I don't have to wrack my brain. In fact, it's a no-brainer in more ways than one. In 1994, the Expos were playing the Dodgers at Dodger Stadium. It marked the first start for Pedro Martinez in LA since the Dodgers had traded him to Montreal, so this was a special night for Pedro, and I'm sure one about which he was really excited.

Unfortunately for Pedro, it ended up being a really bad night for Larry Walker, one of the outstanding players in the game, then an Expo. The first batter for the Dodgers, Brett Butler, hit a double into the right-field corner. Walker retrieved the ball, but, as he turned to throw it back to the infield, it dropped out of his hand and rolled behind him. By the time he'd retrieved the ball a second time, Butler was at third.

Larry Walker is a Gold Glove outfielder with a great arm. This was something you might see in the *Major League* movies—the outfielder cocks his arm and the ball falls out of his hand. But it wasn't a bit funny for Pedro Martinez, I'm certain.

That play was just a precursor of an even more bizarre happening.

Mike Piazza hit a high fly down the right-field line into foul territory. Walker, after a long run, got to it and made the catch. His momentum carried him to the railing. Seeing a kid sitting in the front row, he took the ball out of his glove and handed it to him. "Here, a souvenir for you, little guy." Then he started trotting down the line toward the visitors' dugout, thinking he'd just caught the third out.

Beautiful, except that . . .

It was only the second out!! José Offerman, who'd been at first base, tagged up and began rounding the bases. Suddenly it all became clear to Walker. He'd screwed up again.

It was here that the classic comedy began. Walker backtracked to the railing and demanded the ball back from the kid. "Here you go, Mr. Walker." Larry fired it in. In his panicked state, however, he'd completely forgotten one of the basic principles of baseball: that when the ball goes out of play, it is dead and the runners advance only to a predestined base determined by where they were when the ball was thrown or—as in this case— given away as a gift.

The nice part about it was that in the next inning, Walker went back to the kid, shook his hand and handed him another baseball. No question, one of the most bizarre plays I've ever seen in a baseball game.

When I'm asked why I think Joe has had success as a baseball analyst, I go back to the success Joe had as a baseball player. Joe had a certain amount of talent. Obviously, he had excellent speed. But Joe was always being told he was too small to have a future as a regular in the game. So he always had an incentive to succeed, to prove those people wrong. He studied the game trying to get every edge, and over time, he became the thinking man's player.

The people from his playing days that Joe talks about with fondness are often people who taught him something valuable about the game. For example, the late Nellie Fox, who was inducted into the Hall of Fame in 1997. Fox was the second baseman for Houston when Joe came up to the majors, and he taught Joe about turning the double play, the little techniques of making and receiving throws and turning the pivot.

Nellie Fox is a person revered by Joe—because of that great knowledge, but even more because Nellie was willing to pass on that knowledge to the next generation. Last year, Joe was proud to see that at long last Fox became a member of the Hall of Fame, an honor Joe had lobbied in support of for years.

Johnny Bench is another of Joe's favorites. Joe will tell you that Johnny Bench understood the nuances of the game better than anybody he ever played with.

For all the years they were teammates in Cincinnati, Joe batted in front of Bench. If it looked like a stolen-base situation, they'd set it up with each other before Joe got on base. Joe was going to steal, and Bench would take a pitch or two to allow Joe to do so. Bench also would catch things in a pitcher's delivery, things he picked up even though he wasn't a big base stealer. If a pitcher did something that tipped off a pitch—say, reached into his glove differently for his curveball—Joe said Johnny Bench detected it and shared the knowledge.

Now Joe does the detecting and the sharing. In 1990, the first year of *Sunday Night Baseball,* Gregg Olson was the outstanding closer for the Orioles. Olson wasn't a finesser; he threw two pitches—a good fastball and an outstanding curveball, one of the best in the game.

One Sunday night, the Orioles were playing the Twins, a good Twins team with veteran players like Kent Hrbek, Gary Gaetti, Tom Brunansky, and Kirby Puckett. It was the ninth inning of a one-run game, and Olson was in to close it out for the Orioles.

On the air Joe announced that he knew in advance every pitch Olson was going to throw. Joe had the director get a close-up of Olson looking in for the sign.

"This is going to be a fastball," Joe predicted.

Sure enough, a fastball.

"This one's a curve."

A curve.

Joe had detected a change in Olson's routine: If the pitch was a curveball, Olson would get the sign from the catcher and throw. No hesitation. On the fastball, Olson got the sign, then paused a moment before delivering the pitch. That slight pause was to give the catcher time to signal where he wanted the pitch—inside or outside, up or down. On a curveball the catcher doesn't signal for a spot.

When Joe saw that pause, he knew the fastball was coming.

Apparently the Twins did, too; as Joe was making his point, the Twins lineup was putting together a major rally led by a couple of those veteran hitters, Gaetti and Hrbek. It seemed as if every hitter was sitting on Olson's pitches, as if they knew what was coming next. With Joe in the booth, our viewers had pretty much the same edge.

Over the years, the players themselves have become big fans of *Sunday Night Baseball*. All the other Sunday games are day games, so if they want to watch on Sunday night, they can.

The players also enjoy being on *Sunday Night Baseball* because it's a showcase game, one they know is being watched by a national audience and by many of the other players who played that afternoon.

In 1990, we had a game in Philadelphia between the Cubs and the Phillies. Don Zimmer was the Cubs' manager at the time. Sunday morning, Joe and I were on our way to a production meeting when we saw Zim sitting in the lobby of the Sheraton Society Hill, reading a newspaper.

We stopped to talk. As we spoke, we found out that in the game that night, Zimmer planned to rest the Cubs' biggest star, their biggest name, Ryne Sandberg. Zimmer had a good reason for it—actually, two good reasons. A tough righthander was going for the Phillies that night, and the Cubs were going to be traveling after the game, getting into the next city in the wee small hours.

As we went into our meeting, Joe and I talked about Sandberg. We were ticked. It just wasn't right. *Sunday Night Baseball* is a showcase game. Yeah, Sandberg should play—no question about it. He would want to play, and the fans would want to see him.

And it would be good for us, too. Well, I suppose.

When we left the meeting, Joe and I found Zimmer and attempted to talk him into putting Sandberg back in the lineup. We mentioned it was the one game seen by all the other players and that Sandberg would want to be in the game.

Joe had been reading the out-of-town box scores during the week, and he'd noted that in the first or second game of the Cubs' next series, a tough right-hander would be pitching. If Zimmer played Sandberg in our game, Joe pointed out, Zimmer still could rest him a couple of nights later.

Zimmer listened politely, arms folded, not saying anything.

That night when we got to the ballpark, Sandberg's name was in the lineup. Zimmer had gone to Ryno and asked him how he felt about playing; sure enough, because the game was going to coast to coast, Ryno said, he'd rather take his night off later.

That same year, we went into Pittsburgh at a time when the Pirates were the best team in the National League East, with outstanding players like Andy Van Slyke, Barry Bonds, and Bobby Bonilla—and an unheralded young manager headed for big things, Jim Leyland.

When we arrived at Three Rivers Stadium, we learned that Bonilla was not in the lineup. First thing, I went to Bonilla to find out from him why not.

"Are you hurt?"

"Nope, fine."

"Is there another reason?"

"Couldn't tell you. You'll have to ask the manager."

It was clear that Bonilla was none too pleased to be missing a *Sunday Night* game.

So I went to Leyland. And it was basically the same story

as when Joe and I had encountered Zimmer in the hotel lobby. Leyland said the Pirates would be traveling all night after the game, a sleepless start to a ten-game road trip. Thus, Leyland thought that this would be a good time to give Bonilla a rest, so he'd be strong and ready to go when the Pirates hit the road.

From a baseball standpoint, you couldn't fault Leyland's reasoning, but he'd neglected to take into account that *Sunday Night Baseball* quickly was being seen by the players as the new national game of the week, one they not only wanted to play in but to shine in.

In 1991, late in the season, we were in San Diego for a Sunday-night game between the Padres and Pirates. Before the game, we were setting up to do what we call a "standup," a live shot from the field. We had all this electronic hardware lined up adjacent to the third-base dugout: lights, cameras, a huge umbrella to eliminate shadows, a big reflector to gather up the sunlight and shine it into the broadcasters' faces. It looked impressive, like we were filming a big Hollywood movie. Or as Van Slyke said when he noticed all the equipment, "Wow, this must be the [bleepin'] game of the century tonight!"

Yes, Andy, we like to think so.

Joe and I were going on the air in a minute and a half. All of a sudden Bonilla and Bonds walked over and started chatting us up. We were going live in sixty seconds with nothing particularly profound to say, so I asked them to come on with us. Sure, great. And then . . . we were on.

To this day, I couldn't say whether the meeting was pure serendipity; Bonilla was in the midst of contract negotiations with the Pirates, and that's what we talked about. On national TV.

Bonds made a point about how important it was to keep Bonilla with the ballclub. He also said that if Bonilla left, he'd be very interested in following him to another club when his own contract expired the next year.

Nothing was settled that night. But again it showed that *Sunday Night Baseball* was gaining stature among the players. It continues to this day.

The only player I can think of who might be anti–*Sunday Night Baseball* is Tim Leary.

Hey, I can understand. Sandpaper tastes bad enough when you're *not* on national TV.

2,131, 22:15

Three o'clock in the afternoon on September 6, 1995. In a few hours, barring a cholera epidemic or something of that nature, Cal Ripken would own baseball's all-time record for consecutive games played.

The Late Show with David Letterman was calling.

A *Late Show* producer apologized for contacting me so late, but they needed a favor: Would I play a part in a comedy bit to air on Dave's show that night?

The subject: the streak.

The idea was simple yet funny. Before the game, at about five o'clock when *The Late Show* was being taped for that night, Dave and I were linked up via satellite—Dave from Manhattan, me from in front of the batting cage at Camden Yards.

As it played out on the air, Dave said, "Jon, we're taping our show in the afternoon before Cal breaks Gehrig's record. But the show airs *after* Cal breaks the record. To give our viewers a flavor of what the night was like, could you share with us what you'll say at the moment the record falls?"

"All right, David. Glad to," I replied, expressionless, as agreed upon in the earlier call with the producer. Then in total deadpan, I droned, "Ripken heads out to play shortstop to start the game."

Pause.

"He's there now . . ."

Longer pause.

"And . . . that's the record."

And . . . that was it. The bit got a big laugh up at the Ed Sullivan Theater. And, although it was comedy, I think it really went to the heart of the kind of record Cal was breaking.

Cal's iron-man streak ranks up there with the most prized baseball records. And, truly, it may be the record that will be the most difficult to break.

But the nature of the record precluded a moment of achievement, one when the record was set. This was not Hank Aaron hitting number 715—the drama of the big moment when the ball actually left the ballpark. This was not Pete Rose breaking Ty Cobb's all-time hit record—there it is, number 4,192!

Cal's record arrived right on schedule, like a commuter train. For months, we knew the exact date he'd pass Lou Gehrig's mark of 2,130 consecutive games played. As long as he stayed healthy, stayed in the lineup, and jogged out to shortstop on September 6, he had the record.

To be at the microphone when Cal passed Gehrig was an honor, one any broadcaster would treasure. I know I did, including the inning I shared the microphone with President Clinton. But Letterman had it right: When the big moment arrived, the challenge might have been keeping it from becoming anti-climactic.

Of course, as the evening played out, Cal passing the immortal Gehrig on the iron-man list was a momentous night at the park. Arguably, the nights of September 5, when Cal tied Gehrig's mark of 2,130, and September 6, when he erased the fifty-six-year-old record, were the most emotionally charged evenings at a ballpark in recent memory.

Those games were so magical, sometimes they didn't seem real. I give credit to the Orioles; the front-office staff did a beautiful job.

In late August, two weeks before Cal overtook Gehrig, the

Orioles began to transform this abstract notion, this ephemeral moment of achievement, into something tangible. They accomplished this with two ideas, two strokes of genius.

All baseball statistics and records become official—real—when that game becomes official. If the hometown team is leading after four and a half innings, the game—and its stats—are official. If the visitors are leading, or if the game is tied, everything counts after five innings. The game is official. If a game starts but is called off because of rain before becoming "official," nothing counts—not even a game played in the ironman streak.

So, over those two weeks, whenever a game became official, the Orioles, posted excerpts of baseball rule 4.10C regarding "official games" on Camden Yards's huge Jumbotron screen. This explained to the crowd why this was the relevant moment on the road toward this particular record.

Then, as a buzz went through the crowd, all eyes would turn to the Orioles' second inspired idea—four five-foot-by-ten-foot banners draped from the B&O warehouse, the massive brick backdrop to Camden Yards out beyond right field. Each banner carried a large black numeral outlined in orange. Starting August 13 with game 2,108, the banners kept a daily count of Ripken's streak: 2,109, 2,110, 2,111 . . .

The routine never became routine. At the "official moment," always at the end of an inning or half-inning, the Orioles cued "Day One," an inspiring John Tesh composition, which would echo majestically through the park. And then, as the music reached an emotional crescendo, the banner carrying a new number would unfurl from the warehouse, bringing Ripken and the fans one game closer.

The first night of the streak celebration, Cal seemed put off; it seemed almost an embarrassment to him. Each night as a new banner unfurled, a live picture of him flashed on the Jumbotron. Cal looked away—doing his best, it seemed, to ignore the whole scene.

At the same time, the streak was becoming a national fascination, and Cal couldn't pretend it wasn't so. In early August, the Orioles played three games in New York and four against the Red Sox in Boston. The reception was totally spontaneous and unexpected: In both cities, the fans went nuts, standing, cheering, and paying homage. For an "enemy" player, it was a rare reception.

We had the first taste at Yankee Stadium. Bob Sheppard, the dignified, elegant public-address man, announced "Number eight . . . Cal Ripken . . . shortstop . . . number eight," and the highly partisan Yankee crowd saluted Cal with a standing ovation. There had been no mention of the streak on the scoreboard; the fans just knew, which made the scene all the more heartwarming. There we were, in the legendary Yankee Stadium—Gehrig's stadium—and a man from another team was about to break one of baseball's most cherished records—Gehrig's record—and the fans paid tribute with a loud and long Yankee Stadium roar. It was an emotional moment. There wasn't a dry eye to be found in the visiting radio booth that night.

Then it was on to another of baseball's most famous venues. As Cal came to bat in the second inning of the first game of the series at Fenway Park, another spontaneous ovation erupted. This one stopped the game for two or three minutes, so long that Cal kept stepping out of the batter's box and finally asked Red Sox catcher Mike Macfarlane, "What should I do?"

"Tip your cap," Macfarlane suggested.

After a few tips and a reluctant wave from Cal, the fans finally settled down. It was another misty-eyed moment in a great, historic ballpark, a park in which Gehrig played many times.

Cal now seemed to recognize that the streak was not just a sensation in Baltimore. It was bigger than Oriole fans, bigger than Cal. After New York and Boston, he seemed more at ease with the banners, the dramatic music, and the hoopla. They were becoming much more than marketing gimmicks dreamed up by the front office; they were part of the experience.

On to Baltimore. On September 5, Ripken pulled even with Gehrig. Game 2,130—a moment a mere fourteen seasons in the making.

The honor of throwing out the ceremonial first ball went to Earl Weaver, Cal's first major-league manager, now a Hall of Famer. Weaver tossed a looping strike to Ripken behind the plate. As he met Earl in front of the pitcher's mound, ball in hand, Cal said, "Do you want me to sign it to you, or just to sign it?"

"Just sign the damn ball!" Earl ordered. Even on this night, he was still managing.

The celebration began when Brady Anderson squeezed a fly ball off the bat of the Angels' Greg Myers to end the top of the fifth inning. With the Orioles ahead, that made it official: Cal had tied the "unbreakable record." Tesh's music accompanied the cheers of 46,804 at Camden Yards as the newest number unfurled on the warehouse wall: 2,130.

For almost three minutes, Cal remained on the field acknowledging the ovation. He ducked into the dugout and plopped down on the bench, apparently hoping to end the celebration so that, in the tradition of the Ripkens, the game could go on.

Not this night. Plate umpire Al Clark, let the joyous ovation thunder through the Yards for another three minutes before giving the go-ahead for Jeff Manto to step up to bat and begin the Oriole fifth.

"There's no way an umpire is going to steal from a positive moment that is not just Cal Ripken's, but all of baseball's," Clark told *The Baltimore Sun* after the game.

As he emerged from the dugout to take his position in the sixth, Ripken received another standing ovation. And when he homered in the bottom of the inning, I swear the building shook as yet another celebration began.

It was magic. Cal circled the bases on the ground where Babe Ruth once played as a kid. (Camden Yards was built in the inner-city neighborhood where the Babe once lived.) Ruth, of course, was Gehrig's teammate—and there was Cal producing a Ruthian moment, hitting a homer when everyone most wanted it. Of such moments are legends made.

When the game ended—a rollicking 8-0 Orioles party in which they blasted six home rums—no one left the park. Not a soul. Ten minutes after the game, there wasn't an empty seat at Camden Yards. Finally, the Orioles wheeled a couple of swivel chairs to a spot near the pitcher's mound.

As master of ceremonies for the postgame program, I made my appearance on the field, microphone in hand. My task was to introduce all the luminaries—beginning with Cal—and then an array of celebrities invited by the Orioles to participate in the festivities.

What a lineup. The guests included a rock star, Joan Jett, a Maryland native and a great Orioles fan; an Olympic gold-medal speed skater, Bonnie Blair; and a revered Baltimore sports legend, former Colts quarterback Johnny Unitas. Following them were three baseball Hall of Famers, each in his own way linked to Cal: Frank Robinson, a great Oriole and Cal's onetime manager; Ernie Banks, Mr. Cub, whose record for home runs by a shortstop Cal surpassed in 1994; and Hank Aaron, the man who broke another of baseball's most hallowed and "unbreakable" records.

In the crush of celebrities, somewhat overlooked was what for me qualified as one of the night's most memorable moments. I'm referring here to a presentation made to Cal by Jim Gott.

On May 30, 1982, in what turned out to be Game One of Cal's streak, Jim Gott was the starting pitcher for the Toronto Blue Jays. The Jays won the game and Gott was the winning pitcher—his first victory in the major leagues. Someone had flipped the game ball to Gott afterward, and from that time on, the memento had been on display in his home.

On September 5, Gott came to Camden Yards to deliver the ball to a new owner.

"For thirteen years, I've been holding something on my mantelpiece, not letting the kids chew on it or anything," Gott told Cal and the crowd. "I was willing to give this up for a wonderful thing."

And then he handed the ball to Cal.

I don't remember Cal crying that night, but as Gott handed him that baseball, I could see the tears in Cal's eyes. This was a most generous and touching gesture, from big-league player to big-league player. Here was another player saying, as if on behalf of all big leaguers, "You're something, Cal."

It moved me. And it moved Cal, apparently; he went up to Gott and gave him a big bear hug. He didn't want to take the ball.

Cal repeated several times, "You don't have to do this, you don't have to do this." But Gott insisted the ball remain with Cal. Later, he explained he'd never hesitated giving away the ball.

"I had it for a while," Gott said. "Now it's where it should be, with Cal."

People who know Jim Gott weren't surprised that he'd so willingly handed over a piece of history; sharing is something that comes naturally to Jim. Now retired from baseball and living in Southern California, Jim and his wife own and operate a center for autistic children—two of their children are autistic. Jim directs the center's sports camps, and I bet he's good at it.

We all left the ballpark that night on an emotional high, not knowing what to expect the next night but wondering how what we'd already seen could be surpassed. We needn't have wondered.

The night of September 6 was a collection of incredible

snapshots: Cal's young children, Rachel and Ryan, tossing out the first balls. A forty-second ovation for Cal before his first at-bat. The giant numerals 2,131 being unfurled as the record became official. Cal's famous lap around the field.

Before the game, I remember the sportswriters' jokes about the streak. It was the point of the bit on the Letterman show: We're all here not to see if Ripken *might* get the record on this night; we all *knew* he would get the record on this night. Two thousand one hundred thirty-one *would* happen tonight.

Some of the writers—hundreds from around the world had converged on Camden Yards—tried to imagine bizarre things that could prevent Cal from playing the half inning that the rule book said was required for him to reach 2,131. Pulled hamstring from tripping over the resin bag on his way to short for the start of the game? Maybe a pregame earthquake. Or a tidal wave. Yeah, a tidal wave. They're rare in Baltimore, but hey, you never know.

When the moment arrived and Cal passed Gehrig, then what? I didn't have a clue. There had never been a game quite like this at a major-league ballpark, and so there was nothing in the history books with which to compare September 6.

The game would stop. When Cal officially broke the record, there would be an interruption as the 46,272 fans stood, cheering, whistling, toasting their star shortstop.

But for how long?

Cal was very much opposed to stopping the game to acknowledge the streak, and he told the Orioles just that, just that way: "Don't stop the game when the record is official." He'd given his approval to ceremonies after the game—that was different, Cal said, the appropriate time for such a celebration. But during the game, play on. That was Cal's thing. And, I might add, that's a Ripken thing: Respect the game. The game is the thing. Nothing—not even a great record—is bigger than the game.

Cal Ripken Sr. detests mascots, anything that gets in the way of the game. The San Diego Chicken was a menace as far as Rip Senior was concerned. To him, as to Cal, it was obvious why the fans were there, why the players were there: for the *game.* So, streak or no streak, let's play the game, unencumbered.

The Orioles kept their promise, planning nothing that would stop the game. The fans were another story entirely. They made no deals.

And that's what made the night of September 6 so special— the fans and the impromptu way they made their own celebration. Cal and the fans interacting, feeding off one another's energy, made the night.

It was a night of ovations—so many, they all seemed to blur into one nonstop roar. All told, there were eight times that Cal acknowledged the cheers with a wave or tip of his cap. Once after hitting a dramatic home run in the fourth inning. Seven times in the fifth inning, when the record became official.

I have to add one personal memory; of my inning on the Orioles' radio network with President Clinton.

The White House is forty miles from home plate at Camden Yards. By car, it's an hour up the Baltimore-Washington Parkway, but a mere twenty-six minutes as the helicopter flies. With major-league baseball so near Washington, Baltimore sees a lot of presidential visits. President Reagan had many times come to Memorial Stadium on Opening Day and thrown out the ceremonial first pitch. President Bush and Vice President Quayle were guests on Oriole broadcasts during their administration. Then, when President Clinton was elected, he joined us on Opening Day in 1993. But the most memorable—and nerve wracking—of those White House trips was President Clinton's visit on the night of 2,131.

We were advised that the president planned to stop by for the fourth inning. After the third, I left the booth to visit the men's room, my final preparation.

In a booth next to our WBAL booth, the president was taping a segment for ABC's *Nightline*. Several Secret Service agents stood guard at the door. No problem, I thought as I returned from the men's room. Excuse me, gentlemen. I'll just squeeze by . . .

The agents did not budge.

"Sir, you're not authorized," one of them said, looking at me.

Not that I was looking to pick a fight with a guy carrying a concealed weapon, but, hey, I *had* to get in there.

"I broadcast the ballgames," I said. "The president is coming on with us next inning. I've got to get in there."

The agent didn't move.

My God, I thought, I'll be off the air the rest of the night. I'll miss the president. I'll miss Cal breaking the record.

And all because I had to use the men's room!

Another agent, one who was a great Orioles fan and, as it turned out, a Jon Miller fan, recognized me, fortunately. He took over, escorting me to the booth just ahead of President Clinton and his entourage.

When President Clinton arrived, the nervousness vanished. He smiled and told us he'd been looking forward to the game. He shook hands with everyone; Fred Manfra, my partner on Orioles broadcasts; Paul Eicholtz, our engineer; and Hank Thiel, the longtime caretaker of our hand-operated Fenway Park–style, out-of-town scoreboard.

Finally, the president settled in for what turned out to be the best half inning of the game. The Orioles homered twice in that inning, including Cal's blast.

Before Cal's home run, the president and I engaged in a little baseball banter. The first three pitches to Cal were balls for a count of 3-0. In mock seriousness I said, "On this of all nights, Mr. President, they just cannot walk Cal. Could you send down some sort of presidential order, requiring that Cal be pitched to?"

The president smiled and said, "I know Cal wants to hit one

out. But he's a team player. If they don't throw him a strike, he'll take his walk for the good of the team."

"But if they lay one down the middle—" I started.

"—then he'll hit it," the president finished.

On the next pitch, Cal lined the ball into the seats down the left-field line, a no-doubt-about-it home run. I was excited. The president was beyond excited.

"GO . . . GO . . . GO . . . Yee-ess! Ha-ha-ah!"

At that moment, there was no thought of presidential decorum; the president was just another baseball fan at the ballpark. We all were. How could we not be?

For the second night in a row, in the shadow of the Babe, Cal had done something Ruthian. The ovation was thunderous, but also delirious. He couldn't really have done this again, could he?

That game captured the emotions of everyone in the ballpark, from the fans to the president to the players in both dugouts. Bobby Bonilla, a big star and a veteran ballplayer, carried a camcorder, taping Cal's movements in the clubhouse and on the field.

It seemed like everyone wanted a piece of this historic night. In the fifth inning, Cal was retired on a bloop to short center caught by Angels second baseman Rex Hudler. You've never seen anyone happier to catch a pop fly. To the fans, it appeared that Hudler was showboating, gloating at having retired Ripken. In fact, Hudler was excited because he'd just caught an incredible souvenir.

For the streak-tying and streak-breaking games, Major League Baseball had approved the use of balls bearing a special logo. The balls were printed with the numbers 2,130 and 2,131, and, in the center, Ripken's uniform number—8. It was the first time in major-league history that a baseball with a special insignia had been used in a regular-season game.

A Ripken baseball—especially one used in either of those

games—was a pretty hot souvenir. Hudler not only had one, he had one that had been hit by Cal Ripken on the night he broke the record. Rex was like a little kid. "This one is mine. Cal hit it. I caught it. And now it's going in my trophy case."

After fourteen years, you might think we'd have been prepared for the bottom of the fifth inning on September 6, but no one really was. After the Angels had been retired in the fifth and the game officially was in the books, the giant numbers on the warehouse changed for the first time to read "2,131." Black and orange balloons descended on Eutaw Street. Fireworks lit the night sky.

The place went nuts. Not only was the game stopped, it was stopped for *twenty-two minutes, fifteen seconds!*

Cal did everything possible to get things under control. He came out of the dugout several times to wave and to doff his cap as he touched his heart, as if to say, "you've touched me here."

Finally, Rafael Palmeiro and Bobby Bonilla told Cal, "You've got to take a lap around the field so all these people can see you, or we'll never be able to get the game started again."

According to Bonilla, Cal replied, "I'm too tired. I'll never make it."

"Then walk," said Bobby Bo.

The idea of actually taking a victory lap around the ballpark was totally against the grain for Cal. When you know Cal, your reaction to such an idea is, not in a million years. But the cheering didn't stop, and Bonilla and Palmeiro were not taking no for an answer. Each grabbed one of Cal's arms and literally pushed him out toward the field to start him on his way.

The lap was very emotional. Magic. All along the grandstand, Cal slapped palms and grasped hands. When he passed the Orioles bullpen in left-center, he celebrated with the team's relief pitchers. He stopped one long moment to celebrate with bullpen coach Elrod Hendricks, the only man I can think of—

other than Ripken himself—who witnessed every one of those 2,131 games. Their quick moment made me cry, because Elrod knew better than anyone what it had taken for Cal to reach that milestone.

On the third-base side, Cal shook hands, one by one, with the California Angels. On that night, even they were Ripken fans.

Twenty-two minutes, fifteen seconds. It was unbelievable, Cal and the fans staging their own celebration, each paying tribute to the other. It was the best party I'd ever attended, and I was at work!

After the game, I was co-master of ceremonies for the postgame festivities, sharing duties with Chuck Thompson. One of the first celebrities to be introduced was Earl Weaver. At Weaver's insistence in 1982, Ripken had moved from third base to shortstop, maybe the most successful position switch in history. This night, Earl took Cal by the arm and escorted him from third base to short, symbolizing that move. Oriole players in the lineup on May 30, 1982, assembled on the field. Mike Mussina, Brady Anderson, and Brooks Robinson all made speeches.

As we neared midnight, we were to hear from Orioles owner Peter Angelos, who would make a presentation on behalf of the club. Then, a surprise guest—Joe DiMaggio. And, of course, Cal himself.

It was a tough position for Mr. Angelos to be in. It was late. The fans were understandably restless. They wanted to hear from Cal. But Mr. Angelos's speech lasted fourteen minutes, and during the last three or four many fans began to heckle him. Some boos rained down on the field.

Standing to the left of Mr. Angelos, I couldn't believe the scene. Hey, I'm thinking, we're going to have a riot here.

Finally, Mr. Angelos neared the end of his speech. But instead of handing the microphone to me so I could introduce DiMaggio, he basically introduced Ripken—not a proper introduction, but in such a way that Cal thought he'd been introduced, and so did the fans. They started to cheer as Cal began to stride forward.

I thought, We have Joe DiMaggio here, and he hasn't even been introduced!

I started shouting into the public-address microphone, "Ladies and gentlemen, Cal is going to speak. But first of all, you want to see this next gentleman . . .

"He was Gehrig's teammate. . . . One of the greatest players to ever play the game. Here to honor Cal, the Yankee Clipper, Joe DiMaggio!"

DiMaggio's grand entrance, accompanied by the roar of the crowd, made the ceremony complete. Here was Gehrig's teammate as well as one of the greatest players of all time. Now he was part of this historic night.

Cal finally got his turn at twelve minutes after midnight. He thanked his mother and father, his wife and children, and his friend, Eddie Murray.

Then he thanked baseball.

"Whether your name is Gehrig or Ripken, DiMaggio or Robinson, or that of some youngster who picks up his bat or puts on his glove, you are challenged by the game of baseball to do your very best day in and day out.

"That's all I've ever tried to do."

Leaving
THE ORIOLES

In November 1996, I signed a five-year contract to become the radio and TV voice of the San Francisco Giants. I was happy to be back in the Bay Area, where I'd grown up, and pleased to be working for the Giants, an ascending organization doing some great things. I also was humbled to be following in the footsteps of one of the broadcasting idols of my youth, Hank Greenwald. Hank surprised many people by deciding to retire after the 1996 season, following sixteen seasons at the microphone for the Giants.

As beautifully as things have turned out for me in San Francisco, I can't say that doing the Giants games was originally the plan. For fourteen years, I was fortunate to be the voice of the Baltimore Orioles; it was the best job I had ever had in a city that truly has a love affair going with its baseball team. I'd hoped to spend the rest of my career describing Orioles baseball. Now I have the same hope with the Giants. Why and how that had to change is a story I haven't told until now.

People sometimes ask me what my goals are. Invariably, they're surprised when I answer that, for me, the ultimate would be to broadcast baseball for one team for a long time. It's the career path of most of the great ones in my business: Jack Buck in St. Louis, Harry Kalas in Philadelphia, Ernie Harwell in Detroit, Chuck Thompson in Baltimore. Their voices not only say baseball, they say Cardinals, Phillies, Tigers, Orioles. Vin Scully began broadcasting Dodgers baseball forty-eight years ago; pity the poor broadcaster who has to follow him there.

In 1991, as the Orioles were bidding farewell to Memorial Stadium, I was asked to emcee an on-field ceremony honoring many of the team's radio/TV voices through the years. Among those present was Ernie Harwell, the original Orioles announcer in 1954, and Chuck Thompson, a voice synonymous with Orioles baseball for four decades.

That night, when I introduced Chuck, the reception was overwhelming. A thunderous ovation. Fifty-two thousand fans on their feet, and they would not stop cheering. After I'd passed him the microphone, Chuck said thank you and tried to shush the crowd, as if embarrassed to be the object of such an outpouring of affection.

It was pointless. That crowd loved Chuck. So did another million people listening on their radios and watching on TV. It was the kind of ovation you hear for a great player like Brooks Robinson or Willie Mays, but I had never heard anything like it for a broadcaster. It was an astounding outpouring of affection for one of the great voices of the game.

Standing on that field, with the cheers raining down on Chuck, I thought of all the people who'd grown up listening to him—and of their children who'd also learned baseball from him.

Longevity in the job; it's what I've aspired to wherever the work has taken me in this business. Others might dream of the big national spotlight, the network jobs that take you to the big glamour events. My ambitions are simpler: Find a good club, do good work—and then, God willing, retire from that club a very old man with a towering stack of scorebooks.

Today I have the best of both worlds in my Giants play-by-play job plus my weekly duties with *ESPN Sunday Night Baseball*. For me, it's an ideal arrangement. I've just never wanted to cover the Olympics or to sit between Gifford and Dierdorf on *Monday Night Football.* For somebody else, fine; for me, let it be baseball—and let it last for decades.

In my early years in Baltimore, occasionally *The Baltimore Sun* or *The Washington Post* would run letters to the editor about me. The theme of those letters was a recurring one: "Obviously, Jon Miller isn't going to be here long. . . . He'll be moving to New York."

At times, the comments were laughable. Moving on was never my goal; what I wanted was to put down roots in Baltimore. Before that, when I'd broadcast Red Sox baseball, it'd been to put down roots in Boston. And here's another recurrent theme: before that, Texas. And before that, Oakland. But despite my intentions, I apparently was "Born Under a Wanderin' Star." That's not unusual for a very young broadcaster— remember, I was only thirty when I got to Baltimore. But I was ready for a home that was ready for me.

I've been offered many jobs over the years. After the 1983 season, my first in Baltimore, I received a serious offer from KMOX radio to do the Cardinals on radio with Jack Buck and Mike Shannon. I remember Ron Shapiro, my lawyer, telling me, "I want you to stay in Baltimore. But as your lawyer, Jon, I have to advise you that the Cardinals are making a great offer. You won't get anything near the money to stay in Baltimore."

And I didn't. I ended up staying for a little more than half what St. Louis had offered—but that was fine, because everything was right in Baltimore. The Orioles treated me well. I was able to work the broadcasts following my own vision. I realized that the only reason I would be leaving for St. Louis was for the money, and that had nothing to do with the joy of this job. So I stayed in Baltimore for less money. Contentment 1, Business 0.

The next year, 1984, Ron got a call from the Cubs and their flagship station, WGN. The Orioles had toured Japan after the '84 season, and on the way home I stopped in Chicago to meet with the people from the Tribune Company, owners of the ballclub and the station.

Afterward, when I met with Ron, he told me, "Well, again, Jon, as your lawyer, I have to say this could be the best offer you'll get in your career. It's a lot of money. The Tribune owns the ballclub, the radio station, and the TV station. You certainly won't have to make a deal with a new station every four years."

I turned that one down, too. Contentment was on a roll.

In 1996, my thinking was the same, only more so. Now there were many personal reasons to go along with the professional ones to stay in Baltimore. The Miller clan had put down roots in Maryland. My wife, Janine, and I were married in Baltimore, on a schooner in the Chesapeake Bay—fittingly, on an off day for the Orioles. (Thank God they didn't get rained out the day before!) All of our children have grown up in Baltimore. Two of our children were born in Baltimore. One child is buried there.

Compared to Orioles owner Peter Angelos, the Millers are newcomers to Maryland. Mr. Angelos is Horatio Alger with a Baltimore address; raised in blue-collar Highlandtown, a proud, ethnically diverse neighborhood on the city's east side, he excelled in law school and built a thriving practice. In the 1960s, he dabbled in politics, winning a seat on Baltimore's city council and running briefly and unsuccessfully for mayor.

In the 1980s and '90s, Mr. Angelos recovered hundreds of millions of dollars for shipyard workers and others poisoned by exposure to asbestos. Starting in the early nineties, he has invested heavily in Baltimore, from office buildings to a baseball team—even making a bid for Bethlehem Steel's shipyard.

Baltimore is lucky to have Peter Angelos. I believe that. He cares about the city. He invests in it. And he sure does make Baltimore a more interesting place to live.

Ron Shapiro has been my lawyer for fifteen years. Not only

my lawyer, but also the agent for Cal Ripken, Dante Bichette, and other baseball and broadcasting luminaries.

Over the years, we've worked out procedures for handling negotiations. The first rule is that Ron handles all the actual negotiating. I'm not involved in that. Ron is a superb negotiator, and I pay him for those skills. He's my representative from the beginning of bargaining to the end.

Before the talks begin, Ron and I talk about my objectives, such as salary goals, length of contract, and such. In case negotiations go poorly, we discuss other options; for instance, other teams or networks that might have contacted us or that we've heard might be in the market for a baseball play-by-play man.

Ron is good about keeping me posted; after a meeting, he'll let me know what was offered, then he'll give me his analysis of what the other side is saying and where I should expect the negotiations to go. His instincts usually are right on. Within a few months, we have a deal.

This time was different.

In August 1996, Ron called the Orioles. With my contract set to expire after the 1996 season, he wanted to get negotiations under way on a contract for 1997.

For the next three months or so, until the day the deal with the Giants was done, Ron continued to suggest, then to implore, and eventually to warn that it soon would be too late. But nothing moved the Orioles to action.

At first, Ron didn't seem concerned, so neither was I. But when the season ended on October 13, I wondered what was going on. We should have had a deal—or been close to a deal. Yet Ron was telling me negotiations hadn't even begun.

Ron would make a call and wait a week for it to be returned. Then he'd make another call, and another week would pass before that call was answered. The most perplexing part was that even when Ron and the Orioles were talking, they weren't talking about my contract, only when the Orioles might be ready to begin talking. So the contract itself, which was the whole point of initiating contact with the Orioles in the first place, was never discussed. Was it only me, or did that seem odd?

The only explanation offered was that before talking about my contract, the Orioles preferred to complete negotiations to determine which radio station would broadcast their games in the future. In our three our four previous negotiations with the Orioles, this issue had never come up. If anything, in the past, the Orioles had preferred to complete my contract long *before* they began talks with radio stations.

The Baltimore media began picking up on my contract situation. On October 3, *The Baltimore Sun* quoted an Orioles official saying of the situation, "We want to hear what [Miller is] interested in doing in the future."

Now they had me thinking. Airline pilot? Hey, I'm not even a good passenger! Professional bungee jumper? I'll admit, it would be tempting.

Baseball broadcaster? Oh, yeah, probably that.

OK, the Orioles weren't ready to talk. And they weren't ready to offer assurances either. They might have said, "What are you thinking, Jon? Of course you're our guy. No worries, mate. We just need a little time. Go see a movie, go fishing—relax, it'll get done."

But that's not what they said. Ron and I agreed it would be smart to look at other options (although I wanted to go to the movies first). We couldn't risk letting these nonnegotiations drag on while all the potentially desirable jobs got filled. If we could not get assurances that the Orioles wanted me back, we thought it wise to see if other teams might be interested.

In one of our meetings, I mentioned to Ron that Hank Greenwald had announced his retirement, and so the Giants might be looking for a new voice. We talked about a few other possibilities, but in my mind, we were still planning for a situation that would never occur. If all went well, I'd be back with the Orioles.

In mid-October, after the Orioles had been eliminated from the playoffs by the Yankees, Ron contacted the Giants. The Giants were definitely interested. Later, we had brief discussions with the San Diego Padres and Madison Square Garden, the powerful cable channel that carries Yankees games. Both expressed interest in talking about play-by-play jobs.

For months, Ron's contact at the Orioles was an official responsible for the team's broadcast agreements. With no beginning for negotiations in sight, Ron decided to call Mr. Angelos directly on October 18.

"Other teams are contacting Jon," Ron told him. "If you are interested in Jon, you need to tell your broadcast director to return our phone calls and start negotiating."

Mr. Angelos's answer was interesting—puzzling, but interesting. He explained that he'd been giving a lot of thought to my situation. He wondered why he was paying so much money to someone—me, I guess—who was so negative toward the ballclub.

As he subsequently said on *Sports Forum,* Nestor Aparicio's radio program on WWLG in Baltimore, "I was a little unhappy with . . . his broadcast of the fifth playoff game," when the Orioles were eliminated by the Yankees.

Ron called me and recounted the conversation with Mr. Angelos. We talked about what to do next. Ron offered a suggestion: a one-on-one meeting with the owner. Mr. Angelos and me. Face to face.

My first reaction was, fine. We'll sit down. We'll talk. We'll come to a meeting of the minds. We'll shake hands and that will be that. I wanted to believe that Mr. Angelos was trying to solve a problem.

But the more I thought about meeting with Mr. Angelos, the less I liked the idea. The timing of his expression of dissatisfaction with the broadcasts seemed to me more a negotiating ploy than a real concern. It just didn't ring true.

For the three years I'd worked for him, Mr. Angelos had

never called me, not once, to express unhappiness about something I'd said or done on a broadcast. And yet, with contract talks perhaps about to begin, it was, "Houston, we have a problem."

Surely, I felt, a genuine concern would have been expressed *sometime* during the previous three seasons rather than only now at contract time.

So I went back to rule No. 1, which is "Ron handles all the negotiating."

I called Ron and told him that I had decided against having the meeting. Instead, I asked him to pass along a message to Mr. Angelos. "Tell him it's his ballclub," I said. "And it's his right to have the broadcasts done any way he wants. It's also his right to hire any broadcaster that he desires. I support that right and will have no hard feelings if that's what he decides to do."

Then, on October 20, the day of Game One of the 1996 World Series, Giants owner Peter Magowan called me at home. It was my first conversation with Giants management.

Peter and I had a nice chat. I liked him. He was enthusiastic about the ballclub. We talked a lot about plans for the Giants' new ballpark, on the shores of San Francisco Bay. He'd piqued my curiosity.

Two days later, October 22, the Giants came to Baltimore. Larry Baer, the Giants' executive vice president, met Janine and me in Ron's law office downtown.

I'd expected the meeting to last an hour. We ended up talking almost four. At one point, we realized lunchtime had passed and we'd had nothing to eat or drink. As Harry Caray would say: Holy cow! I was feeling a little light-headed. Even dizzy. It was the middle of Death Valley with an empty canteen. It was . . . all right, enough atmosphere.

We sent for a pitcher of water and kept talking.

Larry's background is in sales, and he was selling that day— a city, a franchise, mostly a new ballpark. Pacific Bell Park opens in 2000, and Larry regaled us with artists' renderings and diagrams of what will surely be a jewel of a ballpark on the edge of San Francisco Bay in the China Basin area of the city.

The architects responsible for Camden Yards in Baltimore are designing Pac Bell Park. Larry and I compared amenities, skylines, even the novelty of home runs at the two parks. In Baltimore, a long homer to right scatters pedestrians on Eutaw Street. At Pac Bell, Larry said, such blasts will dive into San Francisco Bay. Instead of "Barry Bonds goes deep!" it would be "Barry Bonds goes INTO the deep!"

Anyway, it should be fabulous.

The meeting was an eye-opener. Working for the Giants, I decided, could be a great situation. Staying in Baltimore remained my number-one choice, though, and I made that very clear to Larry. "If I can stay with the Orioles, I will," I told him. I was determined that no one would feel misled when this was over.

Before we adjourned, Larry said, "Jon, we don't expect an answer now. But if you're seriously interested in the Giants, we'd like to know soon, by the end of the month."

I agreed.

You see, I knew I wasn't the only broadcaster between contracts in the fall of 1996. After meeting Larry, I had spoken to Joe Angel, the voice of the Florida Marlins and my former partner with the Orioles, a very talented guy and a good friend. He was trying to work out a new deal with the Marlins. Unlike my situation, the Marlins had made Joe an offer, but it was not, at that stage, the "right" offer, apparently. Though he was confident things would come together, he was unsure and a bit uneasy.

"What if they never make the 'right offer'?" I asked. "Do you have a backup?"

To that point, he said, he hadn't spoken with any other teams.

"Maybe you should contact the Giants," I volunteered, trying to help a friend. "They need a broadcaster." Joe did speak with the Giants and, sure enough, there was interest on their part. And why not? They'd received no assurances from me.

Then, on October 24, the day of Game Five of the Yankees-Braves World Series, Mark Maske of *The Washington Post* wrote an article revealing the contacts between me and the Giants. He also referred to the overtures we'd received from the Padres and MSG.

In the article, Maske referred to my situation as "a bidding war," something Ron and I got a kick out of. Hey, I'd have settled for just *one* bid, any reasonable offer from the Orioles.

I was quoted, too: "'My hope is I'll stay with the Orioles,' said Miller."

The next day, the Orioles responded as if they had ongoing discussions with us and were just waiting to hear from me. "The dialogue is good. Jon's a great talent. We have to figure out what he wants to do," an Orioles executive was quoted saying in *The Baltimore Sun* on October 25.

I told Janine, "Maybe they think I might enroll in dental school. No wonder they're confused. They don't know if I want to be a broadcaster or a dentist."

On Monday, October 28, Janine and I joined Ron and his wife, Cathi, for dinner at Tio Pepe, a Baltimore dining institution. Over paella and the famed pine nut–roll dessert, Ron told me about a conversation he had had that afternoon.

A lawyer who knew Mr. Angelos well had called Ron. The lawyer was aware of the troubles we were having with the Orioles and had an idea about getting the negotiations started.

"Jon should show up at Peter's law office first thing in the morning. He might have to wait all day before Peter sees him, because he won't have an appointment. But when Jon gets into Peter's office, the two will talk and get it worked out."

Ron said he wasn't necessarily recommending this approach, but rather just passing along the idea.

Some at the table were offended by the notion that I should have to go beg for my job. After some heated debate, the table voted against this rather novel proposal. "Besides," I said, "Ron does all the begging—er—negotiating."

So here's where we were: From the Orioles, we had been told by Mr. Angelos that I needed to change my style of announcing and approach the task with "a bit of a bias . . . be an advocate for the team . . . bleed a little bit for the Orioles," as he also told *The Sun* on November 3. The Orioles would not make an offer—or for that matter, even hint that they would eventually make an offer later. They would only say, "the club would prefer to settle on a radio carrier for the coming season before choosing its on-air talent," as *The Sun* reported on October 25. Which, as I pointed out earlier, they had never done before.

We were left with a firm offer from the Giants and no offer from the Orioles—only the vague promise of later talks when the Orioles got around to "choosing on-air talent."

Gee, why wasn't I jumping at this great opportunity?

On the afternoon of our dinner at Tio Pepe, I sought counsel from a friend about my failure to elicit a contract offer from the Orioles. He'd been a sympathetic ear as I poured out my frustrations.

"Would you like me to call Peter Angelos? Maybe I could be of some help," he offered.

I didn't mind at all. I thanked him and promptly gave my blessing.

I'd hoped he would report seeing the light at the end of the tunnel—don't you hate it when sportscasters use cliches?—and that he thought things could easily be resolved with Mr. Angelos. When my friend did call back the next day, what he told me was very disappointing.

"I spoke with Mr. Angelos," he said. "My advice to you is— *pack your suitcases!*"

It shouldn't have come as a surprise. There had been too many frustrating phone calls, too many delays in getting down to business. The Orioles had given me all the signals.

But the blunt assessment stung. I was being told it was over. Don't look back. Pack your suitcases.

"Peter is an enormously successful, self-made man," my friend said. "He trusts his instincts. Apparently his instincts tell him the broadcasts should be done a different way."

I sat at home staring at the walls, trying to make sense of the situation. This was real. The Orioles weren't going to make an offer. I wasn't coming back.

No more Esskay hand-operated out-of-town scoreboard, no more Boog's Barbecue, no more, "From beautiful Camden Yards, Orioles baseball presented for your enjoyment . . ."

I was feeling sorry for myself—and I don't mind telling you, I was really good at it! I could have gone for the gold in the self-pity Olympics. "It's a new world's record in the woe-is-me whine-a-thon!"

About this time, Joe Angel called from Miami. His negotiations with the Marlins were still not progressing the way he had hoped. Meanwhile, he said, the Giants had expressed an interest in him, but, "They told me they're trying to sign someone else first," Joe said. "They said that if the deal falls through, they would definitely be interested in talking with me."

Now I understood the Giants' desire to hear from us—one way or the other—by the end of October; if I wasn't going to be their guy, they wanted a chance at making a deal with another of their top choices before that person also signed elsewhere. This was all supposition on my part; the Giants have never told me that's what was happening. But it seemed to me, the Giants' deadline was necessary to give them time to explore other attractive options.

Or, as Joe Angel succinctly put it, "Hurry up and decide, for God's sake!"

Operating on the notion that there might have been a change of heart, Ron spoke again to the Orioles on October 30. There were still no offers, no negotiations. Ron then told them that because of our agreement to inform the Giants of our intentions by October 31, if the Orioles were ever going to make an offer, now was the time. Ron told the Orioles that we intended to contact the Giants at two P.M. the next day.

On October 31, two P.M. passed without any communication from the Orioles. Ron called the Giants and told them we were ready to start serious negotiations. It took four days to hammer out the agreement; the Giants announced the deal on November 4, the same day Janine and I left on a three-week vacation to the Far East.

During the 1997 baseball season, I lived in an apartment on Russian Hill in San Francisco; Janine and the children continued to live in Maryland, as do I during the winter. Our children still go to school in Maryland. I still work out at the Padonia Fitness Center, though not as often as I should!

I guess that explains why we had a laugh when, after I accepted the Giants' offer, Mr. Angelos told the press that Janine's desire to move had been the reason for my change in jobs. "The facts are, Mrs. Miller wanted to return to San Francisco. That's where she's from," Mr. Angelos told *The Washington Post* in an article on March 2, 1997.

That was just one of the many things Mr. Angelos said after the fact that reminded me of what Alice said after going through the looking glass: "Things just keep getting curiouser and curiouser." A few more:

> "If you look at the facts, there's not much control we had over whether he was going to stay or not . . . My speculation . . . is that the San Francisco deal was in the works for some time."
> —PETER ANGELOS IN *THE BALTIMORE SUN,* NOVEMBER 5, 1996
> (By then, sure; for at least five days.)

Angelos said it was "sheer dishonesty" to say Miller was forced to leave Baltimore. "They've gone to great points

to direct the conversation in such a way that the Orioles and I are the culprits."
—PETER ANGELOS IN *THE BALTIMORE SUN,* NOVEMBER 5, 1996

"I would never have given him five years, not for 115 games a year."
—PETER ANGELOS IN *SPORTS ILLUSTRATED,* NOVEMBER 18, 1996
(Since there were no negotiations, the number of games never came up. By the way, I worked 127 games for the Orioles in 1996.)

"Of course we would have kept him."
—PETER ANGELOS IN *THE WASHINGTON POST,* MARCH 2, 1997
(Now he tells me!)

"You are a paid announcer for that ballclub and you should be supportive of that ballclub . . . I want him to believe in the team and to bleed a little bit when we're getting our brains knocked out."
—PETER ANGELOS ON "SPORTS FORUM," WWLG RADIO, MARCH 24, 1997

"I think the most decisive factor was his wife wanted to go back where her family is."
—PETER ANGELOS ON "SPORTS FORUM," MARCH 24, 1997

"I've written this chapter to simply lay out for the record the facts of exactly what happened to bring me from the Orioles to the Giants, and to a new job I really enjoy. I love Baltimore, and I miss working with the team and for the great fans. But sometimes the most surprising career moves turn out to be the best moves."
—JON MILLER, COCKEYSVILLE, MARYLAND, WHERE THE MILLER FAMILY—EVEN MRS. MILLER—CONTINUES TO MAKE ITS HOME, JANUARY 15, 1998

A *Matter of*
TRUST

Baseball broadcasters have without question the best job in the world. My worst fear has always been that I would no longer be able to broadcast baseball and have to actually go to . . . work.

A good baseball broadcaster should have fun and make the broadcast entertaining and informative. A good sense of humor is definitely an asset. But the first responsibility of any broadcaster is to the fans. That responsibility is to report what's going on at the ballpark, vividly, clearly, and accurately. On radio, it's about painting a picture of the action. On television, it's about providing the proper information to complement the pictures.

Professional broadcasters have to build up trust between themselves and the fans. That trust tells the fans that they can believe whatever the broadcaster is telling them, positive or negative. But trust is a fragile commodity; when fans perceive that the broadcaster is less than truthful, they'll stop believing, and the broadcaster's effectiveness is reduced.

In the eighth inning of Game One of the 1996 American League Championship Series between the Orioles and Yankees, a twelve-year-old fan reached over the right-field wall at Yankee Stadium—reached *way* over the wall—and turned a long fly ball off the bat of Derek Jeter into a game-tying home run, one that changed the course of the series.

I broadcast the game on Orioles radio. My description of that disputed play makes a point about the importance of credibility to a baseball broadcaster.

When I saw the ball plucked out of the air, I reported the scene fully: the long drive, Orioles outfielder Tony Tarasco going all the way back to the wall ("He's under it now"), then suddenly the unidentified arm extending beyond the wall and taking the ball into the stands, and umpire Rich Garcia with his hand above his head signaling "home run."

Then I reported something else: that Garcia had made a bad call. The fan had clearly interfered with the play and Jeter should have been declared out, or at the very least been given only a double. On the air, I hit Garcia pretty hard for blowing the call.

When listeners to WBAL in Baltimore, WTOP in Washington, and the entire Orioles' radio network heard my description of that play, I hope they believed it. (If they were Orioles fans, they might even have been outraged by it.) During fourteen years as the voice of the Orioles, I hope I'd established that measure of trust.

But if my listeners' reaction to the description of the play had been one of disbelief—"Here he goes. Miller's crying again. 'The Orioles are getting screwed.' Just like always, oh brother"—then what good would I have been to them, to the ballclub, or to the radio station? What good would I have been to myself?

Television replays later confirmed that I'd accurately depicted the play. That was comforting. But if they hadn't, I'd have reported that, too.

For baseball broadcasters, it all begins with trust. Do your listeners believe you?

Some ballclubs view their radio/TV broadcasts as a propaganda machine, the way the Soviets viewed *Pravda*. In these organizations, the broadcaster's job is not to report the truth about the game, but to report whatever the ballclub wants to project as truth.

To me, this idea is, to put it mildly, misguided. A broadcaster who is perceived by listeners as being biased—justifiably or not—doesn't help his ballclub. He doesn't help in marketing the team, and he doesn't help sell tickets. In fact, his actions are counterproductive to what the ballclub hopes to achieve.

On the other hand, when a broadcaster tells the truth, there's a benefit for the club. A good example is the Cleveland Indians. For decades, the Indians were a bad ballclub—in fact, they were the most consistently bad ballclub in the major leagues. Then, in the late 1980s, the front office developed a new strategy and started to rebuild with young players—Carlos Baerga, Jim Thome, Albert Belle, and Kenny Lofton.

Fortunately for the Indians, they had a fine crew of broadcasters at the time, including the well-established Herb Score and his young partner, Tom Hamilton. If the Cleveland fans hadn't trusted their broadcasters, their reaction to being told the Indians were a team on the rise might have been different: "Yeah, yeah. Here we go again. The same baloney we've been hearing for thirty-five years!"

Instead, Indians fan knew that something good was starting to happen long before the team became a dominating American League power that sold out every game in a gleaming new ballpark. In part, this was because they believed it when Herb and Tom chronicled the exploits of the team's future superstars as the building process was getting underway. The fans obviously believed, as shown by the burgeoning excitement about the team at the same time.

Look at any list of great baseball broadcasters. Each has or had a unique style, a different way of making the broadcasts informative and entertaining. But despite the wide variation in styles, they all come back to the same fundamentals: They tell the truth, give a good, accurate picture of the game, and they earned credibility with the fans.

The Dodgers are one of the premier franchises in the game. Vin Scully is about to begin his forty-ninth season broadcasting Dodger baseball—without ever openly rooting for the Dodgers. Can anyone possibly say the Dodgers have been ill-served by Vin Scully? In a way, Vin Scully means *Dodgers* more than any player on the team. Vin is the backbone of the franchise; people hear Vin's voice and immediately think: Dodgers.

But also, Vin sells the game of baseball. He makes you feel his passion for the game. He makes you feel the fun of baseball, but also the drama and the excitement. And—owners take note—Vin sells tickets.

What Vin tells Dodger fans is happening with the Dodgers, well, that's what's happening. There's never a controversy about whether Vin Scully is telling it accurately. The same with Ernie Harwell in Detroit. The same with Jack Buck in St. Louis. In his day, it was the same with Russ Hodges, and still is that way with Lon Simmons in San Francisco. All these men were very well respected and totally trusted by the fans. And that's the whole point: gaining the trust of the fans.

In some cities, there's a history of the broadcaster assuming the role of "Fan in the Booth." Pittsburgh is one such example. The first full-time broadcaster for the Pittsburgh Pirates was Rosey Rowswell, a legendary fan. Rowswell rooted, he cheered, and when things went against the Pirates, he mourned.

Rowswell was also a performer. His home-run call is one of the classics. On a well-hit ball, he'd shout, "Go to the window Aunt Minnie, here she comes . . ." Rowswell always kept a tape in the booth with a sound effect of glass shattering. When the ball reached the seats, he'd roll the tape and say, "Oh well, Aunt Minnie got there too late again."

Bob Prince, Rowswell's young sidekick and later his successor, felt that Rowswell had created the expectation of a certain kind of broadcast, so Prince tried to fit the same mold—a cheerleader and an entertainer. When Willie Stargell was hitting lots of home runs in the 1970s, he was also owner of a Kentucky Fried Chicken franchise located in Pittsburgh's Hill District; with each home run Willie hit, the restaurant offered discounts on its drumsticks. Prince incorporated the chicken deal into his home-run calls: "Pirate fans, there's gonna be chicken on the hill—with Will!"

As partisan as he was, Bob Prince gave a very accurate, truthful depiction of the game. He simply added another element: portraying himself as a fan of the Pirates. If the Pirates played poorly, he reported it; if the Pirates screwed up, Bob Prince not only reported it, he was as outraged about it as the guy sitting in the grandstand at Forbes Field.

Harry Caray has been a fan in the booth for more than fifty years, first in St. Louis and now for a long time in Chicago. Harry's whole act is centered on him being the fan's representative in the broadcast booth.

When I speak at banquets, I do a bit in which I impersonate Harry doing play-by-play, with a fan's sensibilities. It's a close ballgame, the bases are full, and the hitter is the Cubs' $6 million-a-year star. (When Sammy Sosa signed his last contract, I had to upgrade it to $10.5 million a year.) With the game on the line, Sosa hits a weak pop-up to kill the rally.

Harry—me impersonating Harry—is livid. "He popped it up! Can you believe it, ladies and gentlemen? What's the matter with him? Ten million a year and he . . . POPS IT UP! Hoe-lee cowww!"

Harry has built up so much credibility with his listeners that when he tells them the Cubs stink, they *know* the Cubs stink. Hey, Harry said so! And Harry's not afraid to tell it in just those terms. In fact, Harry has gotten into a lot of trouble for being blunt. Owners have bristled at his comments. Players have been really unhappy with Harry, but Harry never changes his approach—because Harry believes his responsibility is to the fans.

Baltimore, on the other hand, has a different broadcast tradition. Ernie Harwell was the original Orioles broadcaster when the team returned to the big leagues in 1954. Ernie established a tradition of accurate reporting of Orioles baseball without any cheerleading, without openly rooting on the air. Chuck Thompson followed Ernie with pretty much the same approach.

Listening to Ernie over the years, and to Chuck and to his longtime partner, the late Bill O'Donnell, it was quite evident that Orioles broadcasters were not Orioles rooters—at least, not on the air. Chuck was happy to see the team win; that always came through in his voice. But you never heard Chuck say "we" on the air, as in, "We really need a hit right now!" or "We've got a left-hander warming up in our bullpen." Chuck doesn't use that terminology.

Would Harry Caray have been trusted even more if he hadn't been known as the number-one fan? That would be the subject of a good debate. For one thing, it would be hard for Harry to be more popular than he already is. You can't improve on Harry's record of longevity—or his fame. No one, not Vin Scully, not anybody, has become a more recognizable personality as a baseball broadcaster than Harry.

(Some people who know Harry as an avid fan make the mistake of labeling Harry a "homer." He isn't; a homer is someone who is less than honest when things go badly for the home team, and that's not Harry. When the Cubs are bad, brother, does Harry let you know! And the fans appreciate Harry's candor, which is the foundation of his success. The fans trust Harry.)

I remember a conversation I had years ago with Larry King. Larry started out in broadcasting as a disc jockey in Miami Beach. His first day on the air, Larry said, he learned the most important lesson in broadcasting: Be yourself.

That first day, the station manager decided Larry needed a stage name—something with a little more pizzazz than Larry's real name, Larry Zeiger. In search of the perfect name, the station manager opened the newspaper and turned to the used-car ads. He spotted one for a lot called "King's Previously Owned Autos."

"From now on," he announced, "you'll be 'Larry King.'"

What a day for Larry—a new career and now a new identity. Then the big moment arrived; the record that had been playing finished, and Larry was about to speak his first words on the air. But when he opened his mouth, nothing came out. Larry was so overly excited, he couldn't speak. A disc jockey's nightmare—dead air.

At that point, the station manager came into the booth and said, "Radio is a communication business, Larry! Start communicating!"

Larry flipped on his mike and, in desperation, unable to think of anything else to say, began speaking the first thoughts that came to him.

"This is my first day on the radio. It's the realization of my life's dream to be a radio broadcaster. I just received a new name—Larry King. I've never used it before. As you might expect, I'm extremely nervous.

"Now, I hope you'll enjoy my show."

By the end of that first program, Larry felt very comfortable. He'd found his style, which was just being himself. And Larry has never strayed from that revelation, becoming the most famous talk-show host in the world.

It sounds simple. But it's a difficult message to get across to people, especially young people. Often, they have the idea that to have success in this business, they have to develop a showbiz persona—have the biggest hair and the whitest teeth. Larry rejects that; for Larry, the key is being yourself.

Joe Morgan is always himself on the air. It's his greatest asset. I think you could say the same of many of the other top sports broadcasters. Two that come to mind are John Madden and Dick Vitale. Those two guys are totally genuine. John Madden really is a nice, down-to-earth guy; there's no pretension at all about John Madden. The same is true of Dick Vitale—if you run into Dick in a hotel lobby, it's the same Dick you see on television. He's totally genuine.

As for me, I have to be myself on the air. I can't help it. Besides, who would I be if I decided not to be me? C. Everett Koop? (I've always said it's about time we had a former U.S. surgeon general doing play-by-play.)

Baseball fans feel they know the local baseball broadcaster. There tends to be more of an intimacy than exists with other sports. Frequently, I'll meet a baseball fan in an airport or at a restaurant and they'll look at me as if they know me. Not know *of* me, but know me. Initially, my reaction is to feel somewhat inadequate: "Gee, I should remember this person. Why can't I remember?"

People are very nice; when they see the confusion in my face, they set me straight, gently. "Now, Jon, you don't know me. It's just that I feel I know you . . ." That's one of the fun parts of broadcasting baseball on a daily basis, particularly on the radio—there's a chance to build a real rapport with listeners. You're talking with them every day.

Once, I was on an airplane sitting in my seat when I noticed a guy in the aisle looking at me. I thought, "Well, he recognized me. He'll probably come over now and tell me that he's a big fan." I reminded myself to be pleasant, because he'd soon be walking over to spend a moment with such a big star as myself.

Just as I expected, he leaned down and whispered to me. He said, "I don't want to make a big thing about this—but your fly is open."

Fortunately, I didn't blurt out, "Hey, well, thanks for watching!"

In the broadcast business, we deal in the truth. And some-times the truth makes for awkward moments. Occasionally, I'll stroll through the Giants clubhouse at the ballpark in San Francisco. A few players will be watching a videotape of a ball-game three months earlier, a game I worked. Players like to watch tapes of games from the last time they faced a certain pitcher; the tapes help refresh their memories. What did the guy throw last time? How did he pitch me?

They're deep in thought. Then I walk in. My first thought is, "Man, I hope I didn't hammer one of these guys." Even though the game was three months ago, it might be uncomfortable for everyone for me to be standing in the clubhouse as, on the tape, I'm pointing out this guy's base-running gaffe or that guy's weak throwing arm.

Then again, it's a good reminder: Words have meaning. Use them carefully. Up in the booth, it's easy to be critical. Every-thing looks so easy. I try to always treat the players with respect. They're the best in the world at what they do; if they made it to the major leagues, they've reached the top of their profession.

There are times when I'll have to point out a player's mis-takes—that's the nature of the job. But I phrase my observation in a way that isn't belittling to the player. For instance, I wouldn't be comfortable attacking a player: "What's the matter with him? This guy makes too much money to screw up like that." I would never do that. For me, it's enough to say that the man threw to the wrong base and, in turn, that allowed a run-ner to move up an extra base. Or that a left-handed batter should have been looking for an inside pitch, a pitch he could pull to the right side to move a runner from second base to third, but instead hit an outside pitch to the left side: "That just shouldn't happen."

I'm pointing out what happened. I'm reporting. But I'm not taking it personally, as a fan would.

As I mentioned earlier, some broadcasters refer to themselves as fans—but they're really not fans, not the way the guy in Section 336, Row II is a fan. Even Harry Caray, who bills himself as the ultimate fan on the air, is not really a fan. For fifty-three years as a broadcaster, Harry has had the best seat in the house. He's traveled on team charters. He's walked through clubhouses. He's played cards with some of the guys. Harry knows the game, and he knows the people in the game. That's not the life of a real fan. To a regular fan, players are just names on a scorecard. It never enters the mind of a real fan that players are human beings, that players have families, outside interests, and responsibilities.

When you think about it, why should a player's off-field life concern the average fan? When I was a kid, I know it didn't concern me. If, when I was twelve years old, I'd read in the paper that Willie Mays would be out of the lineup for a couple of days because his wife was having a baby, I'd have been outraged. How could he do that to the ballclub? Don't tell me that it's just two games; those two games could cost us the pennant! Hey, I was a fan. Willie Mays was not a human being to me. Willie Mays was 49 home runs and 141 RBIs and the basket catch.

I'm older now, and my relationships with players are a lot more complicated than they were in those days. Now I might sit next to a player on a charter flight. The very next day, I might be pointing out to thousands of viewers and listeners that the same player made a costly mistake.

In my first year broadcasting in the big leagues, Monte Moore loaned me a copy of Red Barber's autobiography, *Rhubarb in the Catbird Seat.* I devoured that book. I was totally absorbed. At the time, I didn't know much about Red Barber. Because I grew up on the West Coast, Red Barber was just a rumor to me. He was that guy who did games back east in the "olden days."

In his book, Barber offered pointers on succeeding as a broadcaster. As someone just starting in the business, I took very seriously his advice not to get too friendly with the players. The job demands that you report on them, and at times, even report negative things about them, Red wrote. And if they're very close personal friends, he warned, that could be difficult.

You need to have relationships with the players. You need to feel comfortable approaching them with questions. But friends? I agree with Red. For a broadcaster, it's a conflict of interest.

I don't speak for other broadcasters, including those who might be very friendly with players; nor do I stand in judgment of them. Everyone makes their own call. But to a twenty-two year old, Red Barber's advice made a lot of sense. I took his words to heart.

I enjoy the company of players, as I do that of managers and coaches. I see them in hotel lobbies, and I've been to dinner with players. Getting to know players, building relationships with them, it's very important.

In 1978, when I was doing the Texas Rangers' broadcasts, I broke Red's rule. I got to be very friendly with Jim Sundberg, and my then, now ex-wife became friendly with Jim's wife. One day, perhaps because we were friends, Jim confided in me that his arm had been feeling a little stiff. This was very bad news for the Rangers, because Jim Sundberg was one of the great throwing catchers in the game. He was a real weapon behind the plate.

One night, Sundberg was catching and a guy on the opposing team stole a base. Sundberg's throw was weak—and, because of my earlier conversation with him, I had a good idea why.

On the air, I said, "Jim has had some stiffness in his shoulder lately. Based on that throw, you'd have to say it's affecting him."

The next day, I got a call from my wife back in Texas. Mrs. Sundberg had called, very upset that I'd revealed Jim's "condition" on television.

Upset? I only knew about the stiff arm because Sundberg told me. He was my source!

I immediately called Sunny—everyone called him Sunny—in his hotel room.

"You put that on the air?" he asked, clearly perturbed.

"Well, yeah," I admitted. "You made a real bad throw and I wanted to explain it. You didn't tell me it was a big secret."

"I just figured you'd know," Sunny said.

This was the conflict I'd read about in Red Barber's book. Hey, right out of chapter nine.

Sunny felt betrayed.

"From now on," I said, "if you tell me something that I shouldn't put on the air, you need to make that very clear. I can't make that decision. All of a sudden there's this terrible throw, what am I supposed to say? 'Gee, it looks like he might have a sore arm on that one—I'll have to ask him tomorrow?' "

Years later, Clyde King, an advance scout for the Yankees, told me that he always carried a small radio with him at the ballpark so he could listen to the local broadcast with his earphones. Monitoring the radio broadcasts, Clyde told me, was an important part of preparing his report; he hoped to pick up bits of information that would make the report more complete.

Once, Clyde recalled, while listening to a ballgame on the radio he'd heard about a catcher having a sore arm. This was not commonly known, and was certainly not known by Clyde. Naturally, this became a big part of his scouting report on this team. As he said, "When the Yankees came to town, it helped us win a ballgame."

I immediately cringed—wondering if it had been Jim Sundberg's sore arm he'd heard about from me! All the more reason why I shouldn't have that information.

Mr. Barber, my favorite author, had a rule he employed to avoid such misunderstandings: When he spoke with managers and general managers, he'd make it very clear they should not offer any information that could not be put out on the broadcast. Don't tell me something if I can't use it, Red would warn; in a live-broadcast situation, where snap decisions must be made, it would be too confusing to have to remember which information can be used and which can't.

I can't say I have some great, elaborate system in place for dealing with such situations. I don't. At times, I'll listen to background information about a certain player, information I know I won't be divulging on the air. Still, such knowledge might be helpful to me in giving a more complete explanation of what is happening on the field. But whomever I am speaking with, I try to have as clear an understanding as possible about what can be put on the air and what can't. Red Barber's rule is a good one, but the world isn't always so black and white.

Still, to all you scouts out there: When you come to Candlestick this summer, leave the Walkman at the hotel. You'll get no state secrets from me!

So now it's springtime, and baseball draws us back again. No surprise there; baseball always draws us back. Baseball is good company. It's everyday. It's dependable. Baseball is like the friend you have for life. Baseball is a vacation from the real world, whenever you want it—fifteen minutes poring over the box scores each morning provides a refreshing respite from the frantic pace of real life. A game on the radio, every day, whenever and wherever you want it—in the car, by the backyard barbecue, at the beach, on the night table beside your bed. (And don't forget, Sunday nights at eight eastern, five Pacific on ESPN—must viewing for a happier life!)

There's room for all of us in baseball, for the fan in the bleachers, the veteran ballplayer—even for the broadcaster who's been labeled "purist." By the way, this "purist" has one last confession to make—I love the DH!

Enough confessions. See you at the game.

EPILOGUE, 2000

As I was saying . . .

Two baseball seasons have come and gone since I completed the manuscript for this book. And by anybody's reckoning—including this baseball purist's—they've been pretty remarkable.

In 1998, all that occurred was the demolition of perhaps the most hallowed record in the annals of sport. And most remarkably, not just once, but twice. Mark McGwire and Sammy Sosa both laid waste to the single-season home-run record of Roger Maris that had stood a mere 37 years.

The 1999 season, though it didn't yield record-breaking individual performances of the same magnitude, was a winner in other, even better ways. Stimulating pennant races in the National League commanded the attention of fans to the season's final day, and beyond, as the Mets and Reds played a tie-breaker playoff to determine the wild card. Later, with an autumn chill in the air, the Braves and Mets treated us to an epic National League Championship Series. (It was a shame that the run of the tenacious, against-the-odds Mets had to end so ignobly on the bases-loaded walk by Kenny Rogers.)

In my mind, these two very different yet similarly entertaining seasons underscore a point made often and, I hope, persuasively, in this book: Baseball is enjoying an era of unprecedented success and health.

It startles me when people comment, as some do, that the game is on the verge of disintegrating. Disintegrating?

The message of the past two seasons is just the opposite: Baseball is the most resilient game, and it will entertain and surprise fans long into the next millennium.

There's a chapter in this book titled, "The Good Old Days Are Now." In it, I make the case that baseball is enjoying a Golden Age. Today's players are equal in many ways to their forebears and superior in others: bigger, faster, and without a doubt in better physical shape. Thank you, Sammy and Big Mac, Griffey Jr., Pedro, Arod, Derek, and Nomar. Over the past two years, you've made my point for me.

I'm fortunate to have been around both Sosa and McGwire a lot during their historic home-run chases of 1998 and 1999. I recall being in St. Louis for *ESPN Sunday Night Baseball* at the end of August in 1998. In the batting cage that night, Big Mac was treating an early arriving crowd to one of the greatest shows in sports: McGwire taking batting practice. (He never disappoints, launching breathtaking, tape-measure home runs one after another.)

As he hopped in and out of the cage, we began chatting about a house he'd bought for his parents near the Pacific Ocean in the San Diego area. He'd read an article that suggested living near the sea was a way to lower blood pressure and bring about a sense of well-being and overall good health. Buying the house, he said, was the best thing he'd ever done for his mom and dad. Since the move, his dad's health and spirits were the best they'd been in years, he told me.

Then Big Mac turned the sales pitch around, urging me to look for a place near the ocean for my family. We had a laugh about it. But maybe this talk had a subtle, and until now, undetected, effect on the Miller clan. Janine and I recently bought a home near San Francisco on the Pacific Coast, with invigorating ocean breezes. (Hey, if I wasn't pretty certain he's financially set for life, I'd have the real estate agent share his commission with

Big Mac, the 70-home-run man *and* home location consultant!)

That night, Big Mac went out and slammed a 500-foot home run to win a game over the Braves, then proceeded on a tear, hitting eight home runs in a torrid nine-day stretch. On ESPN, Joe Morgan and I caught up with him again near the tail end of that home-run spree, as he sat on 60 homers, one shy of tying Maris' record of 61.

It was September 7, Labor Day. Big Mac didn't make the huge crowd at Busch Stadium wait long. In his first at-bat, with Mike Morgan pitching, he slammed a shot down the left-field line. The ball clearly would be gone, out of the park. It was just a question of fair or foul. The answer was fair—the ball slamming against the window of a restaurant beneath the upper deck. Another spectacular blast!

In calling the home run for ESPN, I tried not to deviate from my regular broadcast sensibilities: taking events as they come and trying to make comments appropriate to the moment. After describing the flight of the ball, I did note something I thought as important as the fact that Big Mac had just equaled Maris' record. The home run, coming as it did in the 142nd game of the season, meant McGwire had done something that even Maris had not. He had broken Babe Ruth's record of 60 home runs in a 154-game season. Maris—although he, without question, owned the overall single-season home-run record—had hit his 60th and 61st home runs after the 154th game in the first year the schedule had expanded to its current 162 games. For that reason, I felt McGwire's 61st had broken the Babe's record just as number 62, hit the next night, would break Maris' record.

On the next-to-last Sunday of the season, Joe and I flew to Chicago to work "Sammy Sosa Day" for ESPN at Wrigley Field. There was a beautiful and emotional ceremony before the game, attended by Sammy's mother and several of his siblings. It was the last home game of the year for the Cubs—or so we thought. Unfortunately for Sammy, he wasn't able to deliver the booming home run Cubs fans had hoped to see. And worse, Bret Boone hit three home runs for Cincinnati as the Reds beat the Cubs, who were then in a pitched battle for the National League Wild Card.

As fate would have it, our ESPN crew would return to Wrigley one more time in 1998. The season, which had been made so special by the great home-run race featuring McGwire and Sosa, had been nearly bereft of pennant races. Only the NL wild-card race in which the Giants, Cubs, and Mets battled to the wire, was cause for suspense. The Giants got hot at the end, at one point winning nine of ten to thrust themselves ahead of the Mets. In so doing, they became only the third team in Major League history to be five games out with ten to play, then charge from behind to cause a playoff. (The others are—who else?—the Giants, in 1951 and 1962.)

This time, the Giants and Cubs met in a one-game playoff at Wrigley Field. The Cubs held on for a 5-3 win and the celebrating lasted until the wee hours in Chicago where there hadn't been much to celebrate in the 53 years since the Cubs had last played in a World Series. As things turned out, there would again be no Fall Classic for the Cubbies in '98—they were knocked off three games to none by the Atlanta Braves in the division series. But between Sosa's heroics and a dramatic victory at their great old ballpark in the tie-breaker game, it had been quite a season. Or as the late, great Harry Caray might have shouted: "Hoe-lee cowwww!"

Before moving on, I'll make a final point about the incomparable tandem of McGwire and Sosa. When Sammy followed his 66-home-run season in 1998 with 63 more in '99 (and Big Mac followed up with 65 after his amazing 70) it was said by some that these awesome encores were somehow less interesting than the previous season's record-setting run. One wag wrote that, as with a hit movie, the sequel is never as good as the original. Some said that by surmounting the 60-homer barrier twice, it had cheapened what McGwire and Sosa had done the first time.

For me, this line of reasoning is spectacularly flawed if not just plain preposterous. What Sosa and McGwire did in 1999 was not

Hollywood fiction dreamt up by a screenwriter. What they did was an actual, real-life achievement brought about by a great deal of hard work, dedication, and extraordinary talent. (By the way, don't you think it was significant that nobody else even came close to doing what this extraordinary pair did?)

Baseball records reflect a level of achievement, a level of excellence. The significance of these particular records is known even to the most casual of fans. Hence, the great level of interest and excitement in the pursuit of the record in 1998 by these two remarkable athletes is a phenomenon unique to baseball. The only other player in baseball history to rewrite the home-run records more than once is Babe Ruth himself, the greatest slugger of them all.

And that, my friends, is the comparison that should say it all about the incredible achievements of Big Mac and Slammin' Sammy these last two years. Doing it again in '99 made their achievements in '98 all the greater!

The memorable 1998 season left a lot of breathless fans asking: How can baseball possibly top this in 1999? The answer was by producing perhaps the only thing lacking the previous year: exciting pennant races.

In the National League, the New York Mets and Atlanta Braves battled in the East while, in the Central, a stimulating race developed between the Houston Astros and the amazing Cincinnati Reds, who, with a small payroll, were one of the top stories of the 1999 season.

Wild-card races in both leagues lived up to their birthright—they were indeed wild and unpredictable. In the AL, the youthful Oakland A's staged a surprising run, making their presence felt until deep into September before they finally lost hope of catching the Boston Red Sox. The NL was much more frenetic, a wild-card melee in which the matter wasn't settled until the New York Mets had bested the Cincinnati Reds on the day after the season was supposed to have ended.

Does this sound like an endorsement of the wild-card concept?

I still have some reservations. Yes, the wild-card race in the NL was truly exciting. But the wild card itself didn't add substantially to the excitement already present because, until the season's final nine days, the Mets were in a great race with Atlanta *for first place* in the NL East and the Reds were in an outstanding race *for first place* with Houston in the NL Central. In effect, all that occurred by adding the wild card was to change four teams going for two spots in the postseason to four teams going for three.

On the other hand, the wild card did generate much more excitement in the season's final weekend as the Reds and Mets battled for their postseason lives. (Also, Houston was not assured of making the playoffs until its final-day win at the Astrodome.)

Certainly, the wild card breathed life into the final homestand of the year for the Mets. By this time, the Mets had conceded the NL East crown to the Braves and their only hope was to advance via the wild card. Even that route seemed highly uncertain, though, as they entered the final weekend trailing the Reds by two games with only three to play.

No baseball constituency was more dubious than Mets fans themselves as a crowd of only 29,528 attended a Friday night victory over Pittsburgh at Shea Stadium which, coupled with a Reds' loss, drew manager Bobby Valentine's plucky club within one game of Cincinnati with two to play. Still a longshot, though.

The excitement pitched higher Saturday as the Mets won again. (Many fans were still skeptical however, with 36,878 in attendance, far below capacity.) Cincinnati was a loser for a second straight day at Milwaukee. The two teams were tied for the wild card. Amazingly, what had seemed all but impossible on Friday for the Mets clearly was within reach going into the final day's play on Sunday. The Mets drew a rollicking crowd of 50,111 to Shea for that contest and won a dramatic victory on a wild pitch in the last of the ninth! Late that night after a six-hour rain delay in Milwaukee, the Reds also won to set up a one-game playoff for the wild-card berth for the second straight year. (Al

Leiter completed the Mets' incredible comeback with a two-hit shutout of the Reds before 54,621 disappointed fans in Cincinnati.)

Both clubs had come into the game with 96 wins. Legitimate credentials for a berth in the playoffs. More wins, in fact, than many a World Series team over the years. The Red Sox, the AL's wild-card team, won 94 games. Again, legitimate playoff-team credentials.

In 1999, the new system worked for the Mets and the Red Sox for sure but, more importantly, for the fans. We were treated to the Mets' memorable series with the Braves.

Who'll ever forget Robin Ventura's 15th inning game-winning grand slam?

No!

It was only an RBI single?

Even though it went out of the park?

Man, what a finish. And what a game.

Why, it was one of the best playoff games ever. (That is, until Game Six.)

What a series!

And we were treated to those old rivals, the Yankees and the Red Sox in postseason play for the first time, as well.

There seems no going back to life before the wild card. It'll remain a postseason fixture in one form or another, though that form may well change in 2001, when the National League tries to go to four four-team divisions. That would eliminate the need for a wild card in the National League as the four playoff teams would all be division winners. Another change on the horizon for 2001 in the NL is a possible switch to the so-called unbalanced schedule, which will accent intradivisional rivalries. I love it.

The plan calls for teams to play 18 games against each of the teams within their division, 12 against teams in a designated "sister" division, and six games—three home, three away—against each club in the remaining two divisions.

Giants fans, at last, will have ample opportunities to get revved up for a proper number of Giants-Dodgers wars and, for that matter, Giants-Padres and Giants-Rockies intradivisional series. Teams battling one another for a title, real rivalries being nurtured in the best way possible. A chance to battle real rivals early in the year, again in the summer, and a final showdown in September. Winner take all. Second place, go home.

I like it. Bravo!

The battle for the World Series championship was over in short order in 1999, with the Yankees making quick work of the Braves, sweeping to the title in four games. This series between teams dominant in their respective leagues in recent years spawned a number of newspaper articles discussing whether the Yanks or Braves should wear the mantle: Team of the '90s.

Yankees general manager Brian Cashman, in my eyes, put the issue to rest before the World Series even started when he asked rhetorically, "Aren't the Yankees already the team of the century?" Well, sure. The Yankees' sweep of the Braves was their 25th World Championship—no other franchise in baseball has more than nine.

As for the current Yankees' place in baseball history, consider this: with six consecutive postseason series victories in the last two years, the Yankees have done something only one other team in history has ever done. (The Oakland A's from 1972 to 1974 won three consecutive World Series and also three consecutive League Championship Series—a total of six consecutive postseason series.)

Not even the Yankees of 1949 to 1953, who won five consecutive World Series, still the record, won six straight postseason series. (Not needing to play any playoff series after winning the pennant in the era.)

These present-day Yankees also arguably are the greatest come-from-behind team of all time. Until 1996, only seven times in World Series history had a team gone into the seventh inning or later down by three or more runs and still come back to win the games. So it is obviously not an easy thing to do against that level of competition. Amazingly, the Yankees have managed to win games *four* times against those long odds—three times in the last two years alone—beginning with their historic comeback from a 6-0 deficit which featured Jim Leyritz's three-run homer against Mark Wohlers in Game Four of the '96 series.

What's more, having won each of the past two World Series in a four-game sweep and having an incredible combined postseason record the past two years of 22 wins, 3 losses—and let's not forget three World Series wins in four years, including '96—in my mind makes the case with clarity and eloquence that these Yankees under Joe Torre deserve mention on any short list of the greatest teams ever to play the game.

The award for the most embarrassing press release of 1999 goes to the Baltimore Orioles, who announced the firing of general manager Frank Wren on October 7 in a blistering one-page attack that ended up exposing not Wren, but rather Orioles management, to ridicule throughout baseball.

I'm not here to discuss the merits of whether Wren should have been fired. That's not for me to say and, frankly, is none of my business. But I will say that the indictment of Frank Wren as laid out by the Orioles in this press statement so shook the baseball community that it took Wren all of four working days to land another job (as vice president and assistant general manager of the Atlanta Braves, no less). Obviously, the Orioles' assessment was not taken seriously by Wren's new boss, Atlanta's respected general manager, John Schuerholz.

The Orioles press release recounted Wren's handling of an incident involving Cal Ripken, who'd been late arriving for a charter flight from Baltimore to the West Coast. Cal was stuck in traffic on the Baltimore Beltway and phoned ahead to inform Orioles traveling secretary Phil Itzoe that he would be a few minutes late. Wren apparently made the decision for the plane to leave on time, forcing Cal to find his own way to the West Coast.

"In the opinion of management, there was no need for such an arbitrary and inflexible decision," the Orioles noted in their press release. Cal was apparently unaware that he was about to be dragged into the controversy, and clearly didn't appreciate it. At a press conference about a week after Wren's dismissal, he said he was "uncomfortable" as a main character in "a situation I feel I don't belong in."

Reading about this "controversy," I flashed back to a road trip seven or eight years ago when, because of a terrible traffic tie-up on the Baltimore Beltway, I missed an Orioles charter flight. I arrived at the charter terminal about five minutes after the plane had taken off, then doubled back to the main terminal to make arrangements for a commercial flight to the city in question.

As I took my place at the ticket counter, who should slip into line behind me but Orioles pitcher Storm Davis and none other than Cal Ripken, who together had been caught in the same traffic jam and had also missed the flight. Johnny Oates, then the Orioles manager, didn't hold the plane. Cal didn't make a stink then—as far as I know this is the first time the long-ago incident has been made public—and didn't make a stink this time either. And, oh yeah, Johnny Oates was not fired for leaving Cal behind!

There are long-standing traditions in baseball: The bus leaves on time and the plane leaves on time. It's a player's—and a broadcaster's—responsibility to get there. On time.

During the past two years, baseball gained a permanent commissioner, Bud Selig. I was skeptical of a number of Bud's ideas and approaches during his five-and-a-half years as "acting" commissioner, and have said so elsewhere in this book. Of late, he has taken several positive steps. Appointing a "blue-ribbon" task force to study baseball's economics and propose solutions to the game's financial troubles was a wonderful idea. So was the decision to seek out some of the best and brightest minds from outside the baseball fraternity to serve on the committee, including political columnist and TV commentator George Will, and former Federal Reserve chairman Paul Volcker.

I'm intrigued by one of the ideas to come out of the task force: contraction. There seems to be considerable opposition within the game that could keep this from happening. But the idea is to take two teams in the weakest markets—franchises in Montreal, Oakland, Kansas City, and Minnesota being mentioned most often—and eliminate them.

This would be easier said than done, of course. But it is a sign that some creative thinking is going on with regard to the game's financial disparities between the haves and have-nots.

Finally, it's nice to see some of the proposals mentioned in these pages working their way onto baseball's agenda. Interleague play has moved closer to the "natural rivalry" model tossed out in the book's opening chapter. The unbalanced schedule appears to be in the National League's future. And many owners seem to be heeding Selig's call to keep discussion of their team finances in the boardrooms and away from the fans.

As for "radical realignment," it was dead before the book came out and remains so. I'm thrilled. Never has there been a more ill-conceived plan.

As you no doubt have noticed, much of this new epilogue deals with the drama and excitement of the past two years. But don't mistake these reminiscences for wallowing in nostalgia. Within seconds of Chad Curtis putting the squeeze on the final out of the World Series last October, I was already fantasizing about the beautiful new jewel of a ballpark on the shores of San Francisco Bay where the Giants will make their downtown home in the new millennium: Pacific Bell Park.

Whereas the 20th century belonged to the Yankees, I'm looking inexorably forward to the 21st century, which—who knows?—just might be the century of the Giants!

INDEX